THE TENANTS' MOVEMENT

The Tenants' Movement is both a history of tenant organisation and mobilisation, and a guide to understanding how the struggles of tenant organisers have come to shape housing policy today. Charting the history of tenant mobilisation, and the rise of consumer movements in housing, it is one of the first cross-cultural, historical analyses of tenants' organisations' roles in housing policy.

This book shows both the past and future of tenant mobilisation. The book's approach applies social movement theory to housing studies, and bridges gaps between research in urban sociology, urban studies and the built environment. It provides a challenging study of the ability of contemporary social movements, community campaigns and urban struggles to shape the debate around public services and engage with the unfinished project of welfare reform.

Quintin Bradley is Senior Lecturer in Housing and Planning at Leeds Metropolitan University. He leads research into resident involvement, neighbourhood planning and grass-roots community politics. He has a background in community activism and investigative journalism, and as a housing practitioner he has worked for municipal housing authorities, social landlords and residents' organisations.

Housing and society series

Edited by Ray Forrest, School for Policy Studies,
University of Bristol

This series aims to situate housing within its wider social, political and economic context at both national and international level. In doing so it will draw on the full range of social science disciplines and on mainstream debate on the nature of contemporary social change. The books are intended to appeal to an international academic audience as well as to practitioners and policymakers – to be theoretically informed and policy relevant.

The Tenants' Movement
Resident involvement, community action and the contentious
politics of housing
Quintin Bradley

Social Housing, Disadvantage, and Neighbourhood Liveability
Ten years of change in social housing neighbourhoods
Edited by Michelle Norris

Young People and Housing
Transitions, trajectories and generational fractures
Edited by Ray Forrest and Ngai ming Yip

Housing, Markets and Policy
Peter Malpass and Rob Rowlands

Housing and Health in Europe
Edited by David Ormandy

The Hidden Millions
Graham Tipple and Suzanne Speak

Housing, Care and Inheritance
Misa Izuhara

Housing and Social Transition in Japan
Edited by Yosuke Hirayama and Richard Ronald

Housing Transformations
Shaping the space of 21st century living
Bridget Franklin

Housing and Social Policy
Contemporary themes and critical perspectives
Edited by Peter Somerville with Nigel Sprigings

Housing and Social Change
East–West perspectives
Edited by Ray Forrest and James Lee

Urban Poverty, Housing and Social Change in China
Ya Ping Wang

Gentrification in a Global Context
Edited by Rowland Atkinson and Gary Bridge

THE TENANTS' MOVEMENT

Resident involvement, community action and the contentious politics of housing

Quintin Bradley

Routledge
Taylor & Francis Group

NEW YORK AND LONDON

First published 2014
by Routledge
711 Third Avenue, New York, NY 10017

and by Routledge
2 Park Square, Milton Park, Abingdon, Oxon OX14 4RN

Routledge is an imprint of the Taylor & Francis Group, an informa business

© 2014 Quintin Bradley

The right of Quintin Bradley to be identified as author of this work has been asserted in accordance with sections 77 and 78 of the Copyright, Designs and Patents Act 1988.

British Library Cataloguing in Publication Data
A catalogue record for this book is available from the British Library

Library of Congress Cataloging-in-Publication Data
Bradley, Quintin.
The tenants' movement: resident involvement, community action and the contentious politics of housing/by Quintin Bradley. – 1 Edition.
pages cm. – (Housing and society series)
Includes bibliographical references and index.
1. Rent control. 2. Social movements. 3. Tenants' associations.
4. Housing policy. I. Title.
HD7288.82.B73 2014
363.5'82 – dc23
2013045054

ISBN13: 978-0-415-72026-7 (hbk)
ISBN13: 978-0-415-72025-0 (pbk)
ISBN13: 978-1-315-86708-3 (ebk)

Typeset in Bembo by
Florence Production Ltd, Stoodleigh, Devon, UK

Printed and bound in Great Britain by
TJ International Ltd, Padstow, Cornwall

CONTENTS

FIGURES

ACKNOWLEDGEMENTS

Some people are more to blame for this book than others. I would like to single out, in particular, John Grayson whose adult education classes on the tenants' movement opened my eyes to a hidden history; Murray Hawtin whose commitment to the principles of community action has always been inspirational; the management committees and staff of Kirklees, Leeds and Rotherham tenants' and residents' federations who provided the illustrations in this text, and all the tenants and residents who took part in the research and discussions that have contributed to this book and who gave their time, patience and enthusiasm to this work. I would also like to thank John Flint and Peter Somerville, who, together with John Grayson, read drafts of chapters and made many useful comments and suggestions. My heartfelt thanks go to all who made this work possible.

GLOSSARY

ALHE	Association of London Housing Estates
ALMO	arm's-length management organisation
BME	Black and Minority Ethnic
CCH	Confederation of Co-operative Housing
CDP	Community Development Project
CIH	Chartered Institute of Housing
DCH	Defend Council Housing
DCLG	Department for Communities and Local Government
DETR	Department of the Environment, Transport and the Regions
HARTOE	Housing Association Residents and Tenants Organisation of England
HRA	Housing Revenue Account
IUT	International Union of Tenants
LGA	Local Government Association
NGO	non-governmental organisation
ODPM	Office of the Deputy Prime Minister
PEP	Priority Estates Project
TARA	Tenants and Residents Association
TAROE	Tenants and Residents Organisations of England
TPAS	Tenant Participation Advisory Service
TSA	Tenant Services Authority

1

THE TENANTS' MOVEMENT

Tenants are outsiders in a society fixated on home ownership, and yet a new 'generation rent' finds itself shoe-horned into a private rental sector that is largely unregulated, over-priced, and to a significant extent unfit. High-quality rented social housing – provided by public bodies, co-operatives and not-for-profit organisations – is severely rationed, and everywhere under attack by states enamoured of the illusory benefits of a free market. The question of how tenants can organise collectively, what their aims should be, and how they can achieve them are pressing matters for these times.

This book is about the tenants' movement, the organised and sometimes spontaneous collective action of tenants fighting for a fairer housing system. Tenant protests and campaigns are the inevitable result of the monopoly ownership of property, and its application as fixed capital to levy rents, charge interest and sustain a global financial infrastructure that has extended its influence into every aspect of human relationships (Harvey 2010). The promotion of homeownership as the 'natural' way of life has rendered whole populations vulnerable to the fickle trends and reckless practices of finance capital and staked out a landscape of dramatically widening inequality (Glynn 2009). Residential property sits within an increasingly global market as institutional landlords, public assets and private mortgage portfolios are traded on international finance markets, and local house prices and rents are inflated by the investment strategies of distant speculators (Hodkinson 2012).

Housing policy does not develop in a benign progress of legislative justice but is forged through the social and economic struggles that are inevitable in unequal and divided societies (Johnstone 2000). The provision of decent housing has been fought for and won by thousands of people in grass-roots campaigns, in direct action and protest, over many decades. The tenants' movement was born in a popular struggle to protect housing from the market system, to decommodify it, provide it affordably, and allocate it on principles of need, not greed. It emerged in countries around the world in a wave of mass support for the development of welfare-state systems of redistribution, collective insurance and socialised risk. As the remaining elements of collective protection from the heavy hand of the market are everywhere rolled back, the tenants' movement continues to promote the standards and values of a socialised and fairer housing service and, as a consequence, finds itself opposed to the exploitation of 'the people's home' as a capitalist commodity (Harloe 1995; Peck and Tickell 2002; Harvey 2003).

Recent years have seen a wave of housing protests against the displacement of working-class residents by state-backed regeneration schemes that have raised rents and property values through gentrification (Allen 2008). Homeless encampments have sprouted at the margins of major cities in response to a wave of repossessions and foreclosures following the 2008 subprime mortgage crash. This process of 'accumulation by dispossession' (Harvey 2003) in the global North mirrors the continuing enclosure and privatisation of property in the South to create a newly impoverished industrial proletariat. Housing remains a key question of public policy, not just for the overcrowded megacities of South and South East Asia (Forrest and Lee 2003), or for the slums and favelas of the industrialising global south (Davis 2006a), but for Western countries whose problems of affordability, job insecurity and increased personal risk now force a significant retreat from homeownership among younger generations. In the stark division between those who have capital and those who have none, the growth of the private rental sector across the globe operates as a recognisable marker of injustice. Alongside the land struggles and mass trespasses of dispossessed peasants (Corr 1999) and the protests of the urban homeless (Wright 1997), the tenants' movement is engaged in a Promethean struggle against a housing system that is fundamentally broken.

Tenants' movements remain a potent force across the globe in campaigns for affordable and socially provided housing. The International Union of Tenants (IUT) has 61 member associations in 45 countries, consultation status with the United Nations and the European Union, and is pressing nation states for the implementation of the right to adequate housing, and the adoption of a tenants' charter on standards of affordability, security of tenure and participation in decision-making. While the IUT has its base in Europe, its membership extends to the USA, Canada, Australia and New Zealand, Russia, Japan, India, South Africa, Kenya, Nigeria and many other African countries. In the USA, where the rented sector has been expanding rapidly since 2000 and now makes up over 30 per cent of all homes, tenants' campaigns have successfully pressed for rent controls, opposed state-funded programmes of dispossession and entrenched the principles of residents' action in the political life of many urban centres (Dreier 1984; Somerville 2012), while the National Alliance of HUD Tenants (2013) stretches across thirty states in its campaign to preserve affordable housing and protect the rights of residents housed in private multi-family housing under the US Department of Housing and Urban Development's voucher programme (Hackworth 2009). In Australia, where the size of the rented sector has also increased to nearly 30 per cent, there are tenants' unions in nearly all states providing legal support through tenants' advice and

FIGURE 1.1 International Union of Tenants (IUT): Cora Carter, Secretary of the Tenants and Residents Organisations of England (TAROE), signs an agreement with the Spanish tenants' organisation, the Federació d'Associaciones de Veïns d'Habitage Social de Catalunya

Photo provided by Kirklees Federation of Tenants and Residents Associations

advocacy services, and representing the interests of private renters and social housing tenants, boarders and lodgers. Social housing is at a premium in Australia where it provides scanty protection for the most vulnerable. The Japanese Tenants Union, with 500 local branches, has campaigned against the suppression of social house building and the privatisation of the state housing agency, and advocates on behalf of private renters, who make up 27 per cent of all households. These movements describe themselves as non-governmental organisations (NGOs); they are pressure groups rather than political campaigns and, in an intensely urbanised world where the provision of housing is left to the sleight of hand of the market and distributed regressively, they fight a rearguard action for the recognition of a human right to affordable, secure and decent housing.

Housing is a commodity that can be provided at a profit under capitalism and there are vested interests to oppose any moves to make it affordable. Mass privatisation of state or municipal housing has been enacted across the Russian Federation and the former Eastern bloc, and has spread into Japan and Hong Kong with its large public housing sector, while the provision of social housing in the heartlands of European social democracy is now under threat. In Sweden, where the Swedish Tenants Union still provides the premier model for tenants' movements in other countries, the erosion of the social democratic consensus that combined rent controls with generous subsidies to multi-family housing, municipal housing companies and tenant co-ops has been stark. A public housing sector supposedly open to all has been shrunk to 18 per cent of stock, as homes have been demolished, sold to affluent tenant co-operatives or purchased by sitting tenants. Swedish governments have funded the growth of the private market through regressive taxation and have shattered their policy of tenure neutrality in the promotion of home ownership (Clark and Johnson 2009). Founded in 1923, the Swedish Union of Tenants has over 528,000 individual members, 3,000 local organisations and a national secretariat employing 900 staff. As well as providing housing support and numerous benefits to its members, it is a campaigning organisation that lobbies for the development of affordable homes and tenure neutrality in state policy. It was a central agent in the development of social democratic housing strategy and in securing fairness in the rented sector. The Swedish Union of Tenants won the legal right to negotiate rents in the municipal housing stock, and has agreed the same annual collective bargaining process with landlords across 90 per cent of the private rental sector. Up until 2011, rents in the private sector were set with reference to the rents charged in nearby municipal housing. Property companies mounted the first of several legal challenges to the rent negotiation process and the role of municipal housing in setting limits on private rents in 2005. These challenges resulted in a European Commission anti-competition ruling that forced municipal housing companies to become profit-making and barred them from receiving subsidies, triggering the introduction of market rents in public housing. The effect of this attack by the property finance lobby is also being felt in the Netherlands, where social housing makes up 36 per cent of stock, and the transition from a universal service to a welfare safety net has been speeded by a maximum income limit imposed to restrict access to the poorest and more vulnerable (Turner 2007; Hammar 2013). The global retreat from the provision of social housing as a universal service is a major set-back to the international tenants' movement, which developed in the political ferment and revolutionary spirit of the 1920s to demand 'the introduction of social rent, and housing legislation and for a prompt promotion of municipal and jointly owned housing' (IUT Assembly 1926, quoted in IUT 2013). At a time when the private housing market has demonstrably failed to provide for people's needs, and property speculation has been fingered as the agent of global financial collapse, the raw forces of capitalism are being rolled out remorselessly to maximise profit from the right to shelter. What can the tenants' movement do to resist the state-enforced power of a rapacious property market? What can it do to keep alive a belief in collective and affordable models of housing provision?

In the United Kingdom the assault on social housing is far advanced. The municipal and not-for-profit social housing sector, comprising homes provided by councils, housing associations and co-operatives, has been reduced from 31 per cent of all homes in 1980 to a residual role of just 18 per cent (Wilcox and Pawson 2012). Mass privatisation through the provision of large discounts to sitting tenants under the Right to Buy has removed 2.5 million council houses from public supply, while demolition and under-investment, the withdrawal of security of tenure and the introduction of commercial rents have reduced the role of social housing in the UK to that of an 'ambulance service' or a temporary and increasingly conditional refuge for the most vulnerable (Fitzpatrick and Stephens 2008). Safeguards against homelessness and protection against eviction in the private sector have also been withdrawn and housing allowances capped and slashed (Hodkinson and Robbins 2012). Meanwhile, the provision of new affordable housing has been reduced to a trickle, falling from a 1975 height of 145,000 public, municipal and housing association homes built every year, to 23,000 homes in 2011, with almost all those provided by housing associations operating as semi-commercial companies heavily mortgaged to banks, financial institutions and international bond markets. Although new protest and direct action occasionally shatters its quiescence, the tenants' movement in the UK appears to have been stunned by the scale of this assault. Its small advances have been overshadowed by the regressive direction of national housing policy and the penetration of market exchange into public services based on need. Perhaps the tenants' movement has been co-opted or institutionalised by the torrent of reforms that has transformed the housing system according to the prescriptions of market theory (Mayer 2000; Somerville 2004). This book is an inquiry into a tenants' movement that has become all but invisible as a contentious force.

The idea of a tenants' movement

As in other European countries, the UK tenants' movement emerged in the struggle for social housing and in a series of bitter conflicts with property owners and their organisations, and since those early years it has been associated with the struggle for social citizenship and the demand for a more democratic and participatory welfare state (Grayson 1997, 2010). This is a movement mobilised around a passionate concern for the associational relations of community (Somerville 2012), the resources and facilities of social reproduction and a regard for future generations (Baldock 1982). The idea of a tenants' movement is driven by the organic and seemingly irrepressible dynamic of the neighbourhood tenants' association, or locality-based group (Ward 1974). Tenants associations have been a feature of the English social housing sector since the first estates were built in the 1920s and they continue to emerge in campaigns for improved local facilities, nurtured in partnerships with municipal government and social landlords, elected, accountable and formally constituted. The tendency for these local groups to organise themselves into federations at city or borough level has been the building block from which the notion of a tenants' movement has evolved (Hampton 1970; Somerville 2005b). While national tenant organisations have exercised limited effectiveness, local and federal organisations have proved much more resilient, and many of them are justifiably proud of their longevity; Newcastle Tenants and Residents Federation, for example, has been active since 1977, while others, like Kirklees Federation of Tenants and Residents Associations, were launched in the campaigns of the late

1980s, although the withdrawal of sponsorship by municipal authorities and social landlords in recent years has put an end to a number of other long-lived federations (Morgan 2006).

Neighbourhood tenants' and residents' associations have been cited frequently in community studies since the 1930s, engaged in a range of activities that include negotiating with housing organisations, municipal authorities and other statutory agencies, agitating, campaigning on local issues and promoting 'community spirit' through social activities (Cairncross *et al.* 1992). Some accounts have portrayed tenants' associations as short-lived and fractious (Andrews 1979; Ravetz 2001; Uguris 2004), while others have attributed their tenacity disapprovingly to the pursuit of social welfare aims rather than campaigns and direct action (Sklair 1975; Lowe 1986). The establishment of meeting places, tenants' halls or community centres, and subsequent concerns about their upkeep, facilities and improvement has occupied much of the history of local associations (Ravetz 2001), and these have been the base for social activities aimed at generating 'solidarity around an estate consciousness' (Olechnowicz 1997: 200). A culture of estate newsletters, sports clubs, youth groups, galas, fêtes and social events, food co-ops, parents' and toddlers' groups and lunch clubs has been built up around local tenants' associations and their generation of a sense of place (Durant 1939; Mitchell and Lupton 1954; Jupp 2008). Only about 3 per cent of all social housing tenants are involved in tenant groups but the movement should be conceived as a network that links activists and non-activists within the same geographical community in a cross-cutting pattern of interaction. Around 38 per cent of social housing tenants are aware of their local tenants' and residents' association (TSA 2009); they routinely meet members of the association in public places, at the bus stop or the local shops (Gibson 1979), and are linked by bonds of personal commitment and interdependency, the 'intersecting social networks in which the collective of movement members are embedded' (Stoecker 1995: 12). Lesley Andrews's (1979) fascinating study of a neighbourhood tenants' association revealed the web of family relationships and friendships that extend the activities of the association outside of its formal meetings and committee structure into the wider social networks of the neighbourhood. This diversity in movement participation was expanded beyond the ranks of social housing tenants by the success of policies aimed at promoting homeownership through the privatisation of municipal housing and the development of mixed tenure estates. Social housing now encompasses a range of tenures, including intermediate market rent and shared ownership, and tenants' and residents' associations may include council tenants, housing association tenants, leaseholders, former council tenants who have bought their own home, private tenants and homeowners.

At the centre of this collective culture, the tenants' association has encountered a mixture of patronage and disciplinary intervention from municipal and charitable social landlords, and many supposedly autonomous associations have been initiated and effectively regulated by the landlord as part of their management strategies. The majority of associations, however, are set up by tenants themselves, with or without help from housing or community-work practitioners, and rely on the

FIGURE 1.2 A passionate concern: fancy-dress parade at the tenants' association gala on the Harley estate in Rotherham in the north of England

Photo provided by RotherFed

organisational ability of their members for their effectiveness. They spring up to negotiate with the landlord over issues of local housing management, or to improve local facilities, or to mobilise against potential threats. Even in the turmoil of the rent strikes of the 1960s and 1970s, the primary spark for new tenants' associations was the issue of local housing management and the sense of belonging to a defined neighbourhood (Hampton 1970; Moorhouse *et al.* 1972; Kaye *et al.* 1977). This local focus has led to successful and sustained mobilisation aimed at ensuring participation or greater democratic involvement in housing management. The bitter protests over rents, rebates and security of tenure that have characterised the history of a tenants' movement, the fierce struggles over housing conditions, estate facilities, inadequate heating, damp, system building and alienating estate design, were at their root an enduring campaign for more say in decisions that affect the neighbourhood (Craddock 1975; Rao 1984). The role of the tenants' association in agitating on these issues – some of which became national campaigns, and involved the construction of broad networks and the formulation of joint strategy – has been as the representative of local interests. Tenants' associations are formed in a desire for collective representation and in the need for collective advocacy. They are expressions of neighbourhood democracy; as Ruth Durant (1939: 38) noted so long ago, they virtually form 'a nucleus of local government'. They promote a model of participatory democracy grounded in the routine interactions of place and the formal processes that ensure accountability, and enable redress and renewal. Any failures of tenants' associations to adequately represent varying interests, their propensity to decline into cliques, and to initiate feuds between factions (Andrews 1979; Ravetz 2001) are inevitable outcomes of the democratic process and its recognition of conflicting interests. This focus on collective representation rather than leadership, and on democratic engagement rather than confrontation, is fundamental to the definition of local tenants' organisations, and is one transmitted by their delegates to the federal organisations, ensuring the idea of a tenants' movement is oriented towards social inclusion rather than political antagonism. A denial of political goals is written into the constitutions of tenants' organisations and is seen as an essential mark of their legitimacy. This disavowal of politics dates back to the rent strikes of the 1960s (Kaye *et al.* 1977; Lowe 1986; Grayson 2007) and is a reminder of the marginalisation of social housing tenants from the mainstream concerns of political parties, and the displacement of community and neighbourhood struggles from the workplace agitation of the labour movement. Although widely interpreted as meaning non-party political, this constitutional disengagement from political strategy undermines opposition to state initiatives that are associated with party ideologies. It explains the limited political achievements of national tenants' organisations, and accounts too for the immersion and domestication of tenant collective action in the government-sanctioned policy of public participation.

After forty years of public participation and collaborative governance in social housing policy, it is unclear to what extent there remains a tenants' movement in the UK and what, if anything, it aims to achieve (Ravetz 2001). Tenant activists have been co-opted as surrogate managers (Sullivan 2001) enmeshed in the compromises of governance, while tenants' organisations are increasingly excluded from policy making as the unrepresentative congregation of the 'usual suspects' (Barnes *et al.* 2003, Millward 2005). The strategy of public participation has been a stepping stone for the transference of free market principles to the provision of social housing and public services in the UK more generally. The forces of 'voice' and 'exit' (Hirschman 1970; Paul 1992) have been applied to simulate market dynamics in the distribution of public goods, and where opportunities for exit or competition have been limited, it has fallen to 'voice' or participation to exert consumer pressure and to change the relationship between the public and public services (Barnes *et al.* 2003; Newman and Clarke 2009). Where participation initially generated growth in the number of tenants' organisations (Cairncross *et al.* 1994), more recently it has diminished their influence. In the 1990s, three-quarters of all housing associations supported local tenants' associations, while federal tenants' movements flourished in 20 per cent of local authority areas (Bines *et al.* 1993; Aldbourne Associates 2001). The support for participation evidenced by Conservative and Labour governments from the mid-1970s led to the development of tenants' organisations at both neighbourhood and regional levels. Regeneration monies from government investment programmes like the Priority Estates Programme, Estate Action, City Challenge, Single Regeneration Budget and New Deal for Communities were dependent on the involvement of tenants' and residents' organisations. Compulsory competitive tendering for housing management in 1995, the launch of the Best Value regime and Tenant Participation Compacts in 1998, and the regulatory pressure of the Housing Corporation, Audit Commission and the short-lived Tenant Services Authority all spurred social housing landlords to resource tenants' organisations, while government funding for tenant management organisations was available from 1986 (Furbey *et al.* 1996; Vincent-Jones and Harries 1998; Hickman 2006).

This period of growth was reversed at the end of the 1990s when, under direction from state regulators, social landlords began to adopt market-research techniques to profile their tenants as customers and to dispense with the collective representation of tenants' associations and federations (Cole *et al.* 2001). A number of local authorities and housing associations withdrew financial support from tenants' federations and replaced them with customer forums and consumer panels (Morgan 2006; Grayson 2007). Between 2008 and 2013 five tenants' federations lost their funding or had it frozen pending financial reviews, while government support for a national tenants' organisation was withdrawn. Out of six regional federations set up after 1997 to mirror the Labour government's devolved structure of governance, three had been dissolved, or ceased functioning by 2010 (Housing Corporation 2007; IRIS Consulting 2010). The contemporary tenants' movement in England is represented by a national organisation, Tenants and Residents Organisations of England (TAROE), established in 1997, together with national organisations for tenant management and co-operative housing. While TAROE has only 101 tenants' groups as members (TAROE 2012), the tenant participation consultancy, TPAS, governed by a management board that includes landlords' representatives, has a national membership of 1,195 tenant organisations. There are three regional tenants' federations and a further 37 subregional tenants' federations, 14 of which describe themselves as Tenant Participation Networks or Involvement Groups, and in some cases include landlord representatives on their committees, making clear their function as facilitators of participation with housing companies (IRIS Consulting 2010). At the last outdated count there were more than 10,000 local tenants' and residents' associations on social housing estates (Aldbourne Associates 2001; Cole *et al.* 2000), but these neighbourhood groups are often set up and sponsored by housing organisations to fulfil their requirements for customer involvement. Still more tenant collective action is facilitated, convened and mediated by landlords in constituted or informally assembled panels or forums, while individual tenants are recruited to serve on scrutiny panels, monitor their landlord as tenant inspectors, or become directors of social housing organisations. While some tenant campaigns and protests continue in the defence of social housing, the line between a self-organised urban movement and a landlord-led consultation process is now extremely unclear. Collective action by tenants has been condensed into the rule-governed, reiterative process of participation, the subject of 'how to' manuals for housing practitioners (Cooper and Hawtin 1997). This collective action, however, remains a significant feature of the social housing sector and, according to the most recent Citizenship Survey (DCLG 2009d), membership of a tenants' association is the second most common form of 'civic activism'. It would appear that a tenants' movement still exists in the contemporary landscape of social housing, although perhaps in a new form, and that it is characterised by its participation and partnerships, and not by its direct action.

A domesticated movement?

The tendency for contentious protests to become institutionalised and co-opted by state institutions has haunted the studies of social movements. Social welfare and urban movements, such as the tenants' movement, have been particularly prone to these dynamics, enmeshed as they are in the intricacies of welfare systems and the municipal processes of government (Mayer 2000; Pruijt 2003; Kavoulakos 2006). The restructuring of the welfare state and the outsourcing of the public sector propagated by market theory has provided suitable grounds for the absorption of social movements into new networks of collaboration and partnership (Somerville 2004). Voluntary and community organisations and neighbourhood campaign groups have been recruited as supposed partners or agencies of governance in local economic regeneration programmes, and promoted as models of initiative and enterprise, purveyors of the responsibility and self-help expected of subjects of government (Hamel *et al.* 2000; Fyfe 2005). The domesticating effect of this patronage from local government or institutional authorities on previously disruptive movements has been well documented in studies that have observed the processes of professionalisation, the displacement of goals and the growing influence of 'responsible' approaches in formerly contentious organisations (Zald and Ash 1966; McCarthy and Zald 1977; Piven and Cloward 1977; Jenkins and Eckert 1986, Taylor 1989). The polarity of militancy or quiescence implied in these studies has been challenged by queer theorist and feminist philosopher Judith Butler, who argues that social movements exist in more complex and sometimes co-dependent interactions with established power relations. In her essays in *Contingency, Hegemony, Universality*, co-authored with Laclau and Žižek, Butler (2000) argues that movements attain recognition by replicating norms, thereby reinforcing existing relations of power, and that contentious politics may achieve its aims by exercising regulatory outcomes. Where co-option describes an external collective actor sucked into systems of governance, Butler applies the concept of 'domestication' to signal the continuation of contentious claims from social movements that otherwise appear enmeshed in institutional partnerships (Butler 2000: 157). Domesticated movements may continue to harbour oppositional aims and promote values that challenge the dominant power relations while, importantly, regulatory discourses that seek to co-opt and disarm social movements may give rise to new waves of contentious politics (Cress 1997; Tarrow 1998; Pruijt 2003; Townsend *et al.* 2004).

The theoretical framework that guides this book and its investigation of a tenants' movement is drawn from the work of Judith Butler and will be only briefly introduced here and examined more fully as the argument is developed in subsequent chapters. Butler provides a rigorous approach to thinking about social movements within the constraints of power, and one of her most controversial contributions to academic study is in theorising contestation without attributing to it the traditional agency that allows collective action to appear as a force external to, and independent of, dominant power relations. Judith Butler's theories of hegemony (2000), interpellation and performativity (1990, 1993, 1997a, 1997b) provide interpretive tools to understand the power relations at work in tenant participation and explain the generation of continuing claims to the existence of a tenants' movement from a fragmented and individualised tenant body. Butler's interpretation of the theory of hegemony stresses the contingent and precarious nature of the power exercised by elites and guides her theory of how social change can be achieved by 'domesticated' movements. Hegemony is an attempt by a social group to portray its ambitions in universal terms and to recruit, or 'articulate', other groups to its world view (Butler 2000: 13). The resulting hegemonic discourse takes on the universal status of 'common sense' and offers itself as a surface in which a range of social groups can see reflected their own values and interests. As an operation of power, hegemony is a regulatory process that attributes social identity by establishing norms. In defining normality, it creates and outlaws the abnormal, and for every identity that is attributed there are those that are repudiated as illegitimate, irrational and incoherent (Smith 1998; Howarth and Stavrakakis 2000). Hegemony, then, has what Butler (1993: 3) calls a 'constitutive outside' and the shadows of its excluded identities are a constant reminder of the possibilities that have been foreclosed to impose order, and a constant threat of the return of antagonism. Hegemony remains 'incomplete, open and politically negotiable' (Laclau and Mouffe 2001: 104), threatened by the return of these excluded dynamics. Judith Butler adds considerably to the definition of hegemony formulated in Laclau and Mouffe's (2001) *Hegemony and Socialist Strategy* by theorising the establishment of norms as embodied in the subject and expressed through day-to-day social practice, and she contributes two new dimensions that are particularly useful for applying this concept to tenant participation. The first is an understanding of how normative identities are attributed to individuals and groups. Her theory of interpellation presents personal identity as a social construction assembled and reproduced in daily relations in which the experience of social recognition also acts as a regulatory 'call to order' (Butler 1997b). In everyday interaction subjects cite the norms and regulations of hegemonic power to perform and reproduce a social identity. This identity, a socially sanctioned attribution of permissions and exclusions, must be constantly renewed in 'a regularised and constrained repetition of norms' (Butler 1993: 95). Butler's theory of performativity maintains that this constant process of repetition may not reproduce social identity as an exact copy and instead has the potential to expand the boundaries of what is considered normal and acceptable. By performing identity the subject may change it and the way in which power relations are transformed is through their daily reiteration (Butler 2000: 14). The contentious politics of social movements are, then, projects of repeated erosion, or what Butler (1993: 237) refers to as 'working the weakness in the norm'. They cannot achieve liberation; instead, Butler talks of 'critical subversion' and 'radical resignification' (Butler 2004b: 334). The social change that can be initiated through performativity is for Judith Butler: 'Not a "pure" opposition, a "transcendence" of contemporary relations of power, but a difficult labour of forging a future from resources inevitably impure' (Butler 1993: 241).

Butler illustrates her conception of social change in a study of the rights-claims of gay and lesbian movements (Butler 2000). She argues that to demand human rights for gays and lesbians is to situate a movement within existing dominant conceptions of citizenship, in which the norm is presented as heterosexual, to the exclusion of gays and lesbians. In making a claim on human rights, gay and lesbian movements reiterate the norm of heterosexuality, and by doing so, make their claim intelligible within the existing boundaries of discourse. Yet their claim to rights presents homosexuality as potentially normative, and thereby challenges the limitations of the concept of human rights and the discourse of exclusion it maintains. The successful outcome of gay and lesbian campaigns for human rights will be their absorption into normative discourse; they will be 'liberated into a new mode of subjection that the doctrine of citizenship has in store' (Butler 2000: 40). In Butler's thesis, the acts of resistance of social movements emerge in routine engagement with the exclusionary practices that provide them with intelligibility, and their success is measured in the expansion of what is considered normal or acceptable in hegemonic discourse. In applying Butler's approach, the study of the tenants' movement begins, then, in the power relations of participation and the domestication of tenant collective action in strategies of devolved governance. It does not search exclusively for direct action or confrontation but instead examines the contentious politics that arise from the engagement of tenants with social housing organisations and their partnerships with the agencies of governance.

A tenants' movement in its own words

This book offers the first account of the contemporary tenants' movement in England. Its aim is to investigate the collective action of tenants in the social housing sector; their goals, organisation and beliefs; to evaluate the extent of the movement's 'domestication', and to debate its potential resurgence. The study of the tenants' movement must start in a specific locality and only in the particular and the local does this movement begin to make sense. In the UK, housing policy has been devolved to the Scottish Parliament since 1999, with full powers granted to Wales in May 2011, and the tenants' movement has taken distinctive directions in both countries, and its own trajectory in Northern Ireland. In Scotland a strong labour movement tradition continues to manifest itself in the tenants' movement and in a mutual model of stock transfer. In Wales, a countrywide tenants' federation is resourced by the Welsh Assembly and represented in policy making. The focus of this book is on the tenants' movement of England and the continuing and evolving dynamic of resident involvement, community action and contentious politics in housing in that country. It seeks to uncover the contentions of a popular movement that has been hidden from history and marginalised in contemporary academic debate. It draws on primary research conducted between 2008 and 2012 with residents in council and social rented housing in England active in tenants' organisations and in participation with their social landlords. The participants in this research were drawn from landlord forums, customer panels and scrutiny boards, from tenant directors of social housing companies and board members of tenant management organisations and other tenant-led housing companies, from tenants' association and tenants' federation committees, from regional and national tenants' organisations and tenant campaign groups. The aim was to engage a very broad range of tenants engaged in participation activities with social landlords and achieve a wide geographical spread, and the research involved 151 participants, was carried out in six cities across England, and at three consecutive national conferences of the tenant participation agency, TPAS, an event that draws over 800 attendees and is seen as the principal networking opportunity for the tenants' movement. The research was conducted in fifteen focus groups and ten paired or single interviews, with the average discussion lasting one and a half hours, and with additional data collected in a qualitative survey. The research brought together tenants and leaseholders from housing associations, stock transfer organisations, arm's-length management organisations and retained council housing authorities, along with a number of owner-occupiers active in residents' organisations, although for simplicity the sample are referred to as 'tenants' throughout. Names used in the research are, with some exceptions, fictitious but extracts from conversations and interviews have been transcribed in detail (for a transcription key, see Appendix 1) with deviations, hesitations and repetitions included so that the voices of tenants can be heard without mediation. Where participants are quoted directly, a reference number is included so that they can be identified in the schedule of research (available in Appendix 2).

At this point I should introduce myself as the author, as someone who has worked for tenants' federations, and with tenants' organisations for fifteen years, and has been involved in community action for the larger part of his life. Working under the direction of tenant management committees, I helped established scores of new tenants' and residents' associations, leafleted estates, engaged people on the doorstep, organised public meetings, and helped groups develop their constitutions and action plans. I was unfailingly impressed by the readiness of residents on social housing estates to organise collectively when they could see clear benefits from their action. It was harder to maintain groups once their immediate goals had been achieved, but the commitment of some association members to the improvement of their neighbourhood and its facilities was awe-inspiring. I worked on trail-blazing involvement projects with young people, ethnic minority and refugee groups through which the federations renewed their membership and ensured they represented a diversity of needs. Delegates' meetings, and the conferences and seminars of tenants' federations provided the opportunities for residents to share experiences, argue policy, and make face-to-face representations to decision-makers. I facilitated working groups in which tenant federation members engaged with housing professionals to develop policy or review standards and processes, and organised mystery shopping, scrutiny and inspection services that enabled tenants to hold social landlords to account. I witnessed many times over the process of collective and personal empowerment, a growth in confidence, knowledge and capabilities that involvement in a tenants' organisation brought to its members; the anger too, at the continual stigma, and the government legislation that annulled everything tenants felt was just. I saw also many failings in tenants' organisations; it was very difficult for their management committees to exercise leadership when their only experience was of authoritarian supervision at their former workplaces. Project groups and delegates meetings were successful in enabling tenants to contribute experiential knowledge to policy development by housing professionals, but they were less useful in enabling tenants to develop their own policies by abstracting from their direct experience into more general conclusions. The federations gave some members a sense of limited power, which they were content to enjoy rather than to put to use to pursue their organisation's goals. I noted how senior officials in housing organisations became skilled at cultivating a desire for prestige among the federations' tenant leadership in order to gain approval for, or weaken opposition to, controversial decisions. Although many tenants' associations did extraordinary work in their neighbourhoods, there were some local groups whose main interest was in exerting informal social control over those residents who had attracted their disapproval, and the disciplinary role of these groups existed in uneasy counterbalance to their enthusiastic support for neighbourly relations. Having been inspired to a vocation with tenants' organisations by the example of community workers schooled in the non-directive tradition of the 1970s' Community Development Projects, it was not always easy, while working directly for tenants' federations, to remember why I thought they were a progressive force. In approaching this book I wanted to examine these ambivalent feelings, and to take a fresh look at the role of tenants' organisations and their achievements; to ask whether it is possible to talk about a tenants' movement at all, and if so, whether it can be a force for social change.

The tenants' movement is characterised as one that has rarely spoken in its own words; instead, its story has been told through the accounts of political activists or housing academics. In the face of a 'historically muted subject' (Spivak 1988: 295), the intention behind this book is to let the counter narratives of tenants do much of the talking. The book could not have been written without the active encouragement of its tenant participants, and this has been a collective inquiry into the existence or otherwise of a tenants' movement in which tenants and researcher have been engaged with equal curiosity and interest. Many of the participants of the focus groups expressed their appreciation of the opportunity to debate issues in discussions with other tenants and residents. Four of the focus groups carried out with tenants' federations took place immediately following a formal committee meeting of the organisation and this meant that the group discussion served as a more informal and discursive extension of the organisation's own deliberations.

In these situations the focus group approximated the 'free spaces' or 'havens' of social movement theory (Fantasia and Hirsch 1995; Polletta 1999), a supportive and sheltered environment in which personal experience can be shared and in which one person's opinion can become a general call to arms (Gamson 1992). In conducting the research I tried to reduce the influence of my frame of reference and to adopt a research strategy that aimed to transfer power from the researcher to the participant (Wilkinson 1999). In focus groups I allowed the participants the freedom to lead and direct the conversation to ensure the discussion was influenced by the relationships among the participants and by their responses. I withheld comments that might have influenced the direction of conversation, and waited through momentary silences to encourage further deliberation, deciding not to intervene when group discussions developed into disagreement between individual participants. The analysis of the tenants' movement that emerges is my own and some participants may not agree with my conclusions. My analysis is clearly a construction of the 'truth', an interpretation of findings by a partial and privileged researcher, and perhaps it cannot hope to reflect accurately a movement that exists only in 'the thoughts and practices of thousands of people in a host of localities' (Hague 1990: 245). But this book has been inspired and informed by tenants and their organisations, by people who are subjects in their own right, and who have their own views on the construction of a tenants' movement. I hope that their voices can be heard clearly in the pages that follow.

The trajectory of the book

I argue in this book that a tenants' movement is not a product of material interests, or essential bonds of commonality, but is, instead, a painstaking process of identity work (Snow and McAdam 2000), in which a shared understanding of unity is assembled (Melucci 1989; Gamson 1992). In advancing this argument the book brings housing policy together with social movement studies for the first time since the 1980s to investigate the identity work of tenants and chart the assemblage of the collective identity of a tenants' movement (Melucci 1989, 1996). The search for the contemporary tenants' movement begins in Chapter 2 by exploring the unifying narratives put forward in the literature of urban and community studies and their representation of a radical history of rent strikes and protests, intraclass divisions between homeownership and renting, and the emergence of consumer models of collective action. In the face of the divisions that now characterise the social housing sector, the chapter articulates a new framework through the study of social welfare and urban movements and constructs a rationale in the theory of collective identity to drive its investigation.

Chapter 3 explores the enmeshment of tenant collective action in participation with social landlords, and its submersion in a policy of resident involvement, where all recognition of power dynamics has been removed to make way for market-like models of voice and exit. The chapter examines the enthusiasm with which tenants' organisations initially greeted opportunities for participation, and explains how the policy was applied to introduce market forces into social housing as part of an overall restructuring of public services and the welfare state. Drawing on primary research it charts the exclusion of combative ideas of democracy and equality from the dominant discourse of participation, but evidences too the revelatory effect participation still has for tenants presented with the possibility of empowerment. The chapter advances an innovative framework based on the political philosophy of Judith Butler to interpret participation as a regulatory discourse that attributes identities and engenders subjectivity, and that constitutes a tenants' movement at the same time as it domesticates it.

The awakening of a social movement is the subject of Chapter 4, which demonstrates in the words of tenants themselves how notions of a political public can be articulated from the regulated practices of participation. The chapter explores the reclamation of excluded notions of social rights from market relationships and observes the construction of the boundary markers that delineate a tenants' movement and provide it with a history and a language with which to articulate its vision. Applying the social movement technique of frame analysis, Chapter 4 evidences a convergence of identifications and beliefs among tenants engaged in strategies of public participation. It analyses the construction of collective identity around familiar reference points and storylines with recognisable structures and meanings. The evocation of a combative social movement is assembled around shared belief in the collective provision of housing expressed in opposition to the individualising effects of the market, and reveals the assemblage of common cause in assertions of co-operation and mutual aid and a commitment to the associational relations of community. This theme is developed further in the emergence of antagonism towards the dominance of professional interpretations of need in opposition to the values of experiential knowledge. The chapter evidences the emergence of a contentious belief system that defines the political boundaries of a tenants' movement, marks out its allegiances and identifies its antagonists.

Developing this theme, Chapter 5 charts the construction of interpretative frames around the grass-roots models of participatory and direct democracy that provide a tenants' movement with its distinctive organisational culture. The chapter explores the involvement of tenant organisations in the political strategy of localism, and their cultivation of the discourse of community to invoke an ethic of care around the active production of a sense of place. A commitment to participatory models of governance is shown to motivate collective action in the locality, and provides the structures and democratic principles around which a wider social movement might be mobilised. These collective identity frames challenge the power relations embedded in housing organisations and in the governance of public services more generally and champion a potentially prefigurative model of popular participation in which decision-making is devolved to the locality and rooted in direct experience.

Chapter 6 undercuts the identity work of these collective action frames to investigate their mobilising potential. It points to the failure of assumptions of common cause to generate movement organisation among tenants. Identifications of apathy drawn from divisive strategies of welfare reform are shown to be routinely used to argue against organisation building and block articulations of strategy. The chapter evaluates the extent to which tenant identity work constructs a tenants' movement with aims and action plans, and it presents a vivid picture of its organisational ability, its resources and its ability to exploit its political opportunities. It explores the fragmentation of the contemporary movement, and charts the effect of patronage in the rise of professionalism and the loss of contention, and the challenges facing the mobilisation of national tenants' organisations. The chapter reaches an assessment of the aims and strategic purpose of a tenants' movement and identifies the effect of its domestication and the potential for the resurgence of tenant collective action. Finally, Chapter 7 concludes this exploration of the contemporary tenants' movement and sets out its defining contentions, assessing its successes and limitations, and advancing a framework for understanding the effectiveness of the domesticated social movement. This concluding chapter evaluates the impact of contentious politics in housing within the context of market-oriented regimes and reflects on the development of a distinctive tenant voice and the apparent resilience of ideas of social citizenship in the restructuring of public services. The resurgence of contentious identities among social housing tenants points to the continuing significance of a tenants' movement in housing and community action.

2

THE HIDDEN HISTORY
OF TENANTS

The history of the tenants' movement has never been a value-neutral narrative in which 'what really happened' is uncovered and retold. The tenants' movement is hidden from history, in Sheila Rowbotham's (1973) memorable phrase, rarely able to represent itself, or to make itself heard as a subject. It has expressed itself in the ephemera of leaflets and posters and in a handful of policy documents, but has left little record in its own words (Lowe 1986; Hague 1990; Grayson 1997). Researchers filling this vacuum have conjured a tenants' movement from storylines that reflected their own concerns, or the discourses of the time, constructing narratives of insurgency and resistance, of class struggle and consumer protest. In each of these representations, the tenants' movement emerges as a consequence of 'objective' material interests that motivate and partially determine its collective action. This chapter does not attempt to present a chronological history of the tenants' movement; it is, rather, an analysis of depictions of a tenants' movement contextualised and evidenced from incidents in the movement's history. It first reviews the persuasive characterisation of the tenants' movement as a class struggle for affordable housing, an interpretation that offers a history of rent strikes and protests in which tenants fight for the collective provision of housing as a partially decommodified public service. The weakness of this analysis in accounting for the growth of working-class homeownership or in recognising the importance of intra-class divisions over access to housing explains the emergence in the 1980s of a tenants' movement modelled on conflicting interests of housing consumption. As social housing became subject to market-based strategies of public service reform and privatisation, the tenants' movement was depicted as a consumer group or consumer watchdog, and the study of collective action declined under the pervasive influence of individualising discourses. This chapter critically reviews each of these representations of a tenants' movement and, in the failure of theories of material interest to adequately explain the struggles around social housing, concludes by turning to social movement theory, and particularly to the concept of collective identity to provide a basis for new analysis of the English tenants' movement.

Tenant collective action and class struggle

The identification of tenants' organisations with class interests and class struggle is rooted historically in the campaign for the development of publicly subsidised housing prior to and during the First World War. The Social Democratic Federation, the Workmen's National Housing Council, British Socialist Party, Independent Labour Party, Trades Councils and the Labour Party were all instrumental in the organisation of Tenants' Defence Leagues, rent strike committees and tenants' associations from the 1860s into the early years of the twentieth century, and in co-ordinating tenant agitation over rents and housing conditions for the urban working class that culminated in a series of rent strikes against landlord associations prior to and during World War I (Ginsburg 1979; Englander 1983; Grayson 1997). The influence of socialist groups in channelling these protests into the development of a political campaign for public housing was particularly noticeable in rent strikes in Leeds in 1914 and Glasgow in 1915. There have been some attempts to dispute the class basis of these early rent strikes, and to underline the limited nature of the demand for public housing they championed (Castells 1983; Melling 1983; Bradley 1997), but this tide of militant tenant action, culminating in the threat of a general strike across dockyards and munitions factories, and the spectre of socialist revolution, resulted in the imposition of rent controls on the private rented sector, and has been persuasively credited with the birth of council or municipal housing (Damer 2000).

The Housing Acts of 1919 and 1924 provided central government subsidies and local property tax or rates support for council house building on cottage estates modelled on the utopian design principles of the Garden City movement. This commitment to high standards and substantial public subsidy in the development of working-class housing was a response to the political power and economic muscle of tenants and organised labour evidenced in the rent strikes, as well as to the emergency conditions of the war (Malpass 1990). The new council housing was unaffordable to all but the highest paid and skilled working families, and was seen by most policy makers as a temporary solution in the absence of private market provision for these client groups. The general needs model of council house building was never designed to help those living in the worst housing conditions in the private sector, and high rents and discriminatory allocations policies ensured the exclusion or marginalisation of the unskilled and non-working class, women-headed households and ethnic minority groups from many of the benefits of council housing. It would have required much higher capital subsidies to make council rents affordable for the lowest paid (Glynn 2009). The contention that general needs council housing was intended 'for all' (CDP 1976: 31) indicates the promotion of the specific material interests of the most powerful sector of the working class as universal, and underlines the political and economic powerlessness of the unskilled and unorganised tenants whose exclusion rendered them non-people. When, by the late 1920s, the private house-building market had recovered and organised labour was weakened by mass unemployment, council housing subsidies were redirected away from general needs provision and towards the public health goals of slum clearance. The abandonment of subsidies for general needs housing in 1935 was intended to remove competition with the private sector and enable it to expand to cater for the better-off skilled working-class market. Rents were raised in order to squeeze out affluent tenants while the status of council housing declined with the reduction and targeting of subsidies through means-tested rent rebates aimed at limiting council housing to a welfare safety-net role (Ravetz 2001).

Tenant rent strikes in the 1930s in Leeds and Birmingham (Ginsburg 1979; Finnigan 1984; Bradley 1999) opposed the rent rises and rebates that accompanied the ending of general-needs council housing, and much of tenant collective action since then can be interpreted as defence of the principle of public subsidies for affordable housing that is allocated without a means test (Harloe 1995; Hodgkinson *et al.* 2013). This model of capital subsidy was linked powerfully with the idea of a universal right to housing after World War II when demobilised service personnel and newly formed households encountered a housing crisis worsened by the years of bomb damage and destruction. A mass squatting movement erupted as disused army camps across the country were taken over and run collectively, while empty mansions were occupied by political groups raising radical demands over property rights and challenging the role of the private market in housing the nation (Friend 1980). These mass protests spurred the 1945–1951 Labour government to return to a general needs role for council housing, doubling the size of the public rented housing sector in six years under the championship of its Minister of Health, Aneurin Bevan. Bevan fostered a view of council housing as open to all, providing homes in communities mixed by income and social class. This rhetoric was cemented by the removal of the mention of 'housing for the working classes' from the 1949 Housing Act, appearing to give the impression that council housing was intended as a universal service, alongside the National Health Service, free education and state pensions (CDP 1976: 31; Cole and Furbey 1994). However, no attempt was made to attract middle-class tenants to council housing, while the quality of the new Bevan homes raised the rents out of the reach of poorer households, ensuring they catered mainly for those in well-paid manual work. There was little support within the civil service or the Labour cabinet as a whole for anything other than a temporary public intervention into general house building (Malpass 2005), and in 1956, under a Conservative government, housing policy reverted to promoting private ownership and private renting as the general needs housing solution, restricting the role of local authorities to slum clearance and the provision of a safety net for those excluded from the market.

In 1970 the tenants' organisation, the Association of London Housing Estates, signalled its opposition to these changes in subsidy and rent in a Tenants' Charter that set out a vision of universal council housing, under the leader: 'Housing as a non-profit making community service' (Craddock 1975: 4; Hayes 1988). The

London federation spoke out against government strategy to embed a residual role for council housing and encourage more affluent tenants to exit the sector and enter homeownership (Jacobs *et al.* 2003). Council house rents were increased as subsidies were shifted gradually from affordable house building to means-tested rent rebates that gave conditional subsidies to the poorest as a welfare benefit. Rent rebates were introduced in 1930 to accompany slum clearance, but they became a central plank in the intended residualisation of council housing from the mid-1950s. Tenant rent strikes greeted the return of this welfare policy with violent protests and rent strikes throughout the 1960s, in the London borough of St Pancras, in Sheffield, Walsall, Liverpool, and across the Greater London Council at the end of the decade (Hampton 1970; Burn 1972; Moorhouse *et al.* 1972; Kaye *et al.* 1977; Baldock 1982; Lowe 1986). New tenants' organisations were formed in these protests to lead the campaigns and resist evictions. In the St Pancras rent strike, mass pickets were mobilised through distress rockets and cars equipped with loudspeakers, while bailiffs resorted to tearing off roofs to enter barricaded flats, and police charged protesting crowds outside the town hall. The Greater London Council rent strikes of 1968–1970 witnessed a two-month siege by bailiffs of one fortified property and a mass picket outside the home of the Minister for Housing, while 20,000 tenants and trade unionists demonstrated in Trafalgar Square. In the Housing Finance Act of 1972, municipal rents were placed under central government control and linked to market prices, and a national rent rebate subsidy was brought in, signalling the end of any notion of general needs council housing. The act was met with nationwide rent strikes as 100,000 council tenants protested across the country (Sklair 1975). Tenants in at least eighty local authority areas withheld rent, and rent strikers blocked roads and barricaded factories, bringing traffic and production to a standstill in support of their cause. The failure of most Labour councils to resist the new rents emphasised the isolation of council tenants and led to the collapse of the protests, but the failure of the year-long campaign did not undermine support in the tenant movement for the general needs model of subsidy. Resistance forced a Labour government to modify the Housing Finance Act, and the launch of a new national tenants' organisation was accompanied in 1978 by a Tenants' Charter, which began, 'The right to decent housing is a fundamental right' (Hood and Woods 1994: 64).

It was the practical intervention by socialist campaigners into the housing struggles of the 1970s that helped construct the image of a radical tenants' movement and bequeath anti-capitalist goals to the politics of community action. This engagement in neighbourhood action was associated inspirationally with the Community Development Projects, a Home Office funded programme launched in 1968 that deployed a network of community workers to tackle the social problems of neighbourhoods. These community workers quickly became guided by a class analysis that attributed social problems to structural processes of inequality and oppression rooted in capitalist society as a whole (Loney 1983). Housing provided the focus for much of the community action that developed from these projects, beginning in the inner city neighbourhoods under threat of demolition and urban renewal, and moving in the early 1970s on to the council estates where tenants were organising against rising rents, insensitive housing management and structurally defective homes that were expensive to heat and dripping with damp (Fleetwood and Lambert 1982). Publicised in *Community Action* journal by dissident urban planners, and encouraged by academic texts aimed at the newly minted British Association of Social Work and Association of Community Workers (Baldock 1977), a series of militant campaigns, marches, pickets and occupations followed (Lees and Mayo 1984). In council housing protests, radical community workers thought they had found the class base for a new kind of political movement that would straddle socialist theory and the practice of community action. As Mike Fleetwood and John Lambert (1982: 54) reflected: 'It became feasible to conceive of a broad tenants' movement using a socialist strategy, linked to a form of local organising concerned with short-term objectives to remedy local grievances.'

While in practical terms this attempted mobilisation often disappointed the hopes of the community project teams (Lambert 1981), the framework for their radical practice was provided by Marxist theories of the State and by a classification of tenant struggles as 'objectively, a struggle between capital and labour over the provision of housing' (Clarke and Ginsburg 1975: 4). This attribution to the tenants' movement of a role in the class struggle was inspired by Manuel Castells's (1976, 1977) model of urban social movements and his analysis of the collective means of consumption. Influenced in his earlier work by the Marxist theorist Louis Althusser, Castells interpreted the development of social housing, along with healthcare, education and public transport, as a response by the State to the need to provide the capitalist economy with an adequate labour force. This, he argued, led to the development of a new forum of class struggle in the cities where demands for improvements in public services threatened the authority of the State and the capitalist mode of production it served. Just as industrial production had enabled the collective organisation of a labour movement, so the mass provision of public services within the infrastructure of cities created the possibility of a community movement as an organised opposition to the State from a new front. Castells (1978: 41) identified the tenants' movement with this new arena of class struggle, and community action as the domestic front of class conflict, claiming:

> these demands are expressed on the one hand through the union movement organised at the place of production, and on the other hand, by new means of mass organisation which have gradually constituted a complete network of movements in the sphere of collective consumption, from associations of tenants, to committees of transport users.

In the characterisation of housing struggles as class struggle over the organisation and delivery of public services, tenants were attributed a set of material interests they could mobilise around: the interests of the working class opposed to those of the capitalist class (Bolger *et al.* 1981). The radical community workers who sought to address these interests were following a tradition established by socialist groups who had been attempting for decades to orchestrate tenant collective action in the public and private rented sectors. The Communist Party most famously co-ordinated rent strikes in the East End of London in the 1930s, where they linked tenant collective action to the fight against fascism (Piratin 1948; Srebrnik 1995; Glynn 2005), and helped launch the National Association of Tenants and Residents in 1948, the countywide federation that continued rather inactively into the 1970s. The Communist Party was instrumental, rather controversially, in the rent strike in Sheffield in the late 1960s (Hampton 1970). The International Socialists and other Marxist groups supported the 1972 tenant rent strikes, while libertarian and anarchist groups organised inner-city housing protests and squatting campaigns. Pursuing this tradition, community-action literature celebrated the sporadic rent strikes and incidents of tenant direct action as examples of working-class resistance. The everyday concerns of tenants' associations in local issues such as repairs, environmental matters and their collaboration with local authorities in participation schemes were denigrated as unsatisfactorily lacking in political awareness (Smith 1978). Manuel Castells (1976: 155) had laid the ground rules for this hierarchical structuring of tenant action according to its militancy with his concept of the urban social movement that 'tends objectively towards the structural transformation of the urban system' and his demotion of movements that failed to meet this revolutionary ideal into categories of 'protest', where their actions led to small-scale reforms of the social system, or 'participation', where their efforts merely helped the State to exert social control. In the literature of community action, community workers were urged to be selective about the tenants' associations they helped, and to prioritise only those that were prepared to raise socialist demands about their housing conditions (Corkey and Craig 1978). Many community workers persisted in the belief that neighbourhood struggles were secondary to the 'real class struggle' of trade unions and industrial conflict, and constantly urged tenants to construct alliances with the labour movement (Blagg and Derricourt 1982: 18). They attempted to replicate the structure of the militant shop stewards' committees on housing estates and applied a trade union model to tenant organisations (Foster 1975). The privileging of direct action over negotiation coloured subsequent academic treatment of the development of tenant participation policy. It found expression in Stuart Lowe's (1986: 85) disputed categorisation of tenants' associations into two radically opposed groupings, one a 'politically potent' type of tenants' organisation that pursued a tactic of militant direct action, and the second, the 'established' tenants' association that occupied itself with leisure and social activities, and served unwittingly as a buffer against urban protest. In Lowe's account, the countrywide mobilisation against the 1972 Housing Finance Act was the final act of radicalism of the tenants' movement and was followed by a decline in militancy, corresponding with the rise of tenant participation in social housing. This argument is disputed (Ginsburg 1989; Ravetz 2001), and the rise of the National Tenants' Organisation in 1977 saw the renewal of tenant mobilisation, with thirty federations launched or resurrected, like the Sheffield Federation of Tenants Associations, which had dissolved in the aftermath of failed rent strikes and now reformed to secure involvement in local housing decision-making (Baldock 1982). National progress on a Tenants' Charter was matched by local negotiations to obtain security of tenure from council landlords and rights to consultation on rent and management policy, while rent strikes continued into the early 1980s with Walsall and Coventry resisting rent increases (Savill 1982; Lowe 1997).

The revival of the tenants' movement was made manifest in an upsurge of grass-roots opposition to the Conservative government's 1988 Housing Act with its promotion of council house transfers and the ironically titled 'Tenants Choice' initiative, which raised the spectre of the mass privatisation of public housing (Ginsburg 1989). Important victories were won by tenants in securing democratic ballots before transfers, in making clear the scale of opposition to any private sector involvement, and, in the famous case of Walterton and Elgin, applying the Tenants Choice legislation to defeat Conservative council gerrymandering (Ravetz 2001). The threat to remove six council estates from municipal ownership and place them under the rule of government regeneration agencies as Housing Action Trusts was also successfully resisted by co-ordinated agitation, lobbying and tenant campaigning. Housing Ministers were heckled and jostled at public events, alternative tenant plans for estates were drawn up, pre-emptive referenda held, and new federations

FIGURE 2.1 Repel developers: opposition to the 1988 Housing Act and the planned transfer of municipal housing with a leaflet distributed door-to-door on estates in Huddersfield and district by Kirklees Federation of Tenants and Residents Associations

Photo provided by Kirklees Federation of Tenants and Residents Associations

FIGURE 2.2 Maggie's pride: cartoon opposing the proposals for estate transfers in the 1988 Housing Act produced for tenants' organisations by SCAT (Services to Community Action and Tenants)

Photo provided by Kirklees Federation of Tenants and Residents Associations

born in packed meetings and protest marches (Yelland 1990; Woodward 1991; Karn 1993; Wood 1994), in a show of force that secured the withdrawal, or at least the postponement and revision, of government strategy to remove housing from public services.

The demand for a universal right to housing, and the identification of class struggle with tenants' protest, emerged again in campaigns against the transfer of council housing from municipal ownership that followed the election of a Labour government in 1997 (Daly *et al.* 2005; Ginsburg 2005; Mooney and Poole 2005; McCormack 2008; Watt 2008). These struggles were successful in defeating measures characterised as the privatisation of public housing in 25 per cent of ballots cast by tenants, including high-profile 'no' votes in Birmingham and some of the London boroughs (Ginsburg 2005). Central to these victories was the ability of the campaigners led by the organisation Defend Council Housing to promote a revitalised notion of council housing, constructing a definition of 'public' housing that stressed the advantages of democratic governance through local authority ownership (Smyth 2013). The success of the anti-transfer campaigns in assembling an attractive political representation of council housing was evidenced by their ability to inspire tenants, not only to oppose transfer, but to vote to remain with municipal landlords whose housing management they thought largely incompetent (Daly *et al.* 2005; McCormack 2009). Defend Council Housing and its allies focused on the two exceptional periods of general needs council house building after the world wars to argue the potential for a model of house-building subsidy that enables low rents to be charged for all tenants, and a system of rent pooling according to the historic cost principal (Ambrose 2006), which allows the costs of building to be spread across the whole stock of housing, enabling over time a process of 'maturation', as the cost of building new homes is increasingly offset by surplus from homes whose building costs are fully paid (Kemeny 1995; DCH 2006; Davis and Wigfield 2010). An Early Day Motion on Council House Building (2008), put forward by a group of MPs in support of the campaign, the House of Commons Council Housing Group, makes explicit this vision of council housing as a general needs tenure, one that is accessible to a wide range of occupations and income bands and that is not rationed according to the severity of housing need. In calling for 'a new generation of first-class council housing', the bill depicted a future where local authorities could:

> Open up their allocation policies once again to the wide range of people on council housing waiting lists so that butchers, bakers, nurses and teachers can live together with young families and pensioners thus returning our estates to the mixed and sustainable communities they used to be.

In this political representation of social housing, with its reference to Aneurin Bevan's post-war vision of municipal housing (Foot 1973: 273), there is no mention of the wageless single-parent households, or vulnerable people who might expect to continue to access the sector. In omitting this social group, Defend Council Housing and their supporters were accused of ignoring the failures of municipal housing (Cole 2007): the disasters of system build, the stigmatised and unpopular estates, the coercive and bureaucratic housing management and the divisive, discriminatory and sometimes oppressive manner in which council housing met its public health and welfare goals. The absence of reflection on these less visionary aspects of the tenure reflects a historic divide between the respectable working class and the 'roughs' or undeserving poor (Clarke and Ginsburg 1975; Damer 1989; Watt 2008) who were identified with slum clearance and welfare policy, and who, in popular discourse, are traditionally blamed for the failure of municipal housing as a utopian experiment and its stigmatisation as a tenure of deprivation and moral decline (Card 2006). In the aftermath of the 2008 global financial crash, demand increased for council and housing association renting in response to a crisis of supply and affordability in the private housing market. Both the Labour government and the Conservative-led Coalition government that followed made changes to social housing allocations policies to give preferential access for households in paid employment, and priority to the armed forces (DCLG 2009e; DCLG 2011b). While this representation of social housing as a reward for the deserving ran concurrently with the identification of the tenure as an ambulance service for the poor and needy, it signalled a tension between two models of affordable housing provision (Fitzpatrick and Pawson 2007) and a return to earlier systems of discrimination between the deserving and undeserving (Brown and Patrick 2012). It suggested that social housing was still associated in the popular psyche with 'homes for heroes' (Flint 2008) and with the intraclass divisions of a moralised discourse of conditional access that tenants' organisations, representing the 'respectable' segment of the working class, had failed to acknowledge.

Tenants and intraclass divisions

Council housing tenants have been described as 'unique citizens' (Grayson 2007) who elect not only their local councillors but also their municipal landlord. The association of the tenants' movement with Labour-run local authorities, and with the labour movement as a whole, has been assured by its support for social democratic models of collective housing. Tenants' associations benefited from the devolution projects of Labour-run municipalities in the 1980s (Hambleton and Hoggett 1988; Taylor 1986), while in some Northern boroughs, trade unions and tenants' groups retained strong links (Grayson 2010). But the development of a tenants' movement was a consequence of a growing detachment between the interests of public renters and those of the Labour Party and most trade unions. Tenant loyalty to an ideal of decommodified housing provision has been at odds with the political direction of housing policy since the 1950s, and the rise of working-class homeownership relegated social housing tenants to a backwater that the labour movement largely ignored. The housing struggles that radical community workers hoped would 'build a wider political campaign' (Corkey and Craig 1978: 58) took place, with some notable exceptions, in isolation from the working-class movement. Housing issues were the subject of a compromise between capital and labour that resulted in a housing system that prioritised owner-occupation (Dickens *et al.* 1985), and class struggle appeared an increasingly blunt tool for theorising tenants' struggles (Edgell and Duke 1991). In the urban studies literature of the 1980s, class analysis of tenants' and community protests was replaced by a new theoretical strand that linked collective action to intraclass divisions and the difference between consumption sectors that generated political action.

In developing the theory of sectoral consumption cleavages, Patrick Dunleavy (1980) and Peter Saunders (1981) reflected the erosion of political support for the mass building of public rented housing from the late 1950s, and the increasing cultural and political shift in favour of homeownership that divided working-class homeowners and social housing tenants from the early 1960s (Ginsburg 1979; Malpass 2005). Intraclass divisions appeared to override class consciousness to establish a new set of interests exemplified in the emergence of social stratification based on consumption rather than production. The concept of consumption cleavages, or sectoral divides, was applied to interpret the fracture opening up in the working class between those with capital, or the potential to realise increased value from their ownership of housing, and those who remained in the social rented sector. It reflected too the increasing concentration in the worst council housing of the poorest and most powerless sections of the population, those 'who, through a combination of grading, misfortune or stigmas such as unemployment, single parenthood, illness, old age, large family or black skin, are labelled "undeserving"' (Jacobs 1981: 45). Sectoral theory constructed a thesis of consumer interests taken from Max Weber's sociological theories first applied to the housing market by John Rex and Robert Moore (1967) in their theory of housing classes and the argument that access to housing creates a hierarchical social structure in urban areas. Rex and Moore reasoned that competition for scarce desirable homes had a stratifying effect, and that distribution of housing resources through the market and by local authority allocation established a series of housing classes engaged in struggle over their position on the housing ladder. In particular, Rex and Moore identified the subordinate position of ethnic minority and immigrant communities on the housing ladder as social divisions that cross-cut labour market distinctions. In his criticism of this thesis, Peter Saunders (1981) proposed instead a structure based on the economic interests deriving from a division between homeownership and renting, and asserted that these consumption cleavages generated material interests that did not simply shape the beliefs and voting patterns of those affected, as Patrick Dunleavy (1980) believed, but determined their behaviour. While maintaining that housing was consumed individually, in keeping with Weber's notion of interest groups, Saunders argued that cleavages in housing consumption generated collective action. In making this assertion, he assigned to social rented housing the power to act as a rallying point for political struggle but maintained that collective action in the sphere of consumption was, by definition, always localised and reactive and would not have the transformative qualities attributed by Marxists to class struggle.

Sectoral theory, then, failed to make a definite break with the Marxist concept of class interest but reinterpreted it to acknowledge the intraclass divisions caused by the breakdown of the welfare-state consensus. In his concern with collective action in the sphere of consumption, it could be argued that Saunders was following, however reluctantly, the trajectory of thought taken by Manuel Castells. In its controversial depiction of tenants as agents of class struggle, Castells's early work (1976, 1977) imagined a working class united across the fields of production and distribution, energised by the forces of collective consumption. As he developed his theory to engage with the growing privatisation of consumption that obscured class boundaries, Castells (1978) was to characterise tenants' struggles, alongside other community protests, as the evolution of an urban social movement that crossed class lines and represented the growing centrality of consumption interests to social stratification. In the revision of his earlier thesis, Castells (1983) continued to attribute mobilising effects to consumption cleavages and to assert the local neighbourhood as a field of struggle. Attempting to apply Castells' frameworks to the social housing sector in England, Stuart Lowe (1986) argued for the existence of a working-class social base in council housing that engendered material interests based on class and consumption positions. Lowe theorised that as council tenants were concentrated in defined and distinctive housing estates, they were bound by their shared experience of stigma and conjoined in an overwhelmingly working-class culture. This social base established a set of common cultural and economic interests that enabled council housing tenants to mobilise in collective action, a thesis Lowe applied to his study of protests against the rent rises of the 1972 Housing Finance Act. Even as Lowe was writing, however, the uniformity of council estates was dissolving and the Right to Buy, brought in by the 1980 Housing Act, had begun to fracture the bonds of tenure, culture and place. Tenants were offered massive discounts to buy their council property and in the most significant act of privat-isation of that, and all subsequent governments, more than two and a half million homes in Britain were sold and removed from public stock over a thirty-year period (Malpass and Murie 1999; Pawson and Wilcox 2013). The sale of council houses was to radically reduce the size and status of the social housing sector and speed the residualising effect of a housing policy bias that confirmed its role as an ambulance service for the poorest and most vulnerable, housed in the worst-quality homes (Jones and Murie 2006). In a reassessment of Lowe's profile of the social base of council housing for the much-changed housing system of the 1990s, Cairncross *et al.* (1993) evidenced the numerous distinctions in material interests between tenants of different council estates and different property types, and as recipients of different management processes. Presenting a bleak account of a marginalised and fragmented council housing sector, Liz Cairncross and colleagues trounced the notion that tenants comprised an element within the class struggle, dismissed the suggestion that tenants could be identified as a distinct sector within the structuring of collective urban consumption and debunked the contention that tenants shared any material interests or common issues. The contemporary housing landscape reflec-ted a more individualistic outlook, and with a presumption against the mobilisation of collective action, the tenant interest was reconfigured according to the classical liberal view of the rational consumer.

The consumer voice in social housing

In the programme of welfare state restructuring which began in the mid-1970s, the service user was reborn as a consumer, and the concept of consumer interests was applied as a counterweight to the power of the professional and bureaucratic elites in charge of service delivery (Clarke 2007; Stoker 2004). The classical liberal view of the consumer as a rational, self-interested individual endowed with free choice became transposed to the organisation and delivery of public services, where the supposedly passive recipient of welfare was reimagined as a demanding and sceptical citizen-consumer with an interest in the choice, quality and price of public goods and the accountability of those who supply them (Trentmann 2005). In the Conservative governments of the 1980s and 1990s, and the Labour regime that followed in 1997, the consumer interest was pursued by ushering the market forces of supply and demand into public services through a programme of privatisation, and, where no market was possible, by introducing a range of 'choice and voice' mechanisms through quasi-markets and opportunities for participation, complaint and redress (House of Commons Public Administration Select Committee 2005). The mechanism of voice was fulfilled by the development of policies of tenant participation, or resident, later customer involvement in the social housing sector. Participation came to encompass nearly all tenant collective action and fragmented the traditional organisational structure of the tenants' movement. In the place of tenants' associations it introduced focus groups and market research techniques, while tenants' federations were replaced or replicated by scrutiny panels convened and usually administered by social landlords. Although the voice mechanism of participation was applied with determination to the organisation of public housing in England, and market economics assumed supremacy in the restructuring of welfare services, opportunities to transform social housing tenants into sovereign consumers were limited.

Tenant mobilisation in Britain can be presented as an aspect of the development of a consumer culture, rather than class struggle or the material interests of public renting, a culture in which participation in public services became established as the norm (Potter 1988; Shapely 2006, 2007). The tenants' movement had been depicted as a consumer interest group since the rise of the National Tenants' Organisation (Oxley 1986; Hood and Woods 1994), which was assisted in its development by the National Consumer Council. The individualist persona of the consumer was in sharp contrast to the declining status awarded to social housing tenants as, leached of its best stock and more affluent residents, the sector declined in size sharply through sales and demolition during the 1990s and 2000s, while new social house building was maintained at a very low rate. Even when public investment was made available by the 1997 Labour government it was limited to patching up the damage done to the existing municipal stock by lack of investment under the Conservatives, rather than increase the number of homes (Malpass 2005). By 2005 half of all municipal housing had been transferred to registered social landlords or sold, while half of the remaining stock had been removed to the quasi-market of arm's-length management, and the sector had become even more diversified with the development of new shared-ownership and rent to mortgage housing (ODPM 2004; Ginsburg 2005). Social housing was characterised as intrinsically valueless: the carrier of deprivation, poverty and worklessness (Dwelly and Cowans 2006). Estates with high levels of anti-social behaviour or suffering from marginal demand were demolished to make way for new homes at full market price and for low-cost homeownership (Manzi 2010). It was against this background that a concerted attempt was launched to establish a tenants' consumer organisation or a National Tenant Voice, a project that forged unexpected connections between the concepts of class and consumer, and that demonstrated how supposedly material interests can be adapted to serve competing claims of identity.

In April 2006 a Tenant Involvement Commission led by the National Housing Federation called on government to fund a national organisation to represent the consumer interests of tenants as effectively as the professional bodies and landlord associations defended the interests of service providers. The social housing tenant was characterised as a captive consumer in a service dominated by the interests of producers (Mayo and Tickell 2006). It was argued that the national tenants' organisations were unable to uphold the tenant interest against a well-resourced and articulate producers' lobby represented by the Chartered Institute of Housing, the Local Government Association, and the National Housing Federation itself. This call was repeated by the National Consumer Council in December that year when the Labour government announced a review of housing regulation to be led by Professor Martin Cave. In its recommendations the Cave Review argued for the establishment of a new consumer watchdog organisation to voice the interests of social housing tenants. The model for the National Tenant Voice set out in Cave's report *Every Tenant Matters* (2007) was of a consumer watchdog on the lines of the train passengers' lobby, Passenger Focus, or the OfCom consumer panel, that could collate and research information on landlords' performance at regional and local authority level to influence the national policy agenda. The creation of consumer watchdogs has been a standard feature of the privatisation of regulated public services in Britain, and follows the template of customer advocacy and research originally established in this country by the Consumers' Association in 1956 and the National Consumer Council in 1975 (Hilton 2003).

The idea of the National Tenant Voice imagined tenants in classical liberal terms as a consumer interest, or lobby group, aiming to influence policy from a standpoint of self-interest. This interpretation presupposed a pluralist society and an equality of interests rather than the divided and unequal society of class and sectoral theory (Barnes 1999). In a series of tenant conferences held in the wake of the Cave review, the idea of the National Tenant Voice won widescale support from tenants' organisations but the model to emerge from these workshops was rather different from that of the consumer watchdog imagined by Cave and the National Consumer Council. Tenants pictured a voice that could be a national trade union for tenants, democratically constituted with regional branches and elected officials, holding statutory powers that might extend into the private rented sector, and with the authority to intervene against landlords and resolve complaints (Bandy *et al.* 2007). Responding to proposals for the National Tenant Voice set out in a Tenant Empowerment consultation paper (DCLG 2007a), tenants' organisations called for the new body to have a formal role in government decision-making on housing policy as a representative and democratic organisation led by tenants.

The National Tenant Voice project group was established by the government Department of Communities and Local Government in February 2008 with representatives from national and regional tenants' organisations, and the Tenant Participation Advisory Service (TPAS) sitting alongside the National Consumer Council and the housing trade bodies, with tenants taking the majority of places. By the time the project group issued a consultation paper on its proposals in July 2008, not only had the National Consumer Council been removed from the negotiations, but a shade of antagonism had crept into the imagery of the National Tenant Voice conceived by the group. The voice was to be 'rooted in the tenants' movement, with close working links with representative tenants' organisations' (NTV Project Group 2008a: 2) and, while still imagined as a consumer watchdog with an advocacy and research remit, the new body would help build and strengthen tenants' organisations and be guided by a belief 'that tenants are citizens of equal worth' (2008a: 3). The final report of the National Tenant Voice Project Group, 'Citizens of Equal Worth', made clear the subtle changes to the way a consumer watchdog role was to be envisaged. The core purpose of the new organisation was 'to increase the opportunities for social tenants to have a strong collective influence over the policies that affect them' and it was evident the National Tenant Voice was to be seen as part of a collective movement, strengthening the network of self-organised local and regional tenants' organisations (NTV Project Group 2008b: 14). The role of the new organisation was defined in the Local Democracy, Economic Development and Construction Bill as 'representing or facilitating the representation of the views and interests of social housing tenants in England' and it was to be governed by a council drawn in part from the national and regional tenants' organisations (House of Lords Bill 2008/09: 25). The bill proposed what appeared to be a hybrid of consumer watchdog and political organisation, and, while it appeared to signal one more step in the remorseless marketisation of public services, the proposed model of the National Tenant Voice owed more to collective interests and to a tradition of collective action than to the classic liberal representations of the consumer.

The ability of tenants on the National Tenant Voice project group to apply a consumerist discourse to promote ideas of political representation and collective action importantly reflects the ambiguity of the concept of consumer interest in housing policy. A binary distinction between consumerism and citizenship was erected by Liz Cairncross and colleagues (1997) to categorise the different approaches of social landlords to tenant participation in housing services. Consumerist participation was defined as the publication of performance figures, league tables, and the application of market research methodologies such as satisfaction surveys and focus groups to assess customer views of service quality, while a citizenship view of tenant participation, in contrast, encouraged collective action, and drew links with democratic involvement and self-management. For Catherine Needham (2003), the consumerist approach corrupts the relationship between the citizen and the State, individualising it and turning it into a transaction. It removes the ability of citizens to collectively shape public services or to control directly the way they are delivered. Tracing the history of consumer organisation in the labour movement, and the severing of the vision of co-operative consumption from the producer-centred policy that came to dominate socialist thought, Matthew Hilton argues that the figure of the rational consumer as the keystone of liberal economics was constructed in the face of many other possible consumer identities. 'Consumers were imagined solely as individuals and never as collectives of interested parties and their role in "shopping" was equated with citizenship, thereby excluding many of the agendas that had inspired and fuelled consumer and citizen groups' (Hilton 2003: 266). While consumerism has been applied in social housing, as in other public services, to mould the identity of the welfare service user, a politics of collective consumption has also been utilised to resist these identities and, in the debate over the National Tenant Voice, to construct a contentious political imagery that calls for more democracy and accountability in public services rather than more individual choice (see, for example, Haywood 2007). Commenting on the spread of consumerism into public services and its encroachment into realms of citizenship, Frank Trentmann (2004: 380) warns that the debate concerning the identity of the consumer is far from over, noting that 'consumer identities have become suffused with questions of civic participation, cultural identities, and social and global justice, as well as with a drive to acquire goods.'

The launch of the National Tenant Voice in February 2010, with the election of its fifty-person Tenant Council, was followed swiftly in July by its abolition in the 'bonfire of the quangos' ignited by the Conservative-led Coalition government (Cameron 2009a), and a thirty-year project to transform social housing tenants into sovereign consumers was abandoned. While the identity of the consumer has ushered the transformative dynamics of the market through public housing services, it rested on a charter of tenants' rights enacted in the 1980 Housing Act that provided for security of tenure and the evolution of an expanding range of consultation mechanisms (Lowe 1997). The Coalition government's Localism Act (2011) signalled the end of this project in the removal of security of tenure, the abolition of a consumer-focused regulator and the dismissal of the National Tenant Voice. The 'tenant interest' was located by the Coalition government's Housing Minister, Grant Shapps, only in local issues of individual complaint, and no role was allowed to tenants at a national policy level. Collective action by tenants was limited to the locality and focused on the mechanics of participation over housing standards

FIGURE 2.3 Hands off our homes: tenants protest against proposals to privatise housing management outside the Conservative Party Conference in 1995

Photo provided by Kirklees Federation of Tenants and Residents Associations

FIGURE 2.4 Not for sale: a tenant dressed as Prime Minister John Major at the 1995 protests against privatising housing management

Photo provided by Kirklees Federation of Tenants and Residents Associations

and scrutiny; tenants' federations that continued to campaign around national issues, or to challenge their landlords, were disciplined with threats of, or the actual, removal of funding. An uprising of informally organised tenants' groups united nationally in their resistance to the Coalition government's welfare benefits cuts, and particularly the so-called bedroom tax, emerged in 2013 into the vacuum caused by the withdrawal of formal tenants' organisations from campaigning. This resurgence of tenant collective action over cuts in income subsidies to the low paid and those outside paid employment underlined the continuing relevance of material inequalities and social stratification for collective action in housing. However, it also made clear the cyclic and emergent nature of a tenants' movement and its inextricable connection to social welfare systems and the collective consumption of public goods. It suggested that the consumer model of tenant participation had rendered the formal tenants' movement quiescent, but that a collective identification as tenants could still generate contentious collective action. In the failure of class or consumer theories to adequately explain the basis of the tenants' movement, the final section of this chapter turns to social movement theory suggested as the most relevant framework for analysis of continuing housing struggles (Harrison and Reeve 2002; Somerville 2005a).

Tenants and social movements

Tenant collective action can be seen as one strand in a proliferation of new social movements that arose in the 1960s and 1970s, and that appeared to fragment the traditional distinctions of social class, material interest and consumption (Hewitt 1996). These social movements were labelled 'new' (Habermas 1981) because they seemed to mark a departure from the class-based approach of the labour movement and could not be interpreted through the prism of material interest. In attempting to classify these movements, Alain Touraine (1985) identified their defining characteristic as their concern for cultural issues and their engagement with transforming values and social norms. Movements in the United States and Europe appeared to be championing or rebelling against definitions of identity, striving for civil rights and justice or engaged in defining alternative lifestyles or culture, an approach typified by the women's, gay and lesbian, ecological and peace movements.

New social movement theory posed a challenge to the assertion that collective action is principally propelled by material interests because it focused on the development of consciousness, and the articulation and affirmation of identity rather than on the structural location of interests in a social hierarchy (Pakulski 1995). It directed attention to the assemblage and construction of grievances, and the identification of common issues that enabled social movements to be mobilised. This construction process has been dubbed 'identity work' (Snow and McAdam 2000), and social movement theory developed an approach to analysing frames of identity (Snow *et al.* 1986; Benford and Snow 1988, 1992) to study the assemblage of shared signs and stories that bind participants together and that manifest the beliefs and motivation of a social movement. The concept of collective identity was to become one of the main theoretical frameworks through which this identity work could be studied. In the hands of Alberto Melucci (1989, 1996), collective identity became an incisive analytical tool that focused attention on the relationships developed by individual participants in social movements, and reclaimed a role for emotion, conflict and negotiation in movement construction. Melucci defined collective identity as a continuous process of group debate around the material experiences, grievances and antagonisms of participants that generated goals and strategies and was a fundamental prerequisite for collective action to take place. Collective identity proved an effective and adaptable theory for interpreting the development of the women's movement, and the gay and lesbian movements whose principle objective was to either reclaim a repudiated identity or to assert an identity that had been marginalised or ignored (Bernstein 1997; Taylor and Whittier 1992, 1995). Where the feminist movement, gay and lesbian groups, ethnic minority campaigns and organisations of disabled people and mental health users have all been defined through the concept of collective identity and fixed with the label of identity politics, the tenants' movement, despite sharing many of their characteristics, has remained very firmly an 'old' social movement. The relevance of class-based analysis to housing struggles has continued to be emphasised (Damer 2000;

Johnstone 2000; Somerville 2005a), and the apparent focus of social movement theory on cultural and symbolic concerns rather than the bread and butter of material issues militated against its application to the collective action of tenants.

Two developments in social movement theory served to return class and redistributive concerns to identity politics. One was the re-emergence of interest in urban social movements in the USA and Europe, which, with associated research into 'poor people's movements' (Piven and Cloward 1977), stressed the material demands of collective action; the second was the parallel development in England of the concept of 'social welfare movements' (Williams 1992), a classification that captured the redistributive goals of community-based struggles. New research into urban social movements jettisoned Manuel Castells's (1976) restrictive definition to classify a diverse range of collective action under one grouping, a collection that proved amenable to the inclusion of the labour movement as a social movement and a force for change in the city (Pickvance 2003). In urban movement theory, studies of the desperate mobilisations of homeless people could be considered alongside inner-city squatting campaigns that might in other social movement theorisations have been defined as lifestyle or cultural protests (Nicholls and Beaumont 2004). Studies of urban movements and 'poor people's movements', with their focus on the local rather than the national, appeared well placed to respond to the dilemmas of incorporation and co-option that arose from the 1980s onwards as municipal governments, following liberal market theories, outsourced public services to citizens' organisations or sought to involve them in limited decision-making (Kavoulakos 2006; Pruijt 2003). These increasing threats to welfare systems caused urban movement and 'poor people's movement' theorists to lean towards what had seemed a peculiarly English interest in the role of collective action in shaping definitions of citizenship, universal needs and social welfare (Roth 2000).

In England the new social movements mostly evolved out of community-based struggles (Cowley et al. 1977; Lovenduski and Randall 1993), and their approach to the welfare state and to the issues of housing, health and social care gave them common cause on the question of 'who controlled welfare and in whose interests', as Fiona Williams (1994: 64) put it. Williams sought to reconcile the rivalry between 'old' and 'new' social movements with her concept of the 'social welfare movement' that fused the politics of recognition and redistribution (Williams 1992). These movements shared a common emphasis on participatory involvement and the demand for more control over the everyday environment and were locally based and organised around personal experience (Segal 1979; Lees and Mayo 1984). Through community-based groups and loose networks of local organisations, social welfare movements celebrated their rejection of hierarchical decision-making, experimented with and promoted participative and direct democracy, and endorsed the authenticity of experiential knowledge (Wainwright 2003; Della-Porta and Diani 2006). This wave of community mobilisations directed attention to the welfare state as an area where 'the social relations not only of class, but of gender and "race" – not to mention age, disability and sexuality – are most apparent' (Williams 1994: 64). Women have always played a leading role in the tenants' movement and Peter

Baldock (1982: 123) maintained that the movement was in its origins 'a movement of women', a characteristic that enabled it to develop new ways of mobilising on the housing estates. Cynthia Cockburn (1977b) argued that community action was one element of women's liberation and suggested that the dominant role of women in tenant struggles was the factor that would forge the necessary class links between housing, health and industrial conflict. In its pursuit of participatory democracy, the tenants' movement anticipated the new organisational forms of the women's and students' movements. Similarly, the growth of the disabled people's movement and the development of organisations of people with learning difficulties and mental health service users challenged definitions of need, rights and autonomy that had parallels for social housing tenants (Oliver 1990; Williams 1992; Barnes 1999). The diverse demands of the women's movement, gay and lesbian groups, tenants' associations and ethnic minority organisations all identified gaps in welfare provision brought about by the imposition of restrictive definitions of universal need. The development of refuges for women fleeing their violent partners, for example, highlighted the failure of housing and social services to identify domestic violence as an issue for intervention (Lent 2001), and the work of Women's Aid was hailed as a bridge between the housing struggles of tenants and the women's movement (Hanmer 1977). For Hilary Wainwright (1979: 4), tenants were part of a heterogeneous wish-list of grass-roots upheaval: 'the women's movement, solidarity movements with international struggles, many shop stewards' combines or local action committees, the anti-fascist movement, theatre groups, alternative newspapers, militant tenants, squatters and community groups'.

Studies of social welfare movements (Williams 1992), urban movements (Pickvance 2003), and 'poor people's movements' (Piven and Cloward 1977) provide a legitimate framework in which social movement theory can be applied to understand the collective action of tenants, and to consider the construction of a tenants' movement, not as the property of an essential material interest, but as the development of a collective and contentious identity. An approach to this new analysis might begin in studies of tenants' organisations that reveal something about their shared beliefs and consciousness. An analysis of the East London rent strikes from 1968 to 1970 (Moorhouse *et al.* 1972: 151) found a strong sense of antagonism, of 'them and us', among the rent strikers and their support base, an overwhelming sense that their views were not taken into account and a belief that they had no power or influence in decision-making. The tenants shared a perception that the law was not impartial, and a sense that illegal actions, such as withholding rent or squatting, were justifiable and necessary. The research concluded:

> We suggest that while rent strikes and other varieties of ill-reported urban protest do not involve their participants in a clear vision of a new social order, they do reveal something of that muted, defensive 'counter-ideology' of the working class, which is the basis of the development of class consciousness in the classical sense.
>
> (Moorhouse *et al.* 1972: 153)

These attitudes among the East London rent strikers and their supporters have been represented as 'a kind of folk-Marxism' (McKibbin 1998: 139) generated through the accumulation of grievances in working-class experience and expressed in a muted certainty of continuing injustice. In a study of the mobilisation of tenants' groups against Housing Action Trusts in 1988 and 1989, Rachel Woodward (1991) charted the assemblage of organisational unity that enabled tenants to defeat the threat to council housing from Conservative proposals to remove estates from public ownership. She noted how the divisions between council tenants were overcome and a working unity constructed 'through a continual process of discussion and debate' at tenants' association and campaign meetings (Woodward 1991: 49), and she traced the development of narratives and arguments that patched over the divisions between tenants. What Woodward appears to be describing is the construction of a collective identity robust enough to mobilise a disparate range of tenants' groups and individuals into a movement. These studies straddling two key periods of mobilisation provide a tantalising glimpse of the possibilities of an application of collective identity theory to the organisation of an English tenants' movement. Collective identity offers an analysis of the mobilisation process that does not depend on the identification of objective interests common to all social housing tenants, whether those are understood as class interests or the interests of consumers, but that focuses attention on the actual processes of identity construction or how movements are built from a series of negotiations, narratives, grievances and perceptions. By paying attention to this complex series of interactions and relationships, it may be possible to understand the process whereby disparate individuals are drawn into collective action and the means by which the barriers to mobilisation are overcome, to listen, for once, to the voice of the tenants' movement in its own words, and assess its achievements on its own terms.

Any such interpretation needs to begin with the immersion of the tenants' movement in the complexities and compromises of the public policy of participation. Participation and privatisation have fragmented the tenants' movement, if a movement ever really existed, and individualist discourses, market mechanisms and parables of responsibility are the contemporary location of tenant collective action. Collective identity should not be seen as the 'authentic' voice of tenants, nor should it be portrayed as evidence of resistance or liberation, something of a tendency in social movement theory. To investigate the construction of the collective identity of a tenants' movement it is necessary to listen to the voices of tenants who are enmeshed in the technologies of governance and interpellated by discourses that seek to mould their behaviours and motivations. While these discourses are riddled with ambiguity and can be used to express opposition, any study of the identities constructed in and around the formation of a tenants' movement must situate them as the outcome of a process of regulation and subjection, and interpret the movement as a force for 'domestication' as well as resistance (Butler 2000: 150).

This chapter has explored the construction of the identity of a tenants' movement around the concept of material interest, the collective interest of class position and the individual interest of the sovereign consumer. At different times and in relation to specific forces in housing policy the history of the movement has been presented either as integral to the class struggle for rights to housing, or the consequence of an intraclass division between forms of housing consumption, or as an expression of the market interests of consumers against producers. These narratives of tenants' history have been developed at a careful distance from the study of the social movements with which tenant collective action shares many of its characteristics. The contention put forward in the conclusion of this chapter is that the social movement theory of collective identity provides an analytical tool to understand the organisation, aims and objectives of the tenants' movement. The next chapter begins the investigation of 'identity work' in the policy of public participation and explores the active construction of a contemporary tenants' movement in its partnerships with social landlords, and its domestication in the market mechanics of voice.

3
POWER AND PARTICIPATION

For campaigners involved in housing struggles over rents and urban renewal, property speculation and the crisis of homelessness in the early 1970s, the rise of tenant participation was a predictable attempt to incorporate and disarm a radical social movement that had proved itself capable of major disruption in a countrywide rent strike (Ward 1974; Cockburn 1977a). Housing academics and theorists have shared this viewpoint on the whole, perceiving the growth of participation as a relation of power in which state agencies sought to co-opt tenants organisations, to win their support and shift responsibility for unpopular decision-making on to their shoulders (Saunders 1979; Lowe 1986; Hague 1990; Cairncross et al. 1994; Grayson 1997; Riseborough 1998; Goodlad 2001). Tenant sources, although fully aware of the limitations of participation, appeared, however, to discern some benefits from involvement with landlords, and from the late 1960s onwards in some areas tenant organisations actively pursued a strategy of participation, seeing it as a means to give tenants control over local decisions, with the long-term hope of bringing about a change in the power relations of public services (Craddock 1975: 57; Rao 1984: 102).

As the author of the first manual of tenant participation, Ann Richardson (1983: 5), said: 'If some argue that participation is a significant means of increasing the influence of the new participants, and others contend that it is instead a devious means of decreasing it, someone must indeed be incorrect.' It is clear that any attempt to understand the contemporary tenants' movement must start with an analysis of the power relations of participation, the hopes and possibilities it initially presented to tenants, and the reflections of tenants forty years later on the outcomes of their involvement in housing services. This chapter explores the theories advanced by housing scholars to make sense of the unequal relationship of power between tenants and the authorities. It sets out to understand why, despite that inequality, tenants' organisations have seen opportunities in participation policy to challenge traditional power relations and to advance their interests, and it provides a critical assessment of the impact of tenant participation in social housing and its effect on the power relations of the welfare state.

The rise of public participation in housing

Participation in housing management was the outcome of a tenant campaign for involvement in decision-making, which had its roots in a crisis of identity among residents of council estates in the late 1960s (Rao 1984). It was a continuation by other means of the rent strikes and protests of the 1960s and 1970s, and not, as traditionally viewed, a reversal of strategy or the consequence of the failure of contention. An analysis of the development of tenant participation from its origins in the rent campaign to its evolution as public policy explains what tenants hoped to gain from collaboration and partnership, and brings the successes and failure of forty years of participation into focus. This venture into the past is useful, first because an account of the tenant campaign for participation has never been fully told, and second because it seeks to explain what tenants want from participation and why they continue to pursue it.

It is important to understand the competing pressures on social housing tenants in this period and the way the subsequent evolution of tenant participation and the tenants' movement was influenced by housing policy in the 1960s. Both Labour and Conservative governments were committed to the promotion of home-ownership, and aimed to reduce the role of the council housing sector to a more marginal status as accommodation only for the most needy. A council tenancy was still a prize to be desired, however, and local authority lettings policies had traditionally ensured that the best-quality homes had gone to households judged respectable and hard-working. These homes had, in the main, been built for families in full-time employment; Bevan's vision of 'the doctor, the grocer, the butcher and the farm labourer all in the same street' (Foot 1973: 273) may have remained aspirational but was indicative of both the rise in living standards and the boost in confidence and aspiration among those lucky enough to benefit from general needs council housing. In 1962 the tenure was still seen as the home of a 'labour aristocracy' (Jacobs *et al.* 2003). Municipal housing represented a step up for families moving from the private rented sector where inside toilets and hot running water were by no means readily available (Lupton *et al.* 2009). It was predominantly family housing, with relatively few young or elderly tenants; the average tenants' association member was 'at that time of life when they could most expect to be materially comfortable, who were living in relative affluence' (Baldock 1982: 124). These affluent tenants of post-war council housing were an embarrassment to governments committed to supporting homeownership, and they became the target of state strategies intended to reduce the competitive edge of public rented housing and enable the expansion of the private market. They were accused as a privileged population, undeserving of the subsidies that maintained their rents below market level. Bludgeoned by rent rises and battered into homeownership, those who refused to budge were lampooned in political discourse as 'featherbedded' 'limpets', unfairly clinging on to the benefits of municipal housing (Jacobs *et al.* 2003).

Needless to say, council tenants did not see themselves as privileged. Having submitted to a regime of inspection, selection and, sometimes, disinfection to secure a tenancy, the housing management service they received in exchange was often remote, inflexible and inefficient; the repairs service was sometimes inadequate, while the quality of council homes they were allocated had declined markedly since the mid-1950s and the switch to high-rise system building. Those council tenants lucky enough to be given a tenancy agreement by their local authority found their list of responsibilities long and their rights few, while the landlord's responsibilities went unmentioned. With no protection in statute, council tenants had only common law to defend them from their landlord's unfair practices; they had no security of tenure or rights to succession before the 1980 Housing Act (Lowe 1997). This was a decade of optimism and aspiration, however, and council tenants were less willing to accept an authoritarian management style that required them to know their place (Hayes 1988). Their rejection of what to them was 'a second-class citizen role' (Tenants Charter quoted in Ward 1974) was enabled by a civil rights discourse of rights to public services rather than public hand-outs (Hayes 1989). Although extreme pressure was exerted on them in the form of rent increases, the more affluent council tenants did not choose to buy on the open market. Dissatisfied with their housing management service and the paternalist attitude of their landlord, they nevertheless supported the values of public housing. They wanted to transform the management of council housing rather than turn their backs on it.

The evolution of tenant participation has been best documented in the London boroughs where the drive to establish participation schemes came from the city's tenants' federation, the Association of London Housing Estates (ALHE) and was recorded by Julia Craddock (1975), Nick Derricourt (1971, 1973) and John Hayes (1988, 1989). Exasperated by a bureaucratic and paternalist service, the federation took the desire for participation in housing management and turned it into a co-ordinated and high-level strategy. The London-wide tenants' federation set up four borough co-ordinating committees and a Greater London subcommittee to give strategic direction to the local participation already taking place between tenants' associations and their neighbourhood housing managers. The development of participation as a public policy became the main goal of the organisation (Mayo 1972) and the borough co-ordinating committees drove forward the establishment of consultative structures in council housing decision-making processes (Hayes 1988). As Julia Craddock (1975: 3) explained, they 'assumed the functions of policy making and negotiation, or confrontation, when necessary, with the boroughs and Greater London Council'. Mike Geater, secretary of the London tenants' federation, articulated this drive for participation in explicitly rights-based terms:

> Tenants do have a point of view and as the movement towards tenant participation is gathering momentum [. . .] it is hoped to evolve a process that allows tenants to express those views, that normally no one is prepared

to listen to, a process that will enable them to get their ideas past the bureaucratic barrier to where the decision making takes place, decisions that affect their homes and their lives.

(Foreword, Craddock 1975)

The launch of a Tenants' Charter by the London federation in 1970 trumpeted this growing assertiveness in a manifesto for the new social movement. This declaration of tenants' rights made the demand for participation central to its defence of the ideal of universal provision of council housing 'as a non-profit making community service'. Participation would 'lead to the creation of new relationships between councillors, tenants and housing officers' and the 'rejection of paternalism' (Ward 1974; Craddock 1975). The charter advances a vision of general needs public housing managed in partnership with its tenants, a very different model of public service from the stigmatised and residual tenure intended by policy makers.

While participation was a growing theme in government housing guidance, and a feature of the 1968 Gulbenkian and Seebohm reports into community and social work respectively, and the 1969 Skeffington report on planning, there was little interest among housing authorities to initiate participation schemes with tenants. In 1969, Robert Edward MP tried to introduce a Council Tenants' Charter Bill that would give tenants representation on housing committees, and this was followed by Dick Leonard's equally unsuccessful Council Housing (Tenants' Representation) Bill in 1971 and 1973. It was a recommendation from the National Board for Prices and Incomes in 1967 that tenant participation could soften the impact of rent increases that brought the issue to the attention of housing providers, especially those local authorities where new Conservative administrations were eager to subsidise rebate schemes by raising rents to market levels. Julia Craddock (1975: 14) comments acidly: 'Tenants' participation was not thought necessary by local authorities until it was perceived by some, mostly Tory, councils to be useful to them in trying to introduce large rent increases.'

The development of tenant participation in London did not follow the path hoped for by the tenants' organisations, but there were unexpected and contradictory results. The London Borough Councils showed little commitment to widening democracy in housing decision-making, and it was rare that tenants were granted anything other than consultation rights through the new participation structures. The tenants' federation in the London borough of Lambeth asked their council for control over housing budgets and a decision-making seat on the Housing Committee (Derricourt 1973). Instead, they were given five places on a consultative subcommittee where they could take part in 'council decision-making with tenants' views' (Craddock 1975: 54). It was a trade-off that came to typify the tenant experience of participation and one that provided ample evidence for those who warned of the institutionalisation and co-option of an urban movement. In his eye witness study, Jonathon Rao (1984: 104) concluded participation to be: 'manipulative and concessionary and designed to prevent radical change'. But participating in these limited opportunities seemingly motivated the tenants' organisations to pursue alternative routes towards their goals. This was evident in the significant improvement in co-ordination displayed by the London tenants' federation, the Association of London Housing Estates (ALHE), in its response to the Conservative government's 1972 Housing Finance Bill which formally repudiated a general needs role for social housing and confirmed the shift in policy to a residual sector. It instituted a universal rent rebate scheme and centralised rent setting through a process of mediated market rents. The ALHE's new policy focus enabled it to lead early tenant protest against the bill, and in the process to double its membership, organising protest rallies and lobbying Labour MPs with proposals for amendments. The organisation was, however, refused access to ministers and was denied any consultative role other than the right to submit written comments. This denial of a voice in housing policy triggered the bitter and countrywide rent strike against the Housing Finance Act that confirmed the weakness of the tenants' movement as a national force, and returned it with a renewed commitment to expanding the limited opportunities of formal participation schemes with their council landlords (Hayes 1989).

This reassessment of the early development of tenant participation illustrates how tenants hailed in their aspirations as rights-bearing citizens looked for recognition of this equal status from their local authority landlord, and were confronted with continued inequalities. Council tenants reacted against accusations of being 'featherbedded' and unfairly subsidised, and acted out of commitment to an ideal

FIGURE 3.1 Getting their ideas past the bureaucratic barrier: consultation with tenants' federations on regional housing priorities

Photo provided by Leeds Tenants Federation

of universal public housing that was fast becoming a stigmatised residual sector. The vision they promoted was of a council housing sector managed in partnership with its tenants, a general needs housing service that awarded the recognition of citizenship to its users. In the dismantlement of the general needs model, as the residualisation of council housing gradually branded all tenants as welfare recipients, the only route to escape second-class status appeared to be through participation and the limited social acceptance granted them within the constraints of this particular relationship of power.

Theorising power in participation

Association with the campaigns of a tenants' movement and with the politics of community action enables participation in public services to be conceptualised as a process of empowerment: as a challenge to existing power relations (Somerville 1998; Paddison *et al.* 2008). The perception that participation can be liberatory, that it is about *taking* power (Grayson 1997), connects a radical narrative of the tenants' movement with the ideals of equality and self-determination popularised by the protest movements of the 1960s and the so-called 'new social welfare movements' of the 1970s (Williams 1992). This interpretation of tenant participation through democratic theory depicts it as the pursuit of participatory democracy (Paddison *et al.* 2008), 'perceived as a way to achieve change in a society whose problems are endemic in its very structures' as Cliff Hague (1990: 244) observed. As participatory democracy, tenant participation is presented as a collective process, and it is tenants' organisations, not tenants as individual consumers, who are seen as the main actors. These groups are 'counter-publics' who are able to debate questions of needs and public resources and generate their own strategies for services. They operate as 'parallel discursive arenas where members of subordinated social groups invent and circulate counter-discourses, which in turn permit them to formulate oppositional interpretations of their identities, interests and needs' (Fraser 1997: 81). The goal of participation, understood in this way, is to secure 'a permanent shift in the balance of power from landlords to tenants' (Somerville 1998: 235).

Participation has been recruited into a government project to reinvigorate the processes of representative democracy and to reinspire public interest in politics and public respect for politicians (ODPM 2005). Active citizenship and civic participation have been preached by Conservative, Labour and Coalition governments (Kearns 1992; Imrie and Raco 2003), and the strategies of neighbourhood planning, community rights, participatory budgeting, and community asset transfer have as their apparent goal the empowerment of citizens and their engagement in the tasks of government (DCLG 2008; Localism Act 2011). An upsurge of interest in citizens' juries and other deliberative democratic processes has been accompanied by discussions about co-production or collaborative governance, and tenant participation has been seen as one strand in a wider policy of deliberative democracy (Newman *et al.* 2004). The rise of deliberative processes in government has run parallel to assertions about the failure of representative democracy founded in part on public choice theories in which the ballot box has been equated with the marketplace and voters depicted as consumers choosing between policies (Hirst 1997). The origin of this view lies in the application of market principles to political theory and the resulting assumption that citizens operate as discerning consumers driven by an appreciation of their economic self-interest (Bengtsson and Clapham 1997). In this scenario, participation is envisaged as a market force or an injection of proxy competition into public services in the form of new actors and new tensions. Writing when participation was still a new concept in social policy, Ann Richardson (1983: 27) claimed that any new relationship between service users and service providers creates opportunities and potential outcomes that cannot be pre judged by existing power relations or entrenched interests. Instead, Richardson and later commentators (Cairncross *et al.* 1994; Bengtsson 1995) argued that tenant participation should be considered as a non-zero sum process in which tenants and housing providers both gain from bargaining, though one may gain more, and from which no single outcome can be predicted from the start. In this model, participation in housing becomes a two-way process, bringing benefits to both landlords and tenants, a partnership agreed by all to be 'a good thing' (Riseborough 1998: 221).

These interpretations of the power relations of tenant participation echo a preoccupation in housing policy with the role of 'voice' as a market mechanism (Gilroy 1998; Carr *et al.* 2001). In public choice and rational choice theories, 'voice', famously paired with 'exit' as Albert Hirschman's (1970) twin strategies for preventing the decline of firms and organisations, unleashes the unknown power of the consumer into the previously uncompetitive monopoly of public services. Applied to tenant participation, the invocation of 'voice' signifies a belief that the mere introduction of a new set of people into the decision-making process carries a transformative force that has power to break down barriers and initiate change. While 'exit' has long been a central feature of economics as the response of the market's invisible hand to deteriorating performance or superior competition, Albert Hirschman imported the concept of 'voice' from politics and gave it a free enterprise setting.

> Voice is here defined as any attempt at all to change, rather than to escape from, an objectionable state of affairs, whether through individual or collective petition to the management directly in charge, through appeal to a higher authority with the intention of forcing a change in management, or through various types of actions and protests, including those that are meant to mobilise public opinion.
>
> *(Hirschman 1970: 30)*

The pairing of 'voice' with the free market concept of 'exit' saw it incorporated as a market-like discipline (Stoker 2004), an essential tool for bringing the semblance of competition to public sector monopolies and promoted as such by theorists seeking to apply a neoclassical model of economic behaviour to public goods and services. 'Voice' became enshrined as a transferable suite of participation mechanisms that could be applied to any public sector monopoly or welfare service to trigger consumer pressure as surely and smoothly as market forces (Paul 1992; Rodwin 2000). It has been in this guise, as 'a market-like force' (Hirschman and Nelson 1976: 386), that participation has been ushered through the social housing sector under government edict and managerial reform.

As the wobbly pillar of the welfare state (Torgerson 1987), housing has always been the least decommodified of welfare services, and its public provision has been increasingly rationed to those in extremes of housing need, with the majority of new lettings going to those on the lowest incomes. Social housing has become a marginal and dispensable constituent of the welfare state, providing successive governments with an almost uncontested territory in which to experiment with the introduction of market principles into public services (Malpass 2008). Alongside the privatisation measures of the Right to Buy, the transfer of council housing to registered social landlords, the development of shared ownership and intermediate market renting, the incursion of commercial management practices, and the creation of quasi-markets and choice-based schemes in public sector housing (Malpass 2005), 'voice' has been engineered through the public policy initiative of tenant participation in a menu of involvement processes that includes surveys, feedback, focus groups and customer panels (TSA 2010). The presumptions of market theory that underpin this model of participation assume that the mere presence of tenants in landlord decision-making processes carries the transformative impact of consumer pressure (TSA/Audit Commission 2010). This idealist rhetoric ignores the power of the sponsoring agency to convene the deliberation, select the participants and orchestrate the outcome. Tenant participation, as it is played out by landlords and tenants' organisations, takes place in a space that has been already marked out by discourses that define what services are open to participation, what the aim of that participation should be and what outcomes it is expected to have. This is a public sphere in an increasingly privatised space, where the opportunities for deliberation are narrowed and the range of possible outcomes has been preordained in policy discussions, political discourses and conceptual arenas that are never open to participation (Mouffe 1993; Cooper and Hawtin 1997, 1998). Recent reviews of social housing regulation have confirmed tenant participation as a relationship between consumers and producers over service standards, performance scrutiny and complaint (Cave 2007; DCLG 2010). This conflation of participation with consumer protection appears to signal the closure of debate over the power relations of tenant participation and to establish its 'common sense' definition as a relationship between tenants and housing providers over standards and costs (Audit Commission 2004a). The established belief is that participation serves everyone's interests, that it is the action of responsible parties (Flint 2004a; Paddison *et al.* 2008), and that it takes place in a neutral zone in which the idea of antagonism or conflict has little place (Cooper and Hawtin 1998; Carr *et al.* 2001). In making decisions about goods and services, and in seeking to wield influence over service providers, the tenant as welfare recipient is expected to learn from participation the rules of commodity exchange and to undertake an education in the responsibilities typically associated with property ownership, seen as the hallmark of the empowered citizen (Hart *et al.* 1997).

While Ministers have quoted philosophies that promote the devolution of power to local communities, the actual implementation of participatory democracy as a government project has been unsurprisingly limited and has not been accompanied by any meaningful transfer of power (Marinetto 2003; Taylor 2003; Newman *et al.* 2004). The noticeable failure of participation to bring about fundamental change in who exercises authority and influence has sharpened the scepticism of some commentators and renewed criticisms of it as a mechanism of control and a means of legitimating existing power relations (Riseborough 1998; Carr *et al.* 2001). Participation programmes can be scrutinised and graded according to the extent to which they succeed in transferring power with opportunities for community control or self-management favoured in Sherry Arnstein's (1969) highly charged model of a 'Ladder of Citizen Participation'. Arnstein's assessment of the power relations of participation was shaped by the Community Action projects in the USA during the early 1960s (Marris and Rein 1974), and, as presidential advisor on the later Model Cities Program, Arnstein witnessed the emergence of a powerful movement for neighbourhood control, inspired by the militant civil rights movement and embracing the tactics of direct collective action (Cary 1970; American Planning Association 2005). Arnstein's 'ladder' identified the structural inequalities and power imbalances that restrict the outcomes of participation. She argued that only a transfer of formal decision-making powers to service users, or 'citizen power', could rescue participation from the processes of manipulation, therapy and tokenism (Arnstein 1969: 216). This interpretation was applied by agencies such as the Tenant Participation Advisory Service (TPAS) and the Priority Estates Project (PEP) to evangelise tenant takeovers of the management of council estates in England during the 1980s, and won governmental support as part of a strategy to open up municipal housing to forms of competition, a development that, perversely, reinforced the portrait of participation as a method of social control (Furbey *et al.* 1996; Goodlad 2001). The ease with which participation can be made to serve the strategies of government has confirmed it as a social policy laden with moral and coercive messages, as 'responsible participation' (Paddison *et al.* 2008) or 'responsibilisation' (Clarke 2005), a strategy in which power is increasingly concentrated to shape the behaviour of tenants. Participation has come to mean participation in the marketplace through the consumption of private goods, and as a technology of government it appears intended to encourage entrepreneurial behaviour in responsible citizens (Imrie and Raco 2003). Scholars influenced by Michel Foucault's theory of governmentality (see Rose 1999; Cruikshank 1999; Dean 1999; Flint 2004b; McKee and Cooper 2008; McKee 2009a) regard participation and empowerment as characteristics of governmental practices that seek to structure and shape the field of possible actions (Foucault 1982: 221; Lemke 2002). Participation appears to confer agency and award some limited influence to tenants but does so within parameters that guide and shape their behaviour and reinforce, and effectively perpetuate, unequal relations of power and resource distribution (Cooper and Hawtin 1998: 15). By equating responsibility with economic rationality, participation serves a political programme in which the market is taken as the organisational principle for society, and through which public services, collective insurance and redistributive state functions are intended to be gradually reduced, privatised or withdrawn (Lemke 2001).

While it is reasonable to think of participation as a behavioural strategy of government, and tempting to regard people who are committed to participation as co-opted or deceived, it would be a mistake to imagine that tenants are unable to influence the development and outcome of these discourses entirely. The ability of service users to resist, amend or subvert the disciplinary intentions of governmental programmes that aim to transform their behaviour has been well evidenced (Clarke *et al.* 2007; Barnes and Prior 2009; Newman and Clarke 2009; McKee 2010). The transformation of the welfare state from its post-war settlement has been the outcome of a complex set of political relations in which popular struggle and popular movements have been influential in shaping the development of public services, and of what it means to be 'public' (Williams 1994). The new social settlement is an uneasy assemblage of differing or opposing viewpoints, 'an active process in which positions are negotiated, displaced, subordinated and co-opted' (Clarke *et al.* 2007: 35). Participation was a central theme in the challenge of social movements to the governance of the welfare state but it became a transformative project under the hegemony of neo-classical economics. A dominant social narrative around participation was constructed by recruiting radically different intentions into an assemblage of order, or a 'common sense' definition. The emerging hegemonic discourse becomes an accepted system of thought, beliefs and behaviours that governs our everyday understanding of social relations, and orchestrates the ways in which we consent to, and reproduce particular relations of power in our daily interactions (Butler 2000: 13–14). It is one where market mechanisms of supply and demand, and entrepreneurial notions of responsibility dominate and provide the model for social relations. The concept of hegemony has been applied to the major changes that have taken place since the mid-1970s in the organisation of welfare in Britain, as popular discontent with the paternalism and exclusionary control of public services was harnessed to a project that asserted freedom of choice, an unfettered market and the individualisation of risk (Hall 1988; Torfing 1999). Hegemony offers a sophisticated framework through which to examine the development of tenant participation and its significance in the restructuring of social housing. It is a particularly useful concept to understand how social movements and once-contentious voices can become immersed in these regulatory practices, and how this apparent co-option or absorption can continue to generate collective oppositional identities. In her work on hegemony, Judith Butler (2000) addresses the problem of those 'domesticated' social movements, whose contentious politics have achieved regulatory outcomes and thereby reinforced existing relations of power. Butler's concern stems from an optimism grounded in a specific theory of resistance from

FIGURE 3.2 Standards and costs: enlisting tenants as consumers in the improvement of their landlord's business performance

Photo provided by Leeds Tenants Federation

within power, and she argues that the engagement of social movements in hegemonic discourses can enable them to effect changes in power relations that would not otherwise be achievable. An approach drawing on the work of Judith Butler is therefore admirably suited to an analysis of the role played by the tenants' movement in participation. It allows participation to be understood as a regulatory discourse while maintaining focus on the role of tenants in constructing and changing that discourse through collective action. By drawing on Butler's work on identity construction and the reiteration in practical action of those identities, a tenants' movement can be discerned that is constructed and regulated through participation and that by 'doing' participation subverts it. The next section begins to explore in fieldwork tenants' experience of participation in housing organisations. First, it evidences the revelatory and transformative effect that participation can have for tenants. It then examines tenants' awareness of the limitations of participation as a ritualised and regulatory practice.

Equal citizens?

Stephanie, a tenant director of a social housing company formed in stock transfer from her municipal authority, recounts her positive feelings about the value of tenant participation and the role it plays in her organisation at a discussion at the annual conference of the Tenant Participation and Advisory Service (TPAS) held at the Birmingham International Conference Centre (ID 2). Stephanie feels that because of tenant participation she is, finally, being treated as an equal. The Chief Executive Officer of her housing company has let her know she can call in at any time; her Director of Operations asked her to draw up the organisation's first tenant participation strategy, and, nine years later, that document still forms the basis of the company's way of working. Stephanie says:

> I mean with us, I think it's about attitude and the attitude is, I mean, it's a consultation, it's, I feel when I walk in that company I am on the same level as the housing staff and anybody else. I'm not any better, I'm not any worse, I'm not patronised.

For Stephanie, her experience demonstrates that participation has brought tenants the respect they deserve. The recognition Stephanie feels she receives from the senior managers seems to epitomise everything that tenants wanted in their original desire for participation in housing services. Gina, a committee member of one of the regional tenants' federations (ID 3) expresses this desire succinctly:

> Tenants are equal. It's equal rights, equal citizens and that's how it should be continued to be looked at. We're just as equal as anybody else, we're still people, we're still humans.

This heart felt message is echoed in the title of the report that gave life to the National Tenant Voice in 2008, 'Citizens of Equal Worth' (NTV Project Group 2008b), and the sentiment is expressed by tenants throughout this book. The longing for recognition as an equal citizen may be the passion that drives Gina to travel miles across the country on buses and trains to attend consultation events and voice her concerns about her housing service, but her equal status is conditional on her participation. It is granted to her only in the process of participating, and if she decides not to take part in her landlord's consultation processes, she returns to the status of passive welfare recipient. She becomes again the object of disciplinary interventions intended to modify her behaviour. She will no longer command the status of the active citizen, the possessor of equal rights.

Christine, a member of a tenant management organisation (ID 10), is very aware of these limits to the progress of tenants. She says:

> I just feel myself personally that you're not at the bottom of their list any more. You're not an equal – we'll never be an equal – but I think it's for the better that we are able to come over and speak to them and not be belittled.

The same conclusion is drawn by Susan, at her regional tenants' federation meeting (ID 6):

> The simplest way to describe it is if tenants don't engage with the landlord, then effectively what happens is things get done to them, whether they like it or not. And if they do engage then they can have some say in what the things are.

The concentration of people on very low incomes, often outside the active labour force, in one easily demarcated sector has allowed social housing to become a proxy for government strategies that adopt the concept of empowerment as the cure for a putative welfare dependency (Fraser and Gordon 1997; Somerville 2005a). While homeownership and the consumption of private goods have become synonymous with responsible citizenship under the supremacy of market values, tenants find themselves relegated to the status of flawed consumers whose citizenship is contingent (Bauman 1998), and they remain subject to a range of intensive management processes that are the consequence of their position in the housing market (Clapham *et al.* 2000; Flint 2006). With citizenship defined by homeownership, the participation of tenants grants them only limited recognition. By participating in housing management they display responsibility, but their tenure serves as an indelible stigma of dependence. The experience of stigma, received through attitudes, behaviours and policies, is common to social housing tenants today and provides the motive for participation. The enduring enactment in media representation and government policy of this stigma ensures that participation becomes for tenants a repetitive activity, an unending iteration that promises recognition but never fully delivers. Like Alice's Red Queen, it takes all the participation they can do to stay in the same place, as this reflection among tenants at a TPAS conference (ID 9) makes clear:

YVONNE: We haven't changed the popular image.
CLARE: Not of council tenants.
YVONNE: Not for the politicians and people that think they matter.
LINDA: Those who think they know everything.
WENDY: Hmm.
YVONNE: And the connotations of the word social because the first thing you think of social is you're [on the dole].
CLARE: [You're on the social].
YVONNE: You're on income support.
WENDY: You're a skiver, yes, you're a skiver.
YVONNE: Meaning you've never worked in your life.

The representation of 'council' estates as crime-ridden places and of social housing tenants as morally deviant has been catalogued extensively (see Card 2001; Flint 2006; Johnston and Mooney 2007), and stories of these supposedly dysfunctional families have enlivened film and television fiction and documentary journalism. A survey respondent at the same conference asserted:

> I am a council tenant and proud but I'm treated as a lower class person because social housing tenants are all unemployed, uneducated, single parents, have problem children and so on. Social housing equals social workers equals on the social equals benefits equals deprivation equals crime.

Attempts to transform these imagined welfare tenants into rational consumers by instituting choice in lettings or, through stock transfer, choice of landlord have dominated housing policy for the last two decades, but for Paul (ID 2), a member of a tenants' panel, this free market language merely underlines the sense of prejudice:

> You feel like a beggar some time and as a beggar you have no choice, because if they subsidise your rent, then you've not much to say. Beggars can't be choosers, some people say that.

Discourses of morality have long been prevalent in housing management and have gained new salience (Haworth and Manzi 1999). Anti-social behaviour initiatives have positioned housing management officers as the governors of behaviour (Flint 2006), while the engagement of housing organisations in 'worklessness' programmes, following John Hills's (2007) report, sharpened the focus on the sector as a warehouse for the poor. The majority of social housing tenants depend for their income on means-tested benefits or retirement pensions; their lack of status is matched by the absence of economic power and they are constantly assailed by messages reporting their own failure (Gilroy 1998). For this group of residents from a Tenant Management Organisation (ID 10) the daily reproduction of stigma by housing staff constituted the primary reason they took over the running of their own estate:

JEAN: They used to speak to you as though you were . . .
CHRISTINE: God, yeah.
GARY: Yeah.
JEAN: Dog muck under their feet.

Nor are these attitudes a thing of the past, as Elizabeth (ID 2) maintains in a discussion with tenant directors:

> A lot of them when you go into the offices they still look as if, well, have you just come off their shoe.

The identification of tenants as 'second-class citizens' appears at odds with the dynamics of equality and citizenship that power the interpellative call of participation. The idea of interpellation refers to a process of recognition in which social identity is conferred and the social subject is set in motion. In the work of Louis

Althusser (2001: 118) an individual is granted social recognition only by obeying a call to order from the law. Althusser describes how a man walking away is hailed by a policeman as 'Hey, you there!' and how the man turns, recognising himself in the call. In obeying it he is both given a social identity and called to order as a subject. Judith Butler (1993: 121) explains this: 'The subject not only receives recognition, but attains as well a certain order of social existence, in being transferred from an outer region of indifferent, questionable, or impossible being to the discursive or social domain of the subject.'

The development of participation, and particularly the way in which it has been driven through the social housing sector by government policy and regulation, has brought tenants from an 'outer region of indifferent, questionable, or impossible being' to a position where their views are actively canvassed, and they can sit as potential equals on their landlord's management board. But the abject identification that inspired tenant demands for participation remains a constant accompaniment to their contemporary involvement in housing management. The social recognition they achieve in the act of participation inducts tenants into the subject status that conditioned their original demands for equality. It affirms them as problematic and conditional citizens, and cements this identity as the essential quality of being a social housing tenant. In other words, participation requires that tenants act in the ways in which they are already described. Their very intelligibility, the social recognition that they seek, depends on their reiteration of the norms of this identification. In order to be recognised in their claim of equality, tenants must first accept that they are not and never can be equal. This is a message that tenants hear loud and clear, as this extract from a discussion among members of local residents' groups (ID 4) shows:

GRETA: Well, we're all sort of, you're tarred with the same brush aren't you? You are, you're a tenant and that's it.
BOB: And we're all sinking in the same boat.
GRETA: Yeah.
BOB: [Laughs]
JANE: And we've all got to fight for what
GRETA: And you've got to fight for what you want.
BOB: Yep.
GRETA: And we shouldn't have to fight.
EDNA: Shouldn't be postcoded either.
DEIRDRE: That's life, isn't it?

In this dialogue tenants recognise their exclusion from the equality of citizenship and, in identifying this as an injustice done to them, proceed to make a claim on the concept of universal rights. In resolving to fight for their rights, they reference a history of rights-claiming movements. Tenants are not readily included in the definition of citizens but that does not stop them having recourse to the term. In making a claim on a universal concept that excludes them, they reveal its particularity and challenge its limitations (Butler 2000: 39). This claim to the rights of citizenship is articulated as a basic entitlement in the discourse of participation, expressed here by two members of a tenants' panel (ID 16).

JOHN: A tenant is a tenant when all's said and done. They pay their dues like everybody else.
KEVIN: But I think what it is, is we believe that all tenants deserve the same rights as anybody else.

The contradiction at the heart of participation both reinforces and challenges existing relations of power. Tenants are presented with the possibility of an equality that contradicts their subordination in all other identifications. But that equality is negated by the fact that they are tenants and therefore can never be equal. Chantal Mouffe (2000: 302) dubs this a contradictory interpellation: 'A situation in which subjects constructed in subordination by a set of discourses are, at the same time, interpellated as equal by other discourses'. It is a contradiction that allows tenants to question and to challenge the social identity bestowed upon them. The social recognition inherent in the act of participation cannot then merely reproduce subjection; it constructs a new social subject. This makes the interpellative call of participation – the award of social recognition – a revelatory and transformative moment for tenants, and many in this research cited a particular occasion or circumstance when they glimpsed the possibilities they thought participation could offer. This epiphany may have been a moment when for them injustice came sharply into focus, but it was also a moment in which they felt motivated and inspired. This combination of subjection and subjectivity is integral to the identification of tenants through participation.

'That changed me,' Ron (ID 13) said, describing the moment when he encountered what he describes as the tenants' movement. It was at a meeting convened by his landlord to discuss housing transfer proposals. It was a moment of realisation:

> It was a Sunday morning, I'll never forget it, it was a Sunday morning, and we all sat round a table. I thought, it's funny, we can have a say here, and change our way of thinking.

It was to launch Ron as a social movement activist; within weeks he was elected chair of a borough tenants' panel and, a year later, was one of the founders of a regional tenants' federation.

Michael (ID 17) recounts a similar experience of Damascene conversion in his first encounter with a tenants' federation engaged in participation.

> I found it infectious. Um, that these, this small band of people were on this like mini-crusade to change the way the council were working and they were being restricted on every corner.

Neither Ron nor Michael believed that the participation process was likely to lead to any immediate improvements or that it would benefit them personally. Michael immediately concluded that his landlord had little interest in tenants' views and was unlikely to take any suggestions on board. What attracted him, what possessed him at that moment was not a belief in dialogue or the power of 'voice'. It was the suggestion that change was elusive but attainable.

> We found it hard to walk away, you know, once you were in. It was, and it still is, it's infectious, you know, and I think every little, sort of piece, every small victory still means something even now, you know, it can be just changing a line on a policy or a strategy but it still means something, to sort of, still putting our mark on things.

John (ID 14) saw a television documentary in which councillors 'with clipped accents' were talking about what was best for tenants. Looking back he identifies this as the moment that he became a housing campaigner who went on to become a director of the National Tenants' Organisation.

> It's silly. Something simple like that.

Simple, but life changing; it was an interpellative call that initiated him into the tenants' movement, that constructed a tenants' movement for him. In these three

FIGURE 3.3 Putting our mark on things: glimpsing the possibilities of equality in participation

Photo provided by Leeds Tenants Federation

accounts, tenants were able to glimpse the possibilities of new directions on an occasion when they were also, and paradoxically, reminded of their stigmatised status. These were moments of epiphany in which they were able to question and to rearticulate an identity, 'spots of time' in which they were reminded of their exclusion from citizenship, and yet, simultaneously, directed to their rights as citizens. Tenant participation has become a rights–claiming strategy, a process in which tenants challenge an abject identification and carve for themselves a new and positive collective identity. The strategy they embark on is a journey into the rights of citizenship; they make claims on the equality and status that characterise the lawful bearers of rights (Marshall 1950). The next section explores their encounter with the boundaries of participation and the effects of its hegemonic foreclosure.

The foreclosure of participation

After a committee meeting in their office on a public housing estate, members of a northern tenants' federation (ID 11) reflect on the benefits of participation. They identify four themes:

SANDRA: You've got to talk to your landlord else you'll get nothing.
BERNARD: You can also gain a certain amount of control over what happens on the estate. You don't get the brown and black colours of front doors any more.
FRANK: You get respect as well.
BERNARD: You get an insight into what they're planning and they also get an insight into how you think, so it helps get rid of any bad feeling from the start.

Participation presents itself in each of these aspects; it is a coercive, regulatory framework that impacts on power relations and that appears to reward tenants with improved status, within the semblance of a partnership of shared interests. The hegemonic project to restructure social housing through participation has success-fully articulated assorted strands of democratic concerns, co-operative traditions, consumer values and communitarian beliefs into a coherent discourse that has secured wide commitment to a market-based reform programme. These strands appeared separate and distinguishable when Liz Cairncross *et al.* (1997) from Glasgow University coined their influential appraisal of participation through three ideal landlord types: traditional, consumerist and citizenship models. The traditional model was characterised as a managerial strategy aimed at maintaining the acquiescence of tenants, the citizenship model acknowledged the collective action of tenants' organisations, and the consumer model perceived tenants as individuals engaged in a process of exchange with their landlords. Cairncross *et al.* explained that consumerist housing organisations 'pursue an individualist form of tenant participation as part of the establishment of market relations in council housing'

(Cairncross *et al.* 1997: 42). When Paul Hickman revisited the Cairncross typology in 2006, his analysis confirmed the prediction that the consumer model would become increasingly influential in tenant participation but argued that the three ideal types were no longer sufficient to conceptualise the complexity of tenant participation practices. The scope of participation had widened beyond the narrow landlord–tenant relationship, and opportunities for involvement had opened in areas of management, policy and regeneration. The number of participants had grown and, against the trend, collective tenants' organisations had retained a role in consumerist housing organisations, while landlords following the traditional model had also broadened their approach to participation. Despite this evidence of diversity and expansion, Hickman argued that the meaning and purpose of participation was now almost entirely defined through the traditional and consumerist models. Participation was no longer pursued as an activity that empowered tenants but rather as a mechanism for providing better housing management services. Definitions of participation as a process of empowerment and democracy, associated by Cairncross with the citizenship model, had been excluded from the dominant meaning. Landlords decided when, where and how tenants would be involved in their housing service and the unifying theme among landlords was 'a desire to retain power and control over tenant participation' (Hickman 2006: 222).

These twin snapshots of the development of tenant participation represented by the Glasgow study, conducted between 1987 and 1991, and Hickman's source, the Sheffield Hallam study between 1998 and 2001 (Cole *et al.* 2000, 2001), chart a process of foreclosure. Questions of power, citizenship and democracy were gradually marginalised and then excluded from the practice of tenant participation. Over this period participation policy was centrally driven by the 'exit' strategies of the Conservative governments with their promotion of tenant management and the introduction of compulsory competitive tendering for housing management accompanying the Right to Buy as strategies to purge social housing from public ownership (Gilroy 1998), and Labour's pursuit of 'choice and voice', delivered through the escalation of the stock transfer process and the promise of citizen governance in housing organisations. Peter Malpass (2005: 203) explained how these government policies defined and narrowed the boundaries of participation:

> The big strategic decisions about the future direction of social housing have been made centrally, leaving tenants with the freedom to influence the timing of change at a local level and a choice as to which of the restricted list of (centrally defined) options to adopt.

The aims, processes and outcomes of what participation is understood to be were refined and narrowed in the assemblage of a particular hegemonic relationship of power. Those strands of participation that had the potential to contest that relationship or that did not directly support it were marginalised or excluded outright. These discursive frontiers set limits on what was accepted as participation, and what could be achieved through its practices, and tenants are aware of them as defined boundary lines, as this discussion among members of a tenants' federation (ID 5) shows:

JULIA: I think we are being listened to more, but I think there's only so far we can go and then once we kind of overstep their boundaries and they just put the shutters on us.

TERRI: Yeah.

JULIA: That is, that's the feeling that I get sometimes, I don't know whether [anybody else] =

TERRI: [I agree] =

JULIA: Has the same feeling, you know, that while ever we're saying what they want to hear, uh, but the minute we start pushing against

TERRI: Once we get to a strategic level their views are =

JULIA: And they put the shutters up =

TERRI: We don't know what we're talking about =

JULIA: Keep us at arm's length.

The contemporary definition of participation, with its rituals of practice, is the outcome of forty years of government reviews, performance management initiatives, regulatory injunctions, landlord innovations and tenant pressure. In 2011, the Coalition government withdrew all but the most essential consumer protection from social housing tenants, leaving local authorities and registered housing providers to devise their own participation schemes, while restricting the role of regulation to the policing of economic viability (Localism Act 2011; Homes and Communities Agency 2012). The framework of tenant scrutiny panels initiated by the short-lived consumer regulator, the Tenant Services Authority (TSA 2010), established under the previous Labour government, continued to be encouraged as accepted practice alongside tenant involvement in the arbitration and settlement of complaints (Bliss and Lambert 2012). This role for tenants in inspecting and evaluating their landlords' housing performance to service standards added to a suite of 'voice' measures that provided individual residents or tenants' groups opportunities to be consulted and occasionally empowered, although generally involvement in decision-making was reserved for those taking formal office as tenant directors of housing companies or tenant-management organisations (TSA/Audit Commission 2010; Housing Right to Manage 2012).

What the majority of tenant participation rituals have in common is their focus on enlisting the voluntary help of tenants in the improvement of their landlord's business performance. This is a managerial interpretation of participation with the accent on economy and efficiency, measured through performance indicators, audits and satisfaction surveys (Harries and Vincent-Jones 2001; Flint 2004a), embedded in the social housing sector by Labour governments from 1997 onwards, through the Audit Commission's Housing Inspectorate, supported by the National

Framework for Tenant Participation Compacts (DETR 1999) and mirrored for the housing association sector under the Housing Corporation (1998). The Audit Commission's (2004b) inspection methodology, their Key Lines of Enquiry, centred regulatory attention on the measurable impact of participation on housing service delivery to the exclusion of its acknowledged effects on community action or empowerment (Audit Commission 2004a). The role of participation was delimited to the benefits it accrued for housing organisations. John Flint (2004a: 897) captured this cogently when he stated 'the empowerment and increased autonomy of individual tenants is a method for further empowering the ability of housing agencies to govern successfully'.

At the TPAS conference of tenant participants from around the country (ID 8), Cheryl reflected on the contemporary framework of participation:

> It gives you a voice, but that's all it gives you [. . .] They want to close our housing office down and we've been through the consultation but they will do whatever they want to do anyway. They have to be seen to consult you, it's a legal requirement, but they will move heaven and earth to do what they want to do anyway. So we've got a voice, but we haven't got the power, if you know what I mean.

Despite the range of opportunities apparently open to tenants to influence housing decision-making, tenants remain excluded from participation in certain areas of the landlord business, in all but the most innovative housing organisations. In the discussion at the conference, residents who had asked their landlords for influence over finance and rent setting, staffing issues, investment planning and contractor selection, reported the refusal with which their request had been met. Paul (ID 2), a member of a tenant panel, noted:

> There are some areas where they want to consult tenants. Some other areas they want to make the decisions and they won't share the decisions.

Where tenants are given access to these decision-making realms it is sometimes unclear what influence they are being allowed. Terri (ID 5) recounted her involvement in the selection of a cleaning contractor. Along with fellow tenants, she interviewed the contractors and voted for the one judged best in quality, only to learn that their landlord had awarded the contract to the company with the cheapest bid. Denise (ID 8) said she had been allowed to take part in the initial stage of staff recruitment but had not been given any role in decision-making:

> I've been told that we have no say in the personnel structure and so it is up to them who they employ, how they monitor that employment, and we are only involved in certain participation but certainly not that area.

The introduction of Tenant Participation Compacts at the end of the 1990s was associated with a readiness among landlords to characterise traditional tenants' organisations as unrepresentative. Tenants reported that they were expected to make their organisations 'more democratic than the local authority itself' in order to persuade their landlord to recognise them (Cole *et al.* 2001: 18). Funding and recognition were withdrawn from some self-organised tenants' organisations and landlord consultation forums were established to replace them. Paul Hickman (2006) cited this as evidence of the desire of housing organisations to maintain control over the participation process while landlords justified it with scathing reference to 'professional tenants' and the 'usual suspects' (Millward 2005). Providing regulatory support to this trend, the most significant element in the Audit Commission's foreclosure of participation was the emphasis it placed on ensuring diversity in landlord consultation processes and its implied criticism of representative tenant organisations for failing to demonstrate that they reflected the make-up of their local neighbourhoods (Housing Quality Network 2002). Landlords were instructed to profile their 'customers' and to assess the success of their participation schemes in helping them tailor their services more effectively; no regulatory weighting was accorded to the recognition or support of tenants' organisations, instead landlords were told to enable individuals to voice their opinions through surveys, focus groups and panels (Audit Commission 2004a). The public imagined for these deliberations was modelled on traditional notions of pluralism, recruited on the basis of essentialist identities to achieve a market-research notion of demographic representation (Barnes *et al.* 2003). Spurred on by the Audit Commission's inspection methodology, landlords took the opportunity to replace what were seen as 'difficult' tenants' groups with 'tame' tenant sounding boards (Morgan 2006: 231), while more borough councils withdrew financial support from federated and campaigning tenant organisations (Grayson 2007).

At a meeting of one of the few remaining regional tenants' federations (ID 6), Susan charts the decline of the traditional network of borough tenants' federations that once underpinned a democratic structure. Reeling off three examples of defunct tenants' organisations in boroughs across the London region, closed down because they opposed specific plans that their landlord was determined would be realised, she concludes:

> And then you've got sort of borough-wide tenants' councils or housing panels or a variety of things, and some are kind of anyway much closer linked with the local authority but not necessarily any less feisty, yeah?

Susan is keen to point out that the tenants recruited into these new processes share the same frames of reference as the autonomous federations that preceded them. But even if the tenants involved are no less 'feisty', the withdrawal of support from self-organised tenants' federations, paralleled by the ascent of market research techniques, appears to have undermined confidence in the effectiveness of participation among many. Ron (ID 3), a regional tenants' federation member who chairs a landlord-administered panel, confides:

> Yeah, well, experience is telling me, the longer I serve on these things, is that landlords, uh, in actual fact, don't want to listen to tenants. They think tenants are too critical of the landlord and they don't want to participate with them, never mind this partnership.

In focus groups and tenant panels the agenda is usually set by housing officers, and what is consulted on and what use is made of that consultation are matters controlled by the housing company. This has made transparent the imbalance of power in participation relationships, and highlighted the foreclosure of meanings once associated with democratic theory, something noted in discussion at Ron's regional tenants' federation (ID 3):

TERESA: And what frustrates me is, when they do have a consultation exercise, they don't involve the tenants at stage one.
ANDREW: Hmm.
TERESA: They involve them at stage 'the end'.
RON: Five ((laughs))
TERESA: And, you know, and that's what frustrates me, because us as tenants, we could change the way that thing goes, and I don't think they like that.
RON: No, they've already set their stall out
TERESA: Yes =
RON: Which way they're going and =
TERESA: They don't want =
RON: They don't want to deviate up another path that could be better.

Autonomous and self-determined tenants' organisations are able to 'formulate oppositional interpretations' (Fraser 1997: 81) and devise 'different norms and alternative values' (Barnes *et al.* 2003: 383). They speak of a tradition excluded from contemporary participation policy. In what has been called 'the supermarket model' of social housing (Clapham and Satsangi 1992: 66), in which an idealised free market is referenced to support a package of managerial reforms, autonomous tenants' groups lend themselves to caricature as selfish interest groups disrupting the free exchange of goods and information (Barnes 1999). In this argument the unorganised individual tenant consumer is seen as legitimate, while the collective voice of tenants is excluded for allegedly pursuing a specific self-interested goal that is unrepresentative of the general views of tenants. A definition of the purpose of tenant participation as integral to the business improvement of housing companies clearly frames this contention. It is the housing professional who defines what is legitimate and what is representative by controlling the meaning of participation or, as Nicholas Abercrombie (1994: 50) put it, 'the authority of the producer is sustained by the capacity to define the meaning of the transaction.' A model of participation in which tenants are recruited as data sources (Beresford 1988) so their experience and views can be harvested by experts for the business improvement of housing companies reinforces the power of the landlord or housing provider (Millward 2005). Tenants who contributed to research in this book employed the notion of the 'tick-box exercise' to indicate the exclusion by housing providers of ideas of empowerment, democracy or challenge from the meaning of participation. In a discussion at his regional federation (ID 6), Najinder said:

> Our housing panels are more often a talk shop rather than a consultation or participation so they just, the council just engages us where they want to, er, tick the box. They've done everything what they've decided upon, and they just come and do a presentation at a meeting and say we've consulted you, you didn't ask us any questions, so it's all done, so.

This theme is taken up in discussion (ID 6) as Jean reflects on her attendance at meetings convened by her housing organisation:

> I felt they were telling me what were going to be done, instead of asking us what we thought. And it was just a matter of, er, ticking a box.

Theresa (ID 3) expands the criticism implied in these discussions:

> I think the landlords [. . .] they've got like little sections of tenants that they know they're going to get away with. You know, ticking the box, yes we, we've consulted on this. In fact they haven't consulted, they took a piece of paper, they've said 'right we're doing this; we just want you to agree to it. You've agreed to it and that's consultation.' I hate that. That's dictation to me, it's not consultation.

For all these tenant participants, the landlord's approach to tenant participation is characterised as partial, self-serving and fundamentally flawed. Yvonne (ID 9) and John (ID 13) pour scorn on landlord-administered focus groups and their recruitment of compliant tenants to confirm the decisions of the housing provider:

YVONNE: They ring them up at the last minute, because they know quite a few people have got other commitments, so they'll ring them that they know who don't do anything all day, 'we'll send you a taxi, can you be here in three?' 'Yeah I'll be' and it's just to fill, it's just to fill a space and tick a box. They've fulfilled it; it looks as if they've done.

JOHN: Taxied to, taxied from, and a nice cup of tea and a bun. It allows an organisation to put forward its good news. Does it allow an organisation to address the deeper concerns? No. Because the agenda is set by the organisation, it is focused on the organisation and the feedback is in a form that the organisation chooses.

The potential for participation to change power relations and to widen democracy has been foreclosed to reinforce the power of housing organisations and public officials. This foreclosure of the possibilities of participation has marginalised the voices of 'counter-publics' (Barnes *et al*. 2003: 396) and delineated what it is possible for tenants to say and do, and what actions they may engage in (Norval 1996: 4). This chapter has charted the rise of tenant participation and the outcomes of the engagement of tenants and tenant organisations in partnership with their landlords. It has demonstrated the revelatory and transformative effect that participation can have in awarding tenants the status of citizens. It has also evidenced a process of foreclosure through which a range of differing conceptions of participation has been compressed into a singular definition of 'responsible participation', a regulated and ritualised practice in which market mechanisms offer choice and voice to propagate behavioural norms and embody regulated identifications. The chapter has clearly indicated the willingness of tenants to contest this foreclosure, to reclaim excluded identities and to challenge the ritual iterations of participation. The next chapter begins to explore the contentious claims and collective identifications that emerge from the everyday partnerships of tenant engagement.

4

CONSTRUCTING A TENANT VOICE

This chapter charts the assemblage of the collective identity of a tenants' movement, and shows how tenants construct a unifying package of common interests, shared values and contentious beliefs from the practices of participation. It begins with an exploration of participation as voice, a market force similar in effect to exit or competition. The metaphor of voice encapsulates the dominant definition of tenant participation. Marilyn, the secretary of a tenants' federation (ID 11), says:

> I don't think that being part of a resident involvement or a residents' group is giving you power, it's giving you a voice. I think that's the difference.

Voice, as Marilyn suggests, is participation shorn of all questions of power or democracy. These factors have been foreclosed, marginalised and excluded from the 'responsible participation' that now dominates the practices of social landlords. It is in the return of questions of empowerment and citizenship, the foreclosed identifications and excluded meanings that make up the 'constitutive outside' of participation (Butler 1993: 3), that collective action re-enters the landlord–tenant relationship. This chapter provides a detailed exploration of this return, illustrating how the performative power of voice is harnessed to uncover articulations of democracy, equality and rights from the rituals of participation.

Getting our voice heard

In a reform of housing policies according to the principles of public choice theory, tenant participation was recruited in the form of the quasi-market mechanism of voice to compensate for the absence of the competitive effect of exit or competition (Boyne and Walker 1999). Just as competition supposedly leads to high performance in private markets, the establishment of opportunities for participation in social housing, as in all public sector services, was intended to bring about improvements in efficiency and effectiveness. Voice, originally considered as political action, was adopted in economic theory as a mechanism 'like the market' (Hirschman and Nelson 1976: 386) and conflated with market forces; it was argued that the exercise of voice by consumers or service users affects 'behaviour modification in providers' (Paul 1994: 3). According to this economic model, 'voice' does more than signify a market force; it provides market signals that have an equivalent effect to consumer competition. The belief that voice exerts market-like stimuli that can change the behaviour of providers deeds it with performative power (Finlayson 2003). As a performative, voice or participation is perceived to have power to enact the social relations it describes, so the mere introduction of service users into the decision-making process supposedly carries a transformative effect (Richardson 1983). As a performative, voice does not describe a situation or an action; it makes something happen; as Judith Butler (1997b: 146) says, 'the word becomes the deed'. In John Austin's (1976) examples, performative speech can constitute the institution of marriage by declaring a couple 'man and wife', or bestow identity through the phrase 'I name this ship'. In the social housing sector, performative voice exerts its corrective force through 'an accepted conventional procedure having a certain conventional effect' (Austin 1976: 14). In the menu of participation options, through surveys and focus groups, in tenant scrutiny panels or on estate inspections, the mere presence of tenants in landlord decision-making processes is understood to enact market-like change.

The use of 'voice' appears to be a typical ontological metaphor (Lakoff and Johnston 1980) in which the process of 'speaking' conveys the effect of 'influence'. A 'louder' voice for tenants may be intended to signify that they have more influence in housing decisions; getting your voice 'heard' might mean that decision-makers change their plans as a result of what tenants say. But voice is more than a metaphor. As a performative it does not simply represent consumer influence, it exerts market power. By exercising voice within the accepted conventional procedure, tenants reference an idealised market in which providers are sensitive to consumer needs and participation initiates an automatic process of market readjustment. Tenants describing the process of participation routinely apply the metaphor of voice as a performative and indicate their expectation of quasi-market effects. 'Giving tenants a stronger voice' and 'ensuring tenants' voices are heard' are common expressions used by tenants contributing to this book to describe the aims and action of participation. They convey a direct causal relationship between speaking to decision-makers and influencing their decisions. Stephanie (ID 2), a tenant chair of her housing board, cites the market performative in her description of the process of participation:

> And it is also a question of just – just making them, I mean, yeah like I say, you can't force someone but if you put your case over strongly enough, and reasoned enough and argued enough, then nine times out of ten they will

take a second look at it and say well, well we haven't thought of it that way or and you can actually, you can do quite a lot with just your voice.

Here Stephanie draws out the syllable in 'voice' as if to reinforce her point that tenants need only to articulate their needs in a reasoned and rational manner to have effect. Despite the pretensions of public choice theory, however, not all tenants believe that the performative impact of 'voice' automatically brings about effect. Public choice theory appreciates that service users are the least powerful among all the stakeholders influencing public sector organisations, but it still assumes that the trigger of 'voice' will be enough to adjust management processes (Paul 1992). As Michael Laver (1976: 464) responded humorously to Albert Hirschman's (1970) original formula, 'voice' means 'staying put and shouting' but 'the trouble is, of course, shouting makes us hoarse'. To be effective, voice must be orchestrated collectively, so that it is both loud and untiring, but more importantly, 'voice' must be able to back up its sound and fury with the very practical threat of collective action. The only occasions when organisations or firms have yielded to 'voice' are when 'exit' has also been threatened, or when protest has appeared likely to escalate into a significant threat to the activities of the organisation (Kolarska and Aldrich 1980). Voice is ineffective if it remains a market mechanism and it must take on its political connotations in order to overcome management resistance.

FIGURE 4.1 It gives you a voice but that's all: waiting to speak at a residents' consultation event

Photo provided by Leeds Tenants Federation

Public choice theory equates a quasi-market voice with exit, the choice of the rational consumer to switch products, and similarly envisages voice as an individual response. As a market framework it is founded on suspicion of collective action (Olson 1971), so contemporary tenant participation privileges individual over collective responses in obedience to this free market idealism. But tenants who apply the metaphor of voice to convey a market-like influence can also use it to support the development of organisations that apply political processes to 'get their views heard'. A performative 'voice' can cite notions of collective representation, collective action and participatory democracy. It can be applied to conjure up the imaginary of a tenants' movement and to give that movement substance in its claims to the rights of citizenship. Reflecting on his experience in negotiations with his landlord, Brian (ID 14), a tenant director, explains:

> Not having your voice heard was frustrating; I felt we weren't taken seriously enough. Because we didn't have a big enough voice there was no way for tenants to get their views through.

Here Brian relates the exercise of voice to a collective 'we'; he expresses the notion that tenants share a common identity, and he acknowledges in struggling 'to get their views through' a power imbalance between this collective – tenants – and their landlords. He then goes on to locate this idea of a collective explicitly in a network of local residents' associations all seeking access to decision-making:

> Once the association was up and running I joined the board to get the voice of the association heard. Then I got in touch with other groups with the same problems getting their views heard at board level.

Voice conveys not just the freedom of the market but its civil and political claims to liberty and equality that bring with them a narrative of social justice. In T. H. Marshall's (1950) renowned definition, citizenship entails the possession of three sets of rights: civil rights that provide for property ownership and grant equality before the law, political rights to vote and take part in decision-making, and contested social rights that allow for an equitable distribution of goods. In the discourse of public service reform, rights to property have assumed a privileged position so that the right to participate politically has been elided with the civil rights of the citizen to participate in the market. While the concept of social rights has been whittled away, and the idea of entitlement guaranteed by the State has been all but erased, the exercise of consumer influence and the expectation of service quality have been enshrined as new constitutional rights for the users of public services (Barron and Scott 1992). This confinement of political and social rights within a contractual commodity transaction leaves behind a marker that enables claims to be made on notions of equality and social justice that have been marginalised but not fully excluded (Nicholls and Beaumont 2004). Voice therefore maintains a strong and dynamic discourse of rights that allows it to capture the civil identities of citizenship, to express them as political rights and to reference through them a claim to social rights.

An illustration is provided in this excerpt from a focus group discussion at a national tenants' conference (ID 22) in which two tenants take a linguistic journey from the civil rights of the consumer to the political rights of citizens. Nick, a housing association tenant, begins with the contract between landlord and tenant:

> If you're a tenant you're in a relationship with a, a landlord, you know you're having this, and, um, that, that's a sort of contractual relationship even if you've got other rights, what the tenants' movement has attached to those rights, I think ultimately, originally there was, it was just a you and them relationship, I think the tenants' movement for me is about making links with other tenants who are in similar situations so that sort of one-to-one contractual relationship is, is seen in the context of your, your neighbours and your community because there's usually one landlord for a lot of tenants.

In the first stage in this journey Nick refers to the contract between tenant and landlord, and the rights that contract brings. He then introduces a tenants' movement that is defined as a series of links made with others in order to attach more rights to the contract, to make it a contract between the landlord and a whole community or neighbourhood. Nick breaches the isolation of the individual consumer to establish a collective contract, while implicitly misdirecting the relationship from the housing service to encompass a concept of neighbourhood and community. In developing his argument, Nick uses the rights discourse inherent in 'voice' to affirm the existence of a social movement that goes beyond the confines of a landlord–tenant contract:

> But it's about, it's the struggle to try to win rights that go beyond that original deal, offer from the landlord which is on the landlord's terms, I mean what you're given. I mean the tenants' movement is a kind of self-parodying term, because it's about your home. Tenant is what the landlord calls you, ((laughs)) you know, that's their term for you, you know, you know. It's your home and it's giving, it's working with your neighbours to give yourself rights to stay in that home and to make sure that home becomes a community.

Defined by Nick, the aim of the tenants' movement is to win rights that transform the terms of a landlord–tenant commodity transaction and make it into a social contract in which a tenancy becomes a home and tenants become a community. Here Nick indicates the adaptability of voice's performative power. By accessing a vocabulary of civil rights through voice, Nick is able to exit the market definition of housing entirely and to construct the outline of a decommodified service: housing as a social right. The language of exit and voice appears easily adaptable to the identity talk of social movements, since it can proceed from a lack of choice to an appeal for equality and then on to the vocabulary of struggle, as Steven, a tenant director of a housing association, illustrates in the same discussion (ID 22):

> So movement, the word movement to me suggests where there's an inequality between the person providing the, whatever you want to call it, the service, the object, and the person receiving it. There's an inequality and often the person receiving these services, or whatever it is, may be static in that place, so the only way to change what you have and what you're stuck in, and where you've got no choice, is to coalesce and form with your fellow people and try and band together, and share in a movement, in a, actually act against whoever's providing you with a service, and housing very much fits into that, social housing fits into that, because there virtually is no market, there virtually is no choice.

In his reflection of the idea of a tenants' movement, Stephen uses the civil rights assumption of equality before the law to launch a political critique of the landlord–tenant contractual relationship. He then uses the market discourse of public choice theory to explain the need for collective action. In this realignment of the performative concept, 'voice' applied in the absence of 'choice' signifies collective bargaining and political action rather than an automatic market-like adjustment. Market choice, for Stephen, is to be achieved through the mobilisation of a political and social movement. Once the justification for a social movement is established in the context of performative voice, a new lexicon becomes available to confer common cause on tenants as individual consumers, and to provide a dynamic of social change achieved by the means of collective action in tenant participation, as an excerpt from an earlier TPAS focus group (ID 2) shows:

TED:	I see tenants as a movement
KAREN:	Mm, mm
MODERATOR:	Yes? So why do you think that?
TED:	Well, well we, we want to change things, we want to benefit, that's what, what we're doing
STEPHANIE:	If one person can't do it, then
TED:	We want to have a united front if
KAREN:	Yeah
TED:	If you want to change things.

As voice ranges from consumer rights to social rights and from the commodity to the decommodified, the imaginary of a tenants' movement with a shared vision of purposeful change is enabled, citing political traditions of popular struggle and associations with the trade union and labour movement. John, a member of the national tenants' federation (ID 13) refers to participation through a discourse of popular resistance, constructing a social movement history of tenants, and portraying each advance as a step in a long campaign for social rights.

> People have fought long and hard to raise the profile of tenants and to ensure they get a fair crack of the whip from landlords whatever persuasion. And it's about continuing the work done by previous members of our communities and honouring their achievements and developing on what bricks they put in place and growing the opportunities. There is the class system, stigma, there is the majority of the ruling classes, the Oxford and Cambridge who govern and dictate the rules. So there will always be a ceiling where tenants are allowed to aspire to and they will. Once we reach that ceiling it's up to the next generation of tenants to strive for even greater achievements.

In John's narrative, the vocabulary of consumer voice enables him to portray participation as a political process and to access a language of class and social struggle that conveys the achievements of consumers as a victory for social rights. The language of collective action, with its incantation of political and social rights, is allied to a sense of history and tradition in which progress in housing conditions is attributed to the mobilisation of tenants as a movement, providing a sense of purpose and a dynamic of social progress, as this excerpt from a TPAS focus group (ID 2) suggests:

ELIZABETH: It seems to me, umm, that now, whereas it was like trying to bring tenants trying to get their voice heard, it seems to me as though the, uh, we're now bringing the landlords into the twenty-first century.

MODERATOR: So tenants are making the running?

ELIZABETH: I think so

MODERATOR: They're kind of in charge?

ELIZABETH: I wouldn't say we were exactly in charge but we're letting them know we know, we know our rights now and the land [] well, a lot of the landlords still don't really like it, but, umm, treat them gently and we'll bring them into the twenty-first century.

The speaker, Elizabeth, does not believe that the development of tenant participation as 'voice' has triggered automatic improvements among housing organisations. Instead, change is being brought about as a process of tenant struggle in which claims are made on universal rights. Change is something that has to be fought for and won. This narrative of struggle conflates the implied property rights of the consumer with a tradition of agitation for political and social rights, as can be seen in Carmen's contribution to a discussion group at a later TPAS conference (ID 9):

> I always say it's fighting for the rights of tenants, I don't mean physically in fisticuffs, but it's about fighting. A lot of young tenants come on board and they think this has always been here. It has been a fight and it has been a struggle to achieve what we have achieved.

In this reference to a legacy of struggle and a sense of historical mission, Carmen plucks performative voice from its consumer context and transports it to the manifesto of a social movement. In the same discussion at the TPAS conference, Wendy equates the voice of tenants with nineteenth-century labour movement campaigns:

> Any movement's got to get to the top as they did in Chartism in the Victorian days and, um, you know, to get the movement done at the top level with government as well as with tenants. Because tenants' cries have to be recognised at governmental level in order that action can be taken and then followed through.

Performative voice has been applied to endow tenants with rights, to construct the imaginary of a collective, and to mobilise it, at least in identity talk, as a social movement with the suggestion of aims, objectives and strategy. To sum up, voice,

FIGURE 4.2 Any movement's got to get to the top: lobbying MPs under the banner of Liverpool Federation of Council Tenants and Residents Associations

Photo provided by Kirklees Federation of Tenants and Residents Associations

the market definition of participation, is assumed to have a performative effect in that the mere presence of tenants in decision-making processes influences the outcome. This marketplace definition excludes more political notions of collective action or democracy from the meaning of participation and constructs an identity for tenants around their foreclosed role as consumers within the civil rights of a contract. For tenants in this study, however, the civil rights of voice can be used to reclaim political and social entitlements, to effect the imaginary of a political movement, to envisage housing as a decommodified service, and to assume a package of collective interests that carries with it a historical tradition of struggle for social change. Messages of contentious action can be rediscovered, accessed and performed in a market model of participation to delineate the outline of a tenants' movement.

The imaginary of a movement

The imaginary of a tenants' movement signals the mobilisation of a distinctive and contentious 'counter-discourse' in housing policy. Within the boundary markers erected to outline a movement, 'a set of shared, repeated and meaningful references' (Fine 1995: 128) is generated by tenants engaged in participation to provide a distinctive cultural assemblage of common narratives, traditions and interpretive frames. The generation of these 'collective action frames' (Snow *et al.* 1986) is considered in social movement theory as central to the process of collective identity in which contentious movements piece together the fabric that unites them in protest (Taylor and Whittier 1992). The mechanics of identity work can be explored through the social movement technique of frame analysis (Goffman 1974; Snow *et al.* 1986) to examine the individual narratives and collective contentions that construct the imaginary of a movement and provide it with a package of unwritten and largely unacknowledged beliefs. Robert Benford and David Snow (2000: 615) argue that:

> Collective action frames are constructed in part as movement adherents negotiate a shared understanding of some problematic condition or situation they define as in need of change, make attributions regarding who or what is to blame, articulate an alternative set of arrangements, and urge others to act in concert to affect change.

Three collective action frames are widely shared among tenants active in participation and demonstrate a package of resonant claims, contentions and core beliefs that suggest the construction of a movement identity. These frames set out a package of beliefs that are articulated from shared narratives and that are presented, though not overtly or systematically, as 'what the movement stands for'. They borrow from and seek to bridge and extend elements of dominant discourses to construct new arguments, amplify shared experiences and develop an alternative set of beliefs (Snow *et al.* 1986). They perform core tasks, providing a movement with its causal understanding of where it comes from and what it believes in, making clear the problem the movement seeks to overcome and what it needs to achieve, and finally delivering 'a call to arms' (Snow and Benford 1988: 199) in motivational claims and strategies for change. The tenants' movement imagined in these collective action frames is defined by its passionate commitment to the ideal of social rented housing as a collective and collectivising service. Tenants, otherwise divided and fragmented, are tied together in an oppositional identity through their loyalty to a model of collective housing provision and its associated traditions of mutual aid, co-operation and collective action. These beliefs are sustained by a series of contentious claims made around the power of experiential knowledge, and provided with an organisational structure and movement identity through the promotion of ideas of participatory and direct democracy. These distinctive and consistent packages of belief common to tenants engaged in participation provide the feelings of collective belonging, antagonism and attributions of injustice that sustain an idea of a social movement. The frame of agreement is widely shared between all the tenants who took part in research for this book: individual tenants on focus groups and panels, members of tenants' organisations, tenant directors and members of scrutiny panels. It is an embattled belief system, mobilised around the defence, critique and celebration of a social settlement that has been under sustained political assault for over sixty years. In their vision of a participative social rented housing sector and its communities of democratic and engaged citizenship, tenants demonstrate a commitment to an ideal of public services, and a model of the 'public' in which the collective provision of housing propagates the values of co-operation and inspires neighbourliness and solidarity.

The construction of collective identity around a shared commitment to social rented housing is assembled from a complex discursive frame that presents the tenure as essentially communal and neighbourly, while attributing the negative effects of individualism and social fragmentation to the operation of free market principles in housing. In assembling this collective action frame, tenants reverse the arguments marshalled against social housing and redirect them to oppose the processes of privatisation. In normative housing discourse the entrepreneurial benefits of property ownership have been contrasted with a caricature of social housing associated with the concentration of poverty, disadvantage and deprivation (Manzi 2010). Social housing has been blamed for encouraging welfare dependency and hindering social mobility, and social housing estates, already mixed through the selling of council houses, have been depicted in government studies and popular culture as tracts of uniform concrete blocks, isolated from their surroundings, whose inhabitants fail to share mainstream aspirations or norms (Dwelly and Cowans 2006). Mono-tenure, where that tenure is social rented housing, has been blamed for concentrating deprivation and generating 'deviant' cultures, and tenure diversity has been introduced to former social housing estates through demolition of stock and the development of homeownership aimed at households with more disposable incomes (Hanley 2007; Hills 2007; Hutton 2007; DCLG 2009b). Rebelling against this central tenet of housing policy, tenants reframe communitarian discourse around the breakdown of community (Frazer 1999) to argue that uniformity of tenure, where that tenure is social housing, has the beneficial effect of cementing community bonds and building shared interests. They attribute to policies that have promoted homeownership at the expense of social housing the blame for fracturing the ties of commonality that once united neighbourhoods. The argument can be discerned in this excerpt from a focus group with a regional tenants' federation (ID 3):

RICHARD: Yeah but it's the housing now, on estates, such as there was, going back when everybody was a tenant, a council house tenant, now there is so much interplay.
THERESA: Diversity.
RICHARD: With homeowners, right, that is, they're not doing their input into the estate as what the tenants are through their organisations.
THERESA: Yeah
RICHARD: Right, and there, that is what's letting it down.

In the discussion below members of a regional federation in the South of England (ID 6) attributed the collapse of 'community' on social housing estates directly to a trajectory of public policy that has championed homeownership as the only acceptable tenure and has undermined the public services that once insured against risk.

SUSAN: We've got this kind of situation where, as things kind of deteriorated in terms of the, kind of, funding going into local authority housing and instead of it being seen as a positive thing that it was suddenly we should all own our own home, which came from all parties. That has without doubt divided communities. It's divided young people from old people, young people have had to move away from their families, so you have isolated elderly people, you have new people from new communities who've come in, who have no real resources, and the existing community has no real resources to bring those people together and to make them function well together.
JANE: I think there's a real problem now because breaking up these mono-tenure estates has actually created instability, rather than the other way round.

Jane goes on in this discussion to posit a direct causal link between the privatisation of the Right to Buy and increased turnover on estates, arguing that this creates a sense of dislocation and undermines feelings of community and social harmony:

JANE: The problem we have on a lot of our estates now is, because of the Right to Buy, and because the original Right to Buy people have sold, we now have quite fragmented, um, communities because a lot of them

	are let on, you know, short-term tenancies, six months. I live on a very small estate, there are only sixty-three properties, personally, but, um, you know, you see people walking across the yard and, you know, round [through the estate]
HARRY:	[Don't know them]
JEAN:	You don't know them because they change so, so rapidly. Now the residents, who lived there a long time, whether they're leaseholders or tenants, have a tradition of having organised things regularly on the estate.

What is being advanced in these tenant discourses is a revisionist frame in which a golden age of popular social housing was destabilised by the forces of privatisation with subsequent loss of neighbourhood relations, stability and safety. The impact of the original Right to Buy and subsequent resales on council housing estates has been mixed but, in some cases, dramatic. Low-demand social housing estates have seen substantial redevelopment to create a diverse housing market leading to multiple transactions and the development of transitory populations through an expanding Buy to Let sector. The overall reduction of available council housing and the concentration of 'those with least choice and bargaining power' in the least popular residual stock (Jones and Murie 2006: 148), has destabilised neighbourhoods. There is, therefore, plentiful ammunition to counter the policy aim of mixed communities, and to reassociate community with the consistency and uniformity of mono-tenure social renting.

Far from being the sector of disintegration and neighbourhood breakdown that the dominant stigmatisation discourse depicts, tenants are very aware that social housing is built to high-quality standards and managed by responsive and publicly accountable landlords. They contrast the benefits of social housing with what they claim is the essential isolation of homeownership and the poor management, inflated rents and low standards of repair in the private rented sector. The benefits of public-housing management services are catalogued in this TPAS conference focus group from 2009 (ID 9):

CLARE:	There are a lot of people in the private sector say 'oh, wish we could get that, wish we could have someone come and repair our homes within a few hours of a flood burst' and, I mean I think we're very privileged people
SARAH:	I think we're better off than those in private accommodation to be honest,
CLARE:	To get repairs done, to have someone
LINDA:	You just pay your rent and you get it all done.

The provision of social rented housing is associated with social welfare aims and tenants assert that the tenure encourages the development of bonds of neighbourliness through the experience of a shared landlord, common tenancy agreements and regular contact with housing officers, repairs contractors, or, in supported accommodation, with care staff. In a focus group at the TPAS conference (ID 8), Robert explains that social interaction is intrinsic to the tenure, and alien to the owner-occupied sector:

> Social housing, social as in interacting with other human beings, that's what social means. We are in a great position because we've got a quality of life which is far superior to people stuck in their private bloody little houses.

Yvonne (ID 9) tells a story about the estate where she used to live. She describes it as a mixed community, with social rented, shared ownership and owner-occupied housing clustered along the same access road, each tenure occupying a different section of the road. Yvonne recounts how tenure divisions were visible through the number of children playing in the street.

> On the rented part of the estate the kids all played together, the parents looked out for each other, the second lot [shared ownership], you would see one or two kids playing on their doorstep and in the third lot [owner occupation] never see any at all.

In a meeting with a borough tenants' federation (ID 23), the participants make similar claims for the collectivising effects of social housing:

PAM: I feel as if all my neighbours are the same as me; I feel it's equal. No, but if they're in social housing the same as I am

CHRIS: You all get along; if you run out of sugar

JAN: It's equalising

PAM: I feel the same, everybody's the same

KEITH: What you usually find is people which are working class, like us, or we have been; people who are working class are more sociable with their neighbours than the people who are high and mighty.

PAM: Yeah

KEITH: I think in a community with social housing I think you get more people helping each other socially, you know what I mean, than you do if they live in, er, posh houses. You see the word social means getting on with each other, isn't it? And you usually find on council estates that people are more sociable with each other, because more people are financially in the same boat together, so they know the shortages what they have and what they need. And that's it, I think the social in council property is where you, you know, all your ideas is together, and since there's been tenants' associations, like we're involved with, that's the time when we can all get together, er, and find out certain things like, and help to solve the solutions which is happening around us.

The claim here is that the shared interests established by social housing encourage tenants to care about their neighbours and to work co-operatively to overcome common problems. In the regional tenants' federation discussion noted earlier (ID 6), Jane imbues all social housing tenants with the values of mutual aid and co-operation, identifies these as benefits of the social housing sector and contrasts this with the failures of the private market in the 2008 finance sector crash:

JANE: And, you know, but they also are, in the main, quite *good* about looking after their neighbours, joining in with things and so on, considering the other children on, you know, people's children on the estate and all this sort of thing. So actually they're probably more socially conscious than a lot of people who live outside the council house environment. And, umm, but of course I think we have a big problem of how to, umm, reverse the perception that is certainly peddled in the press and by politicians who, I think, want to just dump council housing, you know, want to get rid of it

NAJINDER: Hmm

JANE: And still despite all the experiences of the last year, couple of years, you know, have this blind faith that the market somehow is going to solve Britain's housing [problem]

SANJIT: [problem]

ALL: ((Laughter))

Jane goes on to contend that the co-operation that is essential to social housing helps to generate collective action in the form of local tenants' associations that mobilise around a sense of neighbourhood, its facilities and services:

> I think our tenants' organisations in our borough, you know, do an *awful* lot of work for the local community because we've been around, we've been involved in the campaign for the local school or whatever it was, over a long period of time.

This is an image of a community whose residents are committed to maintaining their schools and other local services from cut backs and closures, and where a feeling of communal ownership surrounds the local public services because they have been defined as much by the voluntary work of local people as by the resources of public agencies. Tenants' associations are often motivated by issues around the quality and upkeep of the neighbourhood, its facilities and services for children, and they can be involved in a range of local and national campaigns. They have been a seemingly organic development on social housing estates since the 1920s and their aim to 'safeguard and promote the interests of all the tenants on the estate' (Durant 1939: 31) suggests a belief in collective action and an understanding of common interests that have been a tradition of the tenure, one recorded by researchers across the decades (Mitchell and Lupton 1954; Goetschius 1969; Gibson

1979; Cooper and Hawtin 1998; Ravetz 2001). Stuart Lowe (1986) argued that the ability to mobilise support for local tenants' associations stemmed from an awareness of shared interests among residents with a common landlord, as well as from a working-class social base concentrated in council housing estates. This concept of a class united by housing tenure was quick to disintegrate as the rise of homeownership excavated divisions around housing consumption in the working class (Saunders 1990). Tenants contributing to this book, however, appeared able to rekindle ideas of common interest constructed out of common tenure and articulate them to invoke a political constituency. At a borough tenants' federation (ID 13), John attempted to reclaim a sense of commonality in opposition to the divisions of housing consumption that now act as permanent barriers:

> It's about making them see if you live on a mixed estate you all own the estate. They are all of equal value when it comes to community values. They own their community and it's about working together, working in partnership. It's difficult for a tenant that's bought his own home. He may think he's made a vast leap forward; he may think he's better than tenants – it's just a mental attitude.

The desire to foster bonds of mutuality and community can convey a wish for social and political change, and carries with it a long history of political dissent (Taylor 2003). Mutuality can be used as a tool of mobilisation, as the first step in building collective feelings of efficacy, and in developing the relations necessary for more participatory decision-making (Staeheli 2002). Marcie seems to express this at a TPAS focus group in 2009 (ID 8) when she says:

> Community for me means that we are, we discuss with our neighbours, our friends, the people around us the problems we have within housing.

Overt and unspoken class narratives appear within this discourse, as if social housing operated as a metaphor for an imaginary working-class culture founded on the principles of mutual aid (Savage 2000; Watt 2008). Elements of collective ownership and traditions of mutual aid were central to the development of an English working class (Thompson 1968). Eileen and Stephen Yeo (1988) argue that notions of community originated in an oppositional working-class culture of mutuality. This was a 'community made by people for themselves', a social relation that resulted from 'the continual practice of mutual support from the people within it' (Yeo and Yeo 1988: 231). Constructed around informal networks of relatives and neighbours, and led by women, this was a culture that, at its most articulate, expressed a vision of the transformation of social relations on co-operative principles (Williams 1967). The collapse of community is directly attributed by tenants in this study to a trajectory of public policy that has championed homeownership as the only acceptable tenure and has undermined the social housing services that once provided collective insurance against risk. The collective action frame that

FIGURE 4.3 Fair rents and decent homes: Leeds Tenants Federation campaigning for more social housing at a community gala

Photo supplied by Leeds Tenants Federation

unites tenants around their belief in social housing is oppositional in its rejection of the contemporary direction of housing policy and the market-driven individualism brought about through the erosion of support for public housing. As an alternative to these market values it posits collective provision in order to generate a culture of mutual aid and co-operation.

Commitment to an ideal of social rented housing provides a 'collective packaging device' (Snow 2004: 400) that indicates the potential for unity among tenants fragmented by geography, culture and experience. An imaginary tenants' movement is constructed in this oppositional frame but its outline remains ill-defined. A tenants' movement has yet to distinguish itself from 'them': the opposition, the sources of injustice; it has yet to demarcate itself from dominant power relations, to manifest antagonism and display a desire for change. Something more is needed to turn this amorphous assemblage of shared identifications into a social movement with a message. The next section identifies the construction of more antagonistic claims for a reversal of power relations in housing policy.

Experts in the field

A distinctive and recurring theme in the history of social movements since the late 1960s has been 'the questioning and overturning of the character and organisation of what counted as valid knowledge' (Wainwright 1994: 2). This has been especially true in the mobilisation of tenants and other welfare-state users who have championed their experiential knowledge against the professional assessments of need in housing, health and social care. 'These movements questioned the definition of what counts as knowledge, the narrowness of the sources of knowledge considered relevant to public policy, the restricted categories of people whose knowledge was valued and the processes by which knowledge is arrived at,' Hilary Wainwright said (2003: 23). In championing experiential knowledge, social movements began to challenge the authority of welfare-state managers to know what was good for them and to act in their best interests. They sought to speak for themselves rather than let others speak for them (Croft and Beresford 1996). They developed a discursive frame around experiential knowledge that questioned the power relations of the welfare state and the exalted status of professional knowledge. For some movements this frame generated a demand for democratic control over public resources; for others it suggested the possibility of new social relations between users and providers. The dynamic of this challenge to knowledge stemmed from a basis in self-organisation; in constructing a legitimate space for their own deliberation around personal experience, these 'subaltern counter-publics' (Fraser 1997: 81) could begin to frame their own needs, objectives and strategies.

In the dominant discourse of tenant participation the assertion is commonly made that the residents of an area know best about its needs (Mosse 2001). The incorporation of local knowledge into professional decision-making is considered to be a key outcome for participation processes. The extraction of local knowledge, however, takes place within systems and spaces mediated, if not controlled, by professionals, who establish what knowledge is considered legitimate, how it should be communicated, and what uses will be made of it. The development of the 'expert tenant' has been a requirement of the foreclosure of participation as a regulatory project (Millward 2005). Each step in this foreclosure has seen tenants undergo training to achieve certain defined 'competencies' (Furbey et al. 1996). The inculcation of expertise among the minority of tenants taking on specialist roles in a hierarchy of participation has run parallel with the decline in status granted to the experiential knowledge of tenants' organisations as 'counter-publics'. The focus group and customer panel incorporate an amateur disposition among tenants who are asked only to provide the housing professional with their personal experience and opinions to be sampled, quantified and filed (Millward 2005). For tenants to be seen as legitimately 'expert' they must identify themselves with housing professionals and not tenant representatives. They must be trained to be expert in the ways of another identity. Tenants have been eager to acquire this training so that they can be allowed to converse as equals with their landlords. They know that experiential knowledge is little valued in the strategic management of housing organisations, and they are prepared to accept that their language and behaviour must be regulated if they are to make themselves understood by decision-makers, as Michael, the chair of a tenants' federation (ID 17) reflects:

> All the time it was like we've got to find out more, we've got to find out more, you know, 'cause they want, everybody wanted to challenge but if you don't know what you're challenging, then you're just making a fool of yourself, so it was like a, all the time it was like a thirst for information, you know, you'd all get little tasks, read up on this and read up on that, you didn't understand half of it so it was really, really very difficult.

The requirement for tenants to acquire new knowledge and behaviours has been most salient in the promotion of citizen governance in housing organisations (Simmons *et al.* 2007). Tenants currently make up over 18 per cent of directors on the boards of English social housing organisations, and can hold one third of directorships in stock-transfer companies and arm's-length management organisations (Cairncross and Pearl 2003; Ipsos Mori 2009a). To become directors, tenants must assume a regulated identity defined in statute, and the Companies Act 1985 and 2006 sets out their duty to act in the best interests of the housing organisation and not necessarily its tenants. Tenant directors take on a corporate identity in which all board members are assumed to be equal and all are tasked with the same aims and interests, predicated on the assumption that the power relations that reproduce inequality and injustice stop at the boardroom door. Tenants, however, are a demographically distinct group on the management boards of housing companies and appear to adhere to a specific set of values (Cairncross and Pearl 2003). Their fellow governors are drawn from the ranks of highly educated, usually male professionals who are employed in senior management roles, and are likely to serve as directors for a range of quasi-public and private companies, and who operate as a local network of governance (Stoker 2004). When they enter the boardroom, tenants are required to adopt the behaviour of directors who are demographically and culturally 'other'. Tenant directors see the model of their identity in the status and educational attainments of their fellow board members and define themselves, in comparison, through their difference from that image. Since they cannot attain the standards required to be a professional director, they remain for ever tenant directors, 'almost the same, but not quite' as the post-colonial theorist Homi Bhabha (1994: 123) expressed it. Evidence of this failure of identification was provided by the Audit Commission in 2004 when it accused tenant directors of raising 'estate-level issues' at the boardroom table to the exasperation of housing association chief executives (Audit Commission 2004a: 43). As a consequence, the housing inspectorate recommended that tenant board members should be selected by interview, rather than election, to ensure their future compliance with the requirements of governance. Since then tenant directors have mostly been selected on the basis of their ability to make strategic judgements and articulate the language of governance. Tenants who want formal decision-making power in housing companies know they need to acquire a different and higher value form of knowledge to fulfil their duties as directors. Stephanie and Karen, two tenant directors (ID 2), understand there is no role for emotion or personal testimony in boardroom deliberations.

KAREN:	It's all about doing your homework first.
STEPHANIE:	Yes
KAREN:	It's no use going in there full of passion. If you've got no
STEPHANIE:	Yeah.
KAREN:	Reasoned argument.
STEPHANIE:	And that's the key to it, we will go in and we will be well prepared.
STEPHANIE:	You can't just say 'I want'. You've got to back it up with a damn good reason why it's a need and not a want and sometimes they will say that's not very practical and there isn't the money [. . .] You've got to be realistic, you can't stamp your feet every time because they look [. . .]
KAREN:	Umm
STEPHANIE:	People will lose respect.
KAREN:	Yeah.
STEPHANIE:	You've got to be sensible. Not a word I'd use very often in connection with me ((General laughter)).

Although presenting this with humour, Stephanie makes clear that she is not comfortable with the formal approach she has to adopt at board. To influence housing decisions tenants have to learn the specialised language, financial codes, jargon and acronyms used by professionals and argue their case dispassionately. This entails more than just learning to communicate in a different manner; it means acquiring a linguistic code that is the key to inequality and class distinction (Bourdieu and Passeron 1990). Tenants are recruited on to the boards of housing companies partly to legitimise the fragmented new landscape of mergers, group structures and take overs among stock transfer companies and traditional charitable housing associations by rooting them in a defined sense of place. When they are elected, it is usually from defined constituencies (Flint 2003). The constituency model, which guaranteed a third of board places for tenants alongside councillors and independent directors, and became the norm for new stock transfer and arm's-length management companies, was adopted partly as a response to the criticisms of unaccountability levelled at housing associations when they replaced elected local government as the main provider of social housing after 1989 (Karn 1993; Mullins *et al.* 1995). This constituency model created an impression of electoral accountability around the new tenant directors and implied that they served in a representative role (Kearns 1997; Malpass 2000). Tenants were promised more influence over decision-making through access to a seat on the governing body and voted for transfer, and supported arm's-length management companies at least in part because they were offered places on the governing boards of the new organisations (Audit Commission 2004a).

All the tenant board members interviewed for this book joined the board of their housing organisation as an extension of their existing involvement in residents' organisations. As active members of their local tenants' associations, they felt that there were barriers preventing them from accessing the necessary knowledge and influence to bring about the improvements they wanted in their local areas. Admission to the board of directors also presented them with the opportunity to begin to reverse a perceived power imbalance and to assert the experience of social housing tenants against the previously dominant views of housing staff. The chance to make a change became their prime motivation in deciding to join the board, and tenant directors saw themselves as initiating a transformation in power structures. As Brian (ID 14), a tenant board member for an arm's-length management organisation (ALMO), said:

> For some staff, tenants were just a nuisance and that needed changing, that persuaded me more than anything and obviously there were people in the ALMO who wanted things to change if I could do my bit.

These tenants believed that to achieve change in the culture of housing organisations, they had first to achieve positions of status. A directorship put them in a position to encourage the development of responsive estate-level services and to forge relationships of respect between tenants and staff. Michael (ID 17) was encouraged as a new tenant board member to meet the staff at his local housing office and to go to their team meetings. From this point of contact, he encouraged the local housing officer to walk around the estate with him. He then invited the local residents' association members to join this regular walk-about and gradually spread this initiative to neighbouring estates. In Michael's assessment of the impact of tenants on the boards of housing organisations, it is this local achievement he stresses. Like many tenant directors, he actively set out to discover residents' concerns in order to represent them at board level. He saw it as his responsibility to go to the meetings of other residents' associations and take notes of problems raised in order to keep himself in touch with tenants' experiences. To tenant board members like Michael there was no conflict between their sanctioned role in providing a user perspective on the board and their role as a representative raising specific issues on behalf of their constituents, and if they could not resolve an issue through their personal contacts, they were not afraid to raise it at a relevant subcommittee of the board.

Senior officers of housing companies, however, routinely discourage tenant directors from taking an advocacy role at meetings and from speaking on behalf of other tenants, and are particularly concerned to prevent them raising specific cases or bringing unresolved complaints to the notice of the board (Clapham and Kintrea 2000). In 2006 the largest housing companies argued that the behaviour of tenant directors was a hindrance to the efficient business operation of social housing companies. They claimed that a high level of knowledge and skills was necessary to govern effectively and that there was no role for tenants at board level (Appleyard 2006). As a result, a review of regulation launched by the Housing Corporation and headed by Sir Les Elton concluded that tenants would have a more valuable contribution to make on operational committees or area panels with direct service delivery functions, rather than on strategic boards (Elton 2006). Several of the tenant directors interviewed, or taking part in focus group discussions for this book, had previously served on parent boards and had been relegated, or chosen to move, to area-based subcommittees. Kevin was one (ID 16), and he explains that his decision not to continue as a member of the strategic board was taken in frustration at the disciplinary pressure exerted on the tenant directors:

> When I was on the board it were tenant focused. But now it isn't, it's strategic. That's what it is now. Because you can't touch a board member now. Like when I were on the board everybody could talk to me, or we could go down [to HQ] and walk into the [Chief Executive's] office and say, 'can I have a word?' yeah. But I'm glad I didn't go on the board, because I like to be on the ground and doing things and seeing things being done, whereas the board they just look at papers and, and sign them off.

These regulatory mechanisms are aimed at enforcing a clear divide between the identity of the tenant director and the role of the tenant representative in the knowledge that many tenant board members are, or have been, members of local tenants' organisations (Malpass and Mullins 2002). Brian, a tenant director (ID 7), who was also a member of his borough tenants' federation, reported that he was regularly disciplined by the Chair and Chief Officer of his housing organisation for failing to regulate his split identity during board meetings:

> I've got to be careful on Board because here [at the Federation] we fight individually for a tenant but on the Board you fight for them all and I still haven't got that into my head yet because I still start shooting my mouth off about this tenant hasn't got this and this tenant ain't got that. [. . .] And then I get pulled to one side, 'you're fighting for all tenants not just one'.

The requirement on Brian to discipline his behaviour in the boardroom forces him to consciously monitor his identity and to associate it with specific modes of symbolic behaviour; as he explains below, he has to decide 'which cap' he wears. Yet his boardroom identity appears to be play-acting, and beneath the mask he retains a belligerent and stubborn loyalty to a tradition of collective representation:

> This is where the two caps come in, you see, and you've got, oh it's terrible, so I think, 'oh well, we're fighting for all of them, wait till I get in office tomorrow [Tenants Federation office] and I'll show them who I'm fighting for, you know'.

In this example, attempts to discipline the behaviour of a tenant director serve only to remind him of his banished identity as representative of a contentious collective. A memory of excluded possibilities is embedded in the regulated identity of tenant director; a tradition of democratic representation and its association with a legacy of collective action form the 'constitutive outside' of the project to mould the tenant director (Butler 1993: 3). This excluded identity can be evidenced in expressions of unity and shared identity by tenant board members, as this quote from Karen (ID 15) suggests:

> We all encouraged each other. The tenant directors wanted a spokesman and it was me. Some of them were a bit nervous at putting their hands up. They used to pass pieces of paper round to me, 'can you ask this?' Like being in school.

Karen's reference to school days creates a lively image of tenant directors as a group of friends. She depicts the tenant board members as having their own codes of behaviour and their own leadership structures. She expects the other tenant board members always to support her in board discussions and sees tenant board members as a block separate from, and sometimes opposed to, the other directors and officers of the organisation. These references establish the boundary markers (Taylor and Whittier 1992) that define the distinct identity of the group 'us', and declare it as an antagonist to 'them'. Boundary marking by tenant directors creates in symbolic terms a political frontier (Norval 2000); it organises the space of the boardroom by charting new relations of power in lines of opposition and division. Two narratives by tenant board members express this political frontier clearly; both describe a moment of outright conflict in the boardroom when the interests of the tenants diverged from those of the housing organisation. In Karen's account, the directors of an arm's-length management organisation were presented with an officer recommendation to withdraw rent collection services from all neighbourhood offices. Karen provides a bitter commentary on the board meeting:

> Tenant board members thought it weren't right to close cash offices [. . .] It was put to a vote and tenants were outvoted. The majority wanted it stopping and we had to agree with it whether we liked it or no and we had to go out and tell our tenants it was the board decision although we didn't agree with it.

In the second narrative a social housing company proposed to demolish over four hundred homes on the grounds that it was not cost-effective to repair them.

As in the first example, the officer recommendation was passed by a majority vote with all the tenant directors voting against demolition. Michael (ID 17) recalled how the debate brought tenant directors together in their opposition to the plans:

> That was the one that got the quieter ones to found their voice. This was people's homes. It was something like 11 to 7 for. Every tenant voted against.

As a result of these moments of partition, when the unity of the board breaks into divergent interest groups, antagonism becomes the tool by which tenant directors may reinterpret their identity as board members. They are thrown into a position where they must define themselves in opposition to the views of senior managers and the other directors. In these circumstances tenant directors are able to develop the ambiguities of their identity to reclaim exiled traditions of participatory democracy and political struggle. Out of ten tenant board members interviewed for this book, six left the board of their housing company two years later because their desire to act as representatives, and to speak on behalf of a tenants' constituency, had led them into conflict with the discourse of corporate unity. The board members who stayed behind were castigated as 'nodding dogs' by one departing tenant director because of the accommodation they had made with the discipline of the board.

The development of antagonism between local knowledge and the expertise of housing professionals gives rise to a discursive frame in which tenants define themselves as a distinct collective or movement and imagine a reversal of power relations that puts them in charge of the housing service. Here the regulated identity of the 'expert tenant' (Millward 2005) is inverted as tenants claim their lived experience as residents of social housing is superior to that of the housing professional. In claiming that they are best placed to make housing management decisions, they mark out counter-social relations for the production of housing knowledge. At a TPAS conference discussion in 2009 (ID 8), Marcie asserts that the experiential knowledge of social housing tenants makes them best placed to manage their own housing:

MARCIE: The people who know what's happening in social housing are the people who live in it and consequently if they can tell it or show it or deal with it then obviously they're going to be able to fix it.

ELIZABETH: We're experts in the field because we live there.

MARCIE: Well, exactly, we have the experience of living in the houses, of living in the community and, um, I think there can be no one who can know more about the person's home than the person living in it.

The assertion of privileged knowledge by tenants is based on their direct experience of living in a neighbourhood and seeing what goes on both night and day. Housing officers, in contrast, are perceived as office-bound and only on the estate in daylight hours, if it all. Cheryl continued the discussion in the focus group (ID 8) and amplified the frame, saying:

> The thing is the people who are in a community, who live there, they can see what's going on. I mean, we can look across the street and see that there's a gang of youngsters hanging out and, you know, in a certain area. We can see, you know, that people can't walk through an alley way or something, so when it comes to the actual environment or the community as such the people who are the local residents will be the ones who will have more experience of what's going on around there. The professionals will be in their offices wherever that may be so they haven't got the actual knowledge or sight or feeling of what's happening around your community and when it comes to the housing itself the question is, who knows more about the needs of their community than the housing professionals? We do know more because we're actually in that community, living it, as compared to someone who may have had a report from the police or, or a tenants association or something, and hear about an incident, we're there living it 24/7. We do know more.

The claim is further developed through the assertion that tenants display a concern and commitment for the neighbourhood and its well-being that housing professionals do not share. Georgia joins the discussion (ID 8) to say:

> We see what they turn a blind eye to. We see what's wrong with our community and we pass it on to them. They, they, ah, they just say, well they say they listen and it will be done, but it's forgotten about and therefore it gets turned a blind, a blind eye to until we will keep reminding them and we have to keep doing this until we get it done. And that's why we are more experienced than what they are − because we see it all the time.

Participation often results, not in professionals adopting local knowledge in their decision-making, but in locals acquiring professional knowledge to promote their concerns (Mosse 2001: 21). An education in professional discourse can enable tenants to claim both the housing insider's knowledge of systems and the residents' privileged understanding of space (Larner and Craig 2005: 418). Tenants' associations try to build a partnership with patch-based housing staff and 'train them' by inducting them into the domestic knowledge that only a resident can claim. These attempts by tenants' organisations to build deliberative relationships with housing management staff are routinely shattered in the restructures of housing organisations when patch officers are transferred and replaced. Recording the frustration of residents' associations when the partnership they develop with operational staff is broken with such disregard, Barbara (ID 8) says:

I think we know more about our communities because professionals move on and we stay and then we have to start all over again and train, train them into their new position.

Housing officers have previously expressed their social distance from their tenants as if they 'were on two different planets' (Clapham *et al.* 2000:73). In the TPAS focus group, Cheryl agrees that housing staff are spatially separate; they live parallel lives, she claims, unable and unwilling to bridge the experiential gap between them and tenants:

CHERYL: You're dealing with people who have a very good wage coming in; they've never been poor, never been out of work, never had to deal with the benefits system, etc.

MARCIE: I think that all housing officers and especially directors should be forced to live in social housing for at least a month before they take up the positions they've got, so they might see what it's like to live in social housing because a lot of them have not got a clue.

CHERYL: They should go back to the floor.

MARCIE: They've never lived in social housing and they haven't got a clue what it means. They've come into these jobs and they've lived in private houses, they've got good salaries, they don't know what it's like to struggle, they've never had housing benefits, they've never had to claim anything. They don't know what goes on within estates where there are problems, and it would do them good to live there for a month or so and see what the problems are among the people they are working for; at the end of the day, they're working for us.

In this partisan statement the collective action frame sets out its fundamental challenge to the power relations implicit in professional knowledge. It is tenants who commission the housing management service and tenants who know best what they need. They pay for the service through their rents, so why are they not in charge?

CHERYL: We employ them, we employ them, we pay their wages

ROBERT: That's right

CHERYL: We pay their wages; they're accountable to us.

This imagined reversal of power relations provides the motivation behind the establishment of tenant management organisations, where an elected tenant board negotiates a budget for their estate from the municipal authority and directly employs and manages its own housing staff to operate a localised service. Marcie's contribution to the focus group exchange noted earlier was rooted in her ardent endorsement of the Community Gateway Association (CCH 2003), a model of stock transfer housing company committed to exporting tenant management and purportedly tenant-led. The Gateway model was developed in 2003 in response to a growing awareness that tenants were uncomfortable with the loss of accountability inherent in the unrelenting programme of demunicipalisation (Chartered Institute of Housing 2006). Throughout the focus group discussion, Marcie enthusiastically promoted tenant management as a strategy for challenging the power of the housing profession and putting tenants in charge. In taking over the running of their estate, she says that tenants are creating new definitions for themselves, new identities.

> I still think there is that stigma attached to anyone who is in social housing as far as the media is concerned. But I think the very fact that tenants are managing the whole of this, this social housing, will raise the status because it makes everyone realise that we're not fools, we're not, you know, we're not here to live on the government's handouts or we're not irresponsible people, we are intelligent, articulate, educated people and we can do for ourselves what the government and any other association has been doing. We're the ones who pay that rent, the ones, you know these are, these, these are our homes, you know, and why should the money that we are paying not, we don't have any control over how it's being spent?

This challenge to the dominance of professional knowledge speaks of an antagonism that marks the limits of partnership and demarcates tenants as a collective opposition. It is expressed cogently by Gina, a regional tenants' federation member (ID 3):

> We no longer have to tip our forelock, say 'yes sir, no sir, three bags full, sir', because what the government did, they educated us, so now we challenge and we question and that is what the problem is that the government can't accept that we're a bit more educated, a bit more knowledgeable and we have the ability to question and challenge.

Local knowledge appears in this discourse as an unproblematic 'common sense' acquired by residency and it does not admit of the social structures and power relations of the localities through which it is generated (Kothari 2001). How a diversity of local 'knowledges' might be represented by tenants, and how power relations might be scrutinised in housing services are the subjects of the third collective action frame which provides the motivational dynamic for a tenants' movement in the principles of localism and direct democracy and is explored in the next chapter. This chapter has analysed the processes through which tenants construct the outline of a social movement within the regulated rituals of participation. By taking part in the menu of participation practices, tenants are able to recover excluded meanings of collective action, democracy and the traditions of popular struggle. These returning identities provide the outline of a tenants' movement, one that takes on explicit and contentious form in the construction of

FIGURE 4.4 Experts in the field: challenging a professional elite at a public meeting of residents

Photo provided by Leeds Tenants Federation

a collective action frame that provides it with a cause and a sense of purpose. The defining diagnostic frame of this tenants' movement champions social housing as a universal service and opposes the dominant direction of housing policy. It imagines a tenant collective united in its superior experiential knowledge and confronted in antagonistic lines of division by an unresponsive and distant professional elite. The collective identity of a tenants' movement is given content and motivation by these frames of discourse. The next chapter explores the mobilisation of this imagined movement around the principles of participatory and direct democracy and examines the role played by governmental strategies of community and localism in cementing the identity of a tenants' movement.

5

TENANT LOCALISM AND DEMOCRACY

This chapter charts the construction of a tenant movement identity around the values and practices of participatory democracy. It locates the third defining collective action frame of the movement in an organisational commitment to the principles of direct democracy and grass-roots decision-making and the mobilising potential of neighbourhood. At the core of this frame of identity is the potential for autonomous tenant organisations to represent collective needs, to inspire practices of democracy and participation, and to localise decision-making in the delivery of public services. Concepts of participatory or direct democracy (Pateman 1970; Held 2006) are deeply embedded in the practices of tenant participation and convey a radical critique of the bureaucratic organisation and paternal governance of social welfare services. Tenants who seek to gain more power over operational decision-making in housing management and change attitudes among housing staff have traditionally expressed these desires in terms of widening democracy. Their interest in the first participation schemes was expressed as follows:

> It is the democratic right of people whose lives are so fundamentally affected by the actions of public bodies to be able to represent their feelings and to influence, if not make, decisions which affect their immediate environment.
> (Craddock 1975: 20)

In drawing on this language of democratic rights, tenants position themselves in a tradition of direct action by social movements, believing that 'the people themselves must assume direct responsibility for intervening in the political decision-making process' (Della Porta and Diani 2006: 240). Discourses of direct and participatory democracy and collective representation are synonymous with the concept of the tenants' movement and its roots in community and neighbourhood action (Baldock 1982; Bolger et al. 1989; Greg 2004). In recent years these themes have emerged as the defining rationale for governmental strategies of localism that have promised to devolve power to communities and empower community groups as agents of governance. The chapter explores the involvement of tenants' organisations in these strategies of localism and the discourses of community governance as they emerge in the practices of tenant management organisations, tenant co-operatives and tenants' associations.

The politics of localism

Political strategies of localism have been intrinsic to a political restructuring of State institutions and State relations of governance (Swyngedouw 2005; Allen and Cochrane 2010), and have promised 'a reordering of public space' (Mohan and Stokke 2000: 250). A pledge to devolve decision-making to local communities has been the constant theme in this wide-ranging transformation of government, one that attributes political content to a particular spatial form in its conflation of the local with better and more democratic governance (Purcell 2006; Painter *et al.* 2011). In English housing policy, localism emerged in the early 1970s in the form of local tenant management through which elected tenants' organisations could take over the running of their housing estates with delegated budgets and their own staff teams. Tenant management has constituted one of the main drivers for 'exit' in strategies aimed at fragmenting and outsourcing the public ownership of rented housing (Boaden *et al.* 1982) and funding to support tenants interested in exploring management options has been available since 1986, under Section 16 of the Housing and Planning Act. Since 1994 council tenants have had a statutory Right to Manage, and voluntary management options were extended to housing association tenants in 2008 (DCLG 2007a), while housing self-build co-operatives and co-operatively owned housing associations provide other resource-intensive legal entities that enable tenants to take local control (Ward 1974; Cairncross *et al.* 2002; Housing Right to Manage 2012).

Under Labour governments from 1997 to 2010 a programme of centrally driven managerial reforms displaced State functions on to devolved parliaments and regional assemblies, but also on to local strategic partnerships and neighbourhood management boards, ensuring the outsourcing of public delivery to private and community interests through a regulatory matrix of targets and inspections (Newman *et al.* 2004). In this strategy of 'community localism' (Hildreth 2011), limited opportunities for citizen governance were extended to residents through the New Deal for Communities and Neighbourhood Management pilots, and in its 2008 White Paper, Communities in Control, Labour pledged to strengthen local democracy by empowering local communities through a 'new style of active politics' (DCLG 2008: i). Maintaining that an extension of democracy would bring about liberty and justice, the White Paper and the subsequent Community Empowerment Bill provided limited extra rights to community groups to exert consumer pressure on local authorities. These fledgling measures were reinvigorated by the Coalition Government as the Localism Act 2011, a more defined package that conflated the enterprising public imagined under Labour's regime with a liberal belief in associational democracy and the traditional Conservative subjectivity of the active citizen whose responsibility it is to participate in governance. The Localism Act (2011) promised to 'shift power away from central government and pass it to local people and community groups' (Pickles 2010). To this apparent end the act introduced to England four new 'community rights' which presented community groups as the principal beneficiaries of devolved governance and handed them the power to initiate neighbourhood plans, trigger consent for new-build projects, be included as potential bidders for the disposal of public assets, and challenge local authorities to take over public services. Minister of State for Decentralisation in 2011, Greg Clark MP, claimed these measures would promote 'the sense of participation and involvement on which a healthy democracy thrives' (DCLG 2011c: 1).

Localism appears as a scalar construction that addresses community organisations as a model for behavioural change to accompany a societal reorientation towards the market as a model for society (Delaney and Leitner 1997; Raco 2003). The 2011 act enlisted the primacy of local knowledge, the enterprising effect of association and the supposed ethical value of belonging as weapons against collective provision, social insurance and a redistributive state (Hall and Massey 2010; Featherstone *et al.* 2012). The promise to move decision-making closer to the people (Westwood 2011), to 'a spatial scale closer to people's felt sense of identity' (Stoker 2004: 125), provided the rationale for a restructuring of the relationship between the State and public services. The rights of the Localism Act addressed community groups as the potential providers and trustees of public services and assets, although the main beneficiaries were the multinational companies and global finance markets involved in privatisation and outsourcing (Fyfe 2005). The Localism Act presented the shift from a redistributive state to one that celebrates market dynamics as a transfer of responsibility from the public to the community, with community serving as a reassuringly familiar proxy for a residual public sector (Hall and Massey 2010).

Refusing boundaries, extending borders

Localism hails communities as subjects and agents of governance within reiterative practices intended to produce the embodiment of a new public (Gibson 2001; Newman and Clarke 2009). The political and spatial demarcation of 'community' is the artificial outcome of the gendered exclusion of domestic and neighbourly care from the dominant narratives of political economy (Mitropoulos 2005). The segregation of unpaid care work on the other side of 'the international division of labour' (Spivak 2010: 41) creates an exclusion zone with a porous boundary, a destination for the outsourcing of welfare services, and a demarcated territory for the governance of behaviour. In strategies of localism, the concept of community has come to stand for moral order, the locale of social responsibility and behavioural norms (Rose 1999; Cochrane 2003; Clarke 2009). 'Community' marks the place where the domestic economy of housework, parental discipline, the bonds of reciprocity and institutional authority all meet to establish the moral bedrock of society, and communities have become therefore 'the instrument through which governments focus their strategies for controlling and regulating social conduct' (Mooney and Neal 2009: 24). Localism relocates the domestic norms of a gendered private space to the public sphere, while invoking political norms in a domestic hinterland, addressing parenting behaviour and personal health as targets of governance, while promising that politics can be brought within reach and made subject to the rhythms of daily interaction (Jupp 2010).

Community action, or 'the politicised voice of local attachment' (Bulmer 1986: 95), still retains the prestige of a transformative collective strategy despite its entanglement in these governmental strategies (Pinkney and Saraga 2009). Mobilisations around place as community have, if anything, been renewed by the ubiquity of the concept in government discourse (Brent 2009), and the claim to represent, recover or build community legitimises campaigners and interest groups, and lends urban social movements a powerful cultural capital (Cohen 1997). The ability of community organisations, especially those in deprived neighbourhoods, to slip between spatial boundaries and move fluidly from contesting the local to governing it, and back again (Newman 2012), has been a subject of particular commentary among feminist scholars (Williams 1993; Martin 2002; Staeheli 2002). Community action manifests itself as an ethic of care extended into the public sphere, mobilising political power from an authority exercised in the domestic realm, and transforming care-giving from women's alienated reproductive labour into a model of co-operation on which to reconstruct society (Abel and Nelson 1990). It appears to borrow from, or act as a continuation of, an economy of reciprocity (Polanyi 1957) celebrated in the community studies literature of the 1950s (Hoggart 1957; Young and Wilmot 1962) exemplified by the informal provision, most often by women, of material and immaterial help through extended family and neighbourhood networks (Williams and Windebank 2000). The high levels of trust necessary to support this economy of care were founded on the geographical immobility of women (McCulloch 1997), and developed in the absence of alternative means of surviving 'as an extended subterranean chain' of services enabling delayed, transferred or indirect repayment of good deeds (Bulmer 1986: 112). This gift relationship (Titmuss 1970) is what Raymond Williams called 'the positive practice of neighbourhood' that aims to foster the social relations of community as a model for the collective organisation of society; 'the basic collective idea' that 'the provision of the means of life will, alike in production and distribution, be collective and mutual' (Williams 1967: 326). It is also, and paradoxically, a relationship that can be commodified in the form of social capital (Bourdieu 1986; Putnam 2000), that adaptable coinage that awards an exchange value to economies based on use value (Portes 1998), and it has, perversely lent a nostalgic resonance to governmental discourses of responsibility, active citizenship and public order. The principles of co-operation and relations of reciprocity are therefore the starting point, and not the outcome, of a process of transformation. Community action, in its transformative mission, promotes community as a space for democracy, where co-operation designates a method of achieving a shared understanding of the common good

(Staeheli 2003). Community action does not restrict itself to developing private relations of care but addresses the political world; it seeks 'to protect amenities, enhance resources and, to a greater or lesser degree wrench control of the local milieu from outside authorities and vest it in strictly local hands' (Bulmer 1986: 95). It can transform local services, like housing, into co-operative ventures and bring democracy to collective consumption. The political technology of localism gives regulatory licence to community action at the same time as it seeks to embrace communities as the embodiment of a responsible and governable public. In its promise to devolve power, localism employs community as a metaphor for democracy and empowerment, and foregrounds the pivotal role played by place and scale in cementing social differentiation and in naturalising power relations (Marston 2000). Localism authorises an enactment of democracy, citizenship and the 'public' through the lived experience of place (Dikec 2012). In seeking to construct a new order of political space, it provides unbidden a discourse through which socio–spatial relations of power are made vulnerable to reconfiguration (Leitner et al. 2008).

In a city in the north of England, members of a Tenant Management Organisation, running a social housing estate of 2,000 homes on behalf of the local authority, are discussing their plans for the locality (ID 10). Christine, who is in her early fifties, is very clear about what she wants to do as the new chair of the management board:

> I know where I want to be and what I want to do and I won't be side-tracked. I want to get the community to how I remember the community round here being, not like it is now.

The claim Christine makes on space reveals her use of discourses of social order to envisage a process of social change (Clarke 2009). She appears to extend the authority that she might exercise in the family home to a 2,000-home estate, and to cast herself as the regulator of conduct in the street and the neighbourhood. Localism provides the licence for this scalar jump (Smith 1993) from personal ethics into a manifesto for socio–spatial transformation that Christine sets out clearly:

> We should be able to walk out of our front door in comfort and feel safe. We should be able to walk up and down without fear of intimidation, and the elderly should feel safe. And that's what I'm hoping to achieve, to get this community back to how it were where people are not frightened, and I think I might get there eventually.

Tenant management enabled elected residents' groups to take over the running of council estates, if supported by a ballot of residents, to decentralise the delivery of housing services to the locality and make changes to the public realm (Cairncross et al. 2002). The management agreement with the local authority provides the tenants' organisation with its legitimacy, and defines the remit of its delegated authority in the maintenance of homes and the regulation of the behaviour of tenants (Flint 2004a). Christine, however, interprets this remit as the transformation of behaviour in order to recreate the reciprocal networks of community:

> You could at one time rely on your neighbour if you were ill. Um, you can't do that anymore, because they lock themselves in and they don't want to know. And that's not, to me, that's not a community.

Christine's aspirations appear to transcend the remit of estate management to imagine what Mike Davis (2006b) has called 'democratic public space', where an ethic of care and neighbourliness is to be nurtured through the rhythms and routines of familiar interaction. Christine's husband Gary explains the vision that clearly motivates the couple; he uses his hands to express the estate as conceptual space; starting out with a small rectangle, then enlarging it to indicate a breach of boundaries:

GARY: A lot of people now if that's their house [indicates a small space on paper] that's their space inn'it? [He makes a bigger space.] That's not their space anymore [shrinks the space], that's their space in their house. And that's why you go out here on a night, you'll not see anybody walking around, where years ago

CHRISTINE: Yeah

GARY: People used to stand at the gate and talk to other people like,

CHRISTINE: 'Course they did.

Gary articulates a desire to enlarge domestic space and to dissolve the boundary between public and private, expressing this as a strategy to breach the isolation of the home and extend domestic space and its feelings of safety into the street (Clark 1994). This is a negotiation over the limits of scale and the socio–spatial positioning it enforces. In Neil Smith's (1993: 105) words, this community organisation 'refuse to recognise the physical boundaries of the home but instead treat the community as a virtually borderless extension of the home'. Their strategy is to appropriate space and with it power; to upscale from home to the estate. This is a transgression of boundaries that widens the agency allotted to them and enables Christine to claim public space as her field of care:

CHRISTINE: My dad used to stand at the gate, when he retired, and everybody knew him, didn't they? And when my dad died they all rallied round to help me mum. You don't get that any more. [. . .] But I just want everything back to how it were. Not exactly; but to make it better for people.

Christine has mobilised the ethics of domestic and neighbourly care to enlist her tenant management organisation in the promotion of co-operation and

FIGURE 5.1 The gift relationship: a free picnic for elderly people organised by the tenants' federation in Rotherham

Photo provided by RotherFed

solidarity. She can envisage a future when the public sphere is rendered caring and safe. Her intention to 'make it better for people' is a statement of strategy which is licensed by the rationality of localism and yet exceeds its remit. The authority vested in her to manage the housing estate has rendered the social relations of public space malleable and open to change.

Politics into the streets

The key assumption underpinning the rationality of localism is that the smallest geographical unit of governance provides the greatest opportunities for citizens to participate in decisions (Lowndes and Sullivan 2008). There is nothing intrinsic, however, to local-scale decision-making that guarantees greater popular participation (Purcell 2006). Tenants' organisations have been distinctive 'in their concern with democracy from below or direct democracy [. . .] a bottom-up, grass-roots version of democracy' (Greg 2004: 29). Their commitment to participation in housing policy appears motivated by a desire to extend 'democracy into the very nature of welfare provision' (Bolger *et al.* 1981: 26). Tenant opposition to the stock-transfer of council housing focused on the loss of local democratic representation in housing governance (DCH 2006; Smyth 2013). The rise of housing associations as the main providers of social housing has given rise to concerns over a loss of democratic accountability in public services. Even arm's-length management companies, although owned by the local authority, are run by appointed boards, or the new magistracy as these unelected directors have been called (Clarke and Stewart 1994). Ideas of collective representation have been diminished in participation processes, where selection of participants on focus groups, scrutiny panels or on management boards has replaced democratic election (Grayson 2007). At a conference of social housing tenant activists from around the country, a group of resident directors from community-controlled housing associations discussed the need for democratic representation in local services (ID 9). These community companies have applied the rationalities of localism to transfer public housing from state authorities to local trusts, and now manage their estates through elected boards based in neighbourhood housing offices with locally based staff. In their discussion they identified electoral accountability, collective representation and a commitment to widening participation as all essential to the production of democracy through localism.

Sara, whose community-led organisation has taken control over their high-rise estate in the South of England, maintains the importance of democratic accountability and contrasts the elections to her community-led board with the restrictive landlord practices of co-option or selection:

> I was very proud to be elected by, by the tenants of my community and it meant that they could see that they had choice rather than somebody co-opting somebody else on and of course because they're going to have them because they're going to speak, going to be on the side of the local authority, ALMO, housing association, call it what you will. So I was very proud to be democratically elected.

In adhering to democratic principles in housing governance, Sara reflects a continuing debate around electoral accountability in public services. Participation, seen as a mechanism for strengthening accountability through effecting consumer information, representation and redress, is twinned in the discourse of tenants with democracy, and the ability to elect the governing board is seen as choice reinforcing voice. Marcie, a tenant director from a community-controlled housing association, flaunts company law to maintain that the democratic election of tenant board members empowers them as representatives rather than company directors:

> I was elected on to there, which I feel very proud of because I have spoken to residents to represent them, to represent their views and it is absolutely important that they know that when you speak to them you are going to go to the committee and put their views to that committee.

While housing providers have configured the question of representation as one of demographic sampling and the co-option of individuals, tenants argue that being representative is a process of collective representation.

CLARE: If you are elected, you can honestly say 'I am speaking on behalf of'. Well, I hope they are, whereas you are only speaking on behalf of yourself aren't you?

YVONNE: But you've also got the right then to go out and say 'I am your elected representative, can you tell me what you want?'

Being democratically elected is the first stage, but being accountable as an elected representative is a matter of maintaining day-to-day contact with local residents. The constitutional requirement for tenants' associations is that their members must live in the area they represent and this local presence is vital to the ideal of grass-roots democracy promoted in the model of a tenants' movement. It ensures that tenant representatives can be mandated and held to account. Brian (ID 7) says:

> You go home and you've got them knocking on your door. I have to be careful because I'm on call seven days a week, you know, really. I mean, I had a text last night – 'when are you having another coffee morning?' I thought, we've just got over one, give us a chance to pull ourselves together and get organised, you know, but this is how they are.

It is the accessibility of elected tenant representatives that ensures they are accountable; as Sara (ID 9) says, she cannot avoid her constituents; she is always on call.

> I mean, we've only got 394 properties on our estate and everybody knows who's on the board and you get stopped. They knock on your door, they stop you in the street. You cannot get away from them.

Sara's rueful comments here indicate that the accountability of tenant representatives is dependent on a web of routine interactions and daily face-to-face encounters that ensure elected officials remain embedded in the concerns of their constituents. The democracy of tenants' organisations is based on their 'nearness' (Kearns and Parkinson 2001) to the face-to-face contact, regular encounters, routine interactions and local knowledge that invest place with familiarity. Nearness is a spatial construction in which a discourse of neighbourliness is manifested around an invocation of locality. Although posited as actually existing conditions integral to neighbourhoods by the rationale of localism, these everyday relationships have to be constructed in material practice and emotional identification by tenants' groups that strive to generate collective identities around the spatial practices of place (Martin 2003). The first stage in the construction of nearness is the work of place-making or the adoption of place as a shared 'field of care' (Tuan 1974). In this work, effective bonds are generated around the idea of place as territory and around the shared interest of residents as neighbours; shared residence is prioritised over the equally formative experiences that stretch over larger scales of belonging (Massey 1994). The construction of 'nearness' can be a partisan claim of hegemony over the neighbourhood by those who declare themselves as the indigenous people, the insiders with inside knowledge and the ability to distinguish those who are 'out of place' (Cohen 1997; Brent 2009). For tenants from community-led housing organisations it appears instead to promote active involvement and participation in local decision-making on housing issues. In seeking to ensure the widest participation, community-controlled housing organisations can be seen to actively construct a sense of neighbourhood, local knowledge, and therefore of the local scale itself through the promotion of democratic involvement in public services. This is partly a physical transformation. Sara (ID 9) provides an account of how her community board of twelve people tried to ensure that the residents of their high-rise estate are engaged in decision-making. She tells how, prior to community control, housing staff from the local authority would never visit the estate, and residents had to make a long and expensive bus journey into the city; now the community organisation has a housing office in the centre of the estate, and:

> Now the people don't have to go all the way into S[town], you know, £5 bus ride, to report something. They just walk down the stairs, or across the green, into the office.

A sense that the community-controlled housing organisation is at the heart of the estate is reproduced in Sara's words. The office is pictured at the crossroads of every route across the estate. But the 'nearness' that distinguishes the tenant directors from the previous local authority managers is constructed through participatory decision-making processes and by encouraging an ethos that every resident matters, as Sara describes.

> Everything we do we go out to the tenants first and we call them 'You Decides', where we put all our questions round the boardroom and the people come in, if they live in a high-rise block, if they live in a low rise, they all get different coloured stickers and, um, this is how we, we run it. So it does work, it does work if you give power to the people.

The face-to-face encounters and social interaction that constitute the basis for democratic community governance have to be actively constructed through participation in decision-making. Transforming place into 'nearness' means bringing decision-making within reach and embedding it in the rhythms of everyday life. After describing a contested election to the board and the creation of a series of subcommittees to involve a wider range of local people in the decisions, Sara explains that participation also involves 'neighbouring' work (Bulmer 1986), or the active fostering of bonds of reciprocity and neighbourly care.

> We have people with special needs and that, two of those go around with one of the, um, Service and Performance [subcommittee] and they do a block inspection, so, it's integrating those people to make them feel 'yes you are

FIGURE 5.2 Constructing 'nearness': RotherFed organise an estate litter-pick complete with prizes from the Easter Bunny

Photo provided by RotherFed

valid'. I mean, we have a lady who comes to our board meetings, she's in her fifties with, er, learning difficulties but she makes the tea and her highlight last meeting was because we gave her a badge with her name on, you know. So it's trying to accommodate everybody, making everybody feel that yes, you have got something to do, you are a valid member of society.

Localism provides this community organisation with the regulatory framework to take decisions on behalf of their housing estate. In delivering its authority, the community organisation makes practices of neighbouring and domestic care central to their estate-management function (Jupp 2008). Participation in decision-making appears here as the outcome of neighbouring and as an active process of inclusion in which democracy is an essential component of the construction of the local. The rationality of localism, with its problematic assertion that the local is inherently more democratic, has authorised spatial practices through which space can be constructed as both local and democratic.

Democracy from below

Localism owes a debt to the tradition of participatory democracy and embeds this uncomfortably within centralised and hierarchical systems of governance (Brownhill 2009). The central direction of localism and the strengthening of State power it conceals (Fuller and Geddes 2008) ensure that participatory democracy is subordinate to the representative democracy of the State and, more frequently, is subsumed by the managerial discourses that have depoliticised the governance of public services and legitimised their outsourcing and privatisation (Swyngedouw 2004; Wallace 2010). The community is construed as a natural territory with a latent capacity for self-government and an innate common sense which enables its residents to reach consensus decisions without interference from big government (Durose and Rees 2012; Hancock *et al.* 2012), but community groups wishing to benefit from the rights of localism are dependent on the local authority for their right to become agents of governance (DCLG 2011c). Their boundaries and constitutions must be designated by state power in order to use the powers of the Localism Act 2011, and their remit is tightly constrained to ensure their subordination to a hierarchy of decision-making (DCLG 2012). Far from being natural entities, community groups may be conjured up to parallel the abstract geography of dispersed state powers, or slotted into existing state structures without developing lines of accountability or adapting any of the core processes of State power to enable wider participation (Taylor 2007).

In a restructuring that has drawn attention to the role of government at regional and local levels, and celebrated the smallest scale as the most democratic, community organisations are encouraged to consider what decisions should be taken locally, and what systems of democracy would deliver the 'empowered participatory democracy' (Fung and Wright 2003) that localism celebrates but fails to implement. London Tenants Federation is a community organisation engaged in the devolved governance arrangements of the English capital. It draws together delegates from formally constituted organisations of social housing tenants in each borough of the city and co-ordinates resident involvement in the London Mayor's housing strategy. A group of those delegates, all council tenants, were engaged in a discussion about how the federation can remain accountable to its borough groups while operating at regional scale (ID 6). In the extract below they sketch out the processes of participatory democracy that ensure that decision-making at regional level stays rooted in the familiarity of place.

JANE: I also think that, um, there actually has to be a democratic structure
SANJIT: Hmm
JANE: So the people who are speaking know they're accountable to the people they're speaking for. I mean, for example, we, nobody in our borough can get to the tenants' council without having been elected first from their tenants' association, then from there to their area forum, from their area forum they go to, so there's a democratic structure and every year you have an AGM, every year you have to show your accounts, every year you have to, [. . .] and then, you, you speak, and if you continually speak for yourself you won't get elected next time round, you know, or if you speak for yourself and people quite like you speaking for yourself

because they agree with you, well, then that's alright, do you know what I mean? You can't necessarily consult on every question at every moment with the people on the ground but you represent them and you go back to them and say, 'I said that and do you agree, and do you support me?'

The scalar decision-making process outlined by Jane begins at the local tenants' association, an elected body with local autonomy, which sends delegates to a tenants' federation in order to co-ordinate federal or borough-wide decision-making. Tenants' associations have evolved a model of participatory democracy in which constituted local groups, elected at annual meetings open to all residents, assume a mandate to speak on behalf of their defined social housing estate. The emphasis on grass-roots democracy and collective representation may appear somewhat ironic given studies of tenants' associations that have identified the splits, feuds and lack of support received by local committees (Ravetz 2001). It is clear that some association committees only represent the views of their extended network of families and friends, and that some tenants elected to represent a defined constituency may only ever speak for themselves (Andrews 1979). Criticisms of tenants' organisations as unrepresentative have accompanied the rise of market research methodologies among social housing providers, and have usually centred on the make-up of tenant committees, which often appear not to mirror the diversity of their neighbourhood, being 'highly ethnocised and gendered' (Uguris 2004: 123) and characteristically made up of older residents, with most being over the age of 50. In contrast, a more useful indicator of diversity might be a focus on the steps taken by residents' organisations to remove barriers to wider involvement on the grounds that 'it is impossible to get everyone involved or to have a single truly representative organisation' (Millward et al. 2003: 39). Although some tenants' associations may in practice represent only specific constituencies, a reflexive discourse of accountability and involvement has attached to the organisational structure of collective action in social housing, as Jane explained:

> Like all those, like all situations how much you actually get down to the roots on the ground is dependent on the people who are doing the representing, or have been elected. You know, some tenants' delegates try very hard to take it back, and then consult up, and what we basically try and do in the Tenants' Federation. [. . .] The thing about a tenants' association is that everybody on the estate potentially can come to the tenants' association, so potentially you are consulting with all of them and you're their voice and you're answerable to them. Even if we know when we turn up they're probably going to nominate the same old people. If they really disliked what we were doing, they wouldn't. They'd get us out, if we were advocating things that weren't in their interest.

In Jane's interpretation the tenants' association brings decision-making into reach and locates it in the space of 'nearness'. Residents 'turn up' routinely, and the familiarity of the 'same old people' is rendered democratic by the routine that ensures that 'everybody can potentially come' and change it. Jane indicates the opportunity for residents to pack a meeting, express their dissatisfaction and obtain redress. In this model being 'answerable' means to be within calling distance and implies being subject to face-to-face challenge. The organisational structure of local tenants' associations and tenants' federations reflects at its core the ethos of direct democracy where the guiding principle is the need to ensure that the local constituents have direct control over the aims, actions and activities of the leadership. This is a characteristic of tenants' organisations that ensures 'working-class interests can both be mobilised and remain dominant in the carrying out of a particular campaign', as Steve Bolger and his radical social work colleagues maintained (Bolger et al. 1981: 144).

The model of direct democracy presented by Jane is one where decisions are made deliberatively at the most local level, and the authority delegated to other scales is limited and subject to recall. Not all decisions can be taken at neighbourhood level, and questions of decision-making at more distant scales of governance and the role of delegation or representation are always problematic in direct democracy. Tenants' federations and some community-controlled housing organisations have adopted a constitutional model that distinguishes between representation in the political meaning of taking decisions at a higher level, and 'functional' representation (Somerville 2005b) where the purpose of higher-level bodies is to support and resource local decision-making. In the co-operative housing movement, secondary co-operatives may provide administration, finance and legal services to the primary co-operative whose members make decisions directly. The tenant-led housing association Watmos, based in Walsall in the Midlands, exemplifies this direct democracy in the tenants' movement. It provides an asset ownership structure, and financial, legal and administrative support to eight tenant management organisations who each retain autonomy over housing management decisions in their neighbourhood areas (Watmos Community Homes 2010). This model of functional representation in housing service delivery enables tenants' organisations to apply the principles of direct democracy to the organisation and governance of public services more generally. Continuing their discussion, London Tenants Federation (ID 6) members begin to imagine what multi-scalar decision-making structures might be like if modelled on the principles of participatory democracy:

NAJINDER: So what I feel is, if there should be a general trend is, the consultation process, or whatever is to be agreed upon, should start at the grass roots and then be taken forward as we go along, then you, you will get effective participation.

SANJIT: The ideal would be that there would be some sort of organisation that was based on delegates from area tenant federations like ours. Everybody here is an elected representative of a residents' association or a tenants' association somewhere. And we come together and we agree things by consensus. I like to use my old, I used to be a shop steward in the film technicians union and I always used to say in meetings: 'I'm sorry, I can't take that back to my members' [laughs]. So whenever I'm in meetings I always try and think like that, okay, can I get, would I, can I get anybody else on my estate to agree to this, no? Well I can't agree to it, even if I think it's a good idea ((laughs)). That. That's real democracy.

JANE: It should be a bottom-up process like we are; it should work by consensus rather than, um, you know; it should recognise regional differences, because there are, you know, the problems of London are unique to London, for example.

The idea of a tenants' movement has been associated with 'prefigurative politics' (Breines 1989: 6) where the political practice of the movement prefigures the desired society they aim to bring about. Relations of equality and democratic participation are practised now, in the locality, while also advocated as long-term strategic objectives on a wider stage. This was an explicit theme in the writings of the New Left in the 1960s and in the organisations of the women's movement through the 1970s and 1980s, where the focus was on developing relationships and organisational forms that were egalitarian, non-hierarchical, and developed the confidence and efficacy of participants to envisage a future society that was organised according to those principles. It has been argued that the same themes are visible in the tenants' movement (Polletta 1999), and that tenant management organisations, co-operatives and tenant-owned housing associations 'experiment with structures which might in some way fulfil some of their longer term goals and prefigure the kind of provision they anticipate may result from wider structural change' (Wood 1994: 154).

In the discussion at London Tenants Federation (ID 6) the delegates speculate about the scalar restructuring of democratic governance that could achieve popular engagement in decision-making. They sketch out a participatory process that attempts to reconcile recognition of difference with the need for consensus in a system of delegation that prioritises local knowledge. The active process of constructing place as nearness that is observed among tenants' organisations empowered under localism is here translated into a spatial structuring of politics imagined to bring supra-local decision-making into reach and to root power in the routine face-to-face interaction of neighbouring. The next section examines how this spatial reimagining of democracy is applied by tenants to debates about governance at national scale.

Bringing it all back home

Despite the spatial transformations of governance in most Western countries, social movement theorists have emphasised the comparative irrelevance of place-based contentious action and characterised campaigns at national and global scale as best placed to achieve social change. A lively debate on the scalar organisation of protest has ensued, examining how urban movements, campaigns and community groups negotiate space and scale, and organise themselves around an awareness of global as well as local influences (see Massey 1994; Harvey 1996; Routledge 2003; Featherstone 2005; Cumbers *et al.* 2008; Leitner *et al.* 2008; Nicholls 2008). Tenants are organised at local, borough-wide and sometimes regional scale by associations and federations, such as the one considered in the previous section, and are networked weakly at national level through the Tenants and Residents Organisations of England and other national groups. The federation acts as an umbrella body of tenants' and residents' associations (sometimes known by the acronym TARAs) that provides them with functional representation at the scale of the borough municipality. Neighbourhood tenants' and residents' associations are the governing bodies of the federation, and the federation executive or management committee is elected and held accountable by the membership through regular general meetings. An idealised reflection on this scalar organisation is provided by the vice chair of a tenants' federation in discussion with another member of their management committee (ID 7).

BRIAN: It's the tenants out there what voted for each and every member on this federation for them where they are today so it's up to them to represent the tenants out there of the whole of [. . .] borough for putting them where they are today
EILEEN: It's not what we want
BRIAN: It's what they want.

These principles of direct democracy operate between the local association and the borough federation, and, as Brian proclaims below, extend on to the national organisation and from there to the international tenants' body, the International Union of Tenants, which has consultative status in the housing, planning and regional economic work of the United Nations.

BRIAN: If you're a TARA you've got a bigger voice; instead of one tenant shouting you've got the whole TARA, and not only that with the TARAs being affiliated to the association, because this office here isn't our office we only manage it on behalf of the TARAs, it's their office really. And we pay a donation to what you call TAROE, that's Tenants and Residents of all England. They pay a fee to the European one which covers the whole of the world, so the tenant's voice will be heard all over the world, you see, so it's a good thing. That's why we push for TARAs, you know.

Brian here describes the federal structure of an international social movement, one that represents a 'scaling-up' of the democratic principles of election, accountability and commitment to grass-roots decision-making. This scalar confederation provides solidarity to the local associations but also, potentially, enables them to maintain a contentious mobilisation that recognises and shares experiences and issues that would otherwise remain parochial and particular (Harvey 1996; Somerville 2005b). No national tenants' organisation has ever received more than partial support from the network of local tenants' associations, however, and most have been established in a top-down manner. The successful national organisations have been those that developed from the regional alliances of local campaigning groups or federations (Grayson 2010). In a movement that privileges 'nearness' in order to ensure direct democracy, suspicion surrounds the suggestion that any decision-making functions should be taken away from the reach of the locality. A debate over the function of the national organisation can be examined by revisiting the northern tenant management organisation featured earlier in this chapter (ID 10). Jean, a member of the tenant management board, is keen to promote the benefits of the National Federation of Tenant Management Organisations to her colleagues.

JEAN: I do think national tenants is a very good thing because everyone's telling one another their little tips. It's like you read in newspaper, um, somebody'll tell you tip how to get lipstick out of your thing or some chewing gum off things, it's word of mouth and little tips like that I think help you

CHRISTINE: Yeah

JEAN: With what you are doing; and I think that is important. And you only get that by meeting other people and hearing what they're doing and things like that. Yeah, I'm a big believer in national tenants' movement.

Jean characterises the role of a national organisation as one of providing 'little tips' and sharing experience; the symbolic language she uses here will be examined later. Gary, Christine's husband, intervenes at this point to challenge the relevance of a national movement to the locality, saying:

GARY: But should we mirror other tenants' associations? You know, should we work same way as them, or should we try and find better ways of working? You know what I mean? If they come out with ideas should we take their ideas, use their ideas?

JEAN: Well, they come along and use yours as well; it's a movement that's a mixture.

GARY: I, I

JEAN: You learn and they learn.

GARY: I don't believe in, er, mirroring other associations, I think we should build us own way, and make us name in it, we should find us own ways.

For Gary, even the idea of networking with other organisations threatens to push decision-making out of reach, as if accountability rooted in 'nearness' necessitated the exclusion of wider mobilisation. Jean counters this challenge by returning to the gendered language of the example she used before, and explicitly appealing to Christine's experience, to explain why a national organisation is beneficial.

JEAN: Yeah, but what I'm saying, finding your own way actually, what I'm saying it's, it's like I've just been saying about lipstick and tips, so, you don't, your wife don't want to know how to get lipstick out of her top, she needs to find it out herself, but no, she would be grateful for that little tip

CHRISTINE: Yeah, I would

JEAN: Wouldn't yah? So this is what I'm saying. Tips from other people – you don't have to do what they do. Just like you pass your tips what you found on to other people, you're not mirroring them, because although you've got that tip, you might find a better way round it

CHRISTINE: Yeah, yeah.

The domesticity of Jean's analogy of removing lipstick from clothes, and her appeal to Christine, Gary's wife, to support her in this gendered knowledge, recalls a debate among radical community workers in the late 1970s and 1980s about the mobilisation potential of the tenants' movement they were determined to effect. Peter Baldock (1982) attributed the ability of the tenants' movement to establish new organisational models based on participatory and direct democracy to the leadership role of women. The symbolic importance of mutual aid and co-operation in the framing activity of tenants was a result of 'new modes of organisation based on local housewives' networks, modes that were more informal, put more emphasis on mutual support, were more openly democratic than the models imposed by men' (Baldock 1982: 124). The domesticity of the movement proved its strength in generating distinctive values, but, as John Cowley (1979: 133) noted, 'places of residence fragment people, each behind their own front door'. In his account of the tenants' rent protests in Sheffield from 1967 to 1968, Baldock envisaged the tenants' movement developing from a 'revolt of women, the managers of working class consumption, against an attack on their ability to do that job of managing consumption' (1982: 124). Tenants' action begins in the kitchen, for Baldock, and spreads to the street, but it remains an issue of household management and is therefore constitutionally unable to become a national movement. Steve Bolger and the co-authors of *Towards Socialist Welfare Work* (1981: 143) supported this view:

> If locality based community groups have a strength it stems from the immediate, material relationship the constituents have to the issue; a direct material relationship that can, if developed, contradict a subordinate and social democratic consciousness. However, a direct material relationship cannot of, and by itself, construct a political understanding which expands beyond the issue in question to a wider political perspective.

In discussion over lipstick traces and national movements, Jean used the immediate and material analogy of household management to convey the benefits of national mobilisation. The example of swapping tips on how to remove lipstick from clothes shifted the debate into a gendered space, and appealed to the scalar jump that is essential to community action: the extension of domestic agency into the public sphere. Jean has moved the space of the discussion, metaphorically, from the board-room of the tenant management organisation – a public body operating under delegated powers from the municipal authority – to a domestic setting, where women exchange tips on household management. The national organisation is transformed accordingly from a distant and potentially intrusive entity into an informal exchange (perhaps over an imagined fence or garden gate) of household news and views. In this discussion Jean and Christine have begun to negotiate 'a politics of scale from below' (Escobar 2001: 161) through the language of domesticity and neighbouring. They suggest, contrary to the views expressed by Steve Bolger and Peter Baldock, that national (or international) political mobilisa-tion can be envisaged as a reciprocal process of neighbourly exchange, and networks and solidarities may be constructed through the parallel connection of domestic spaces. This is an imaginary in which power is embedded within face-to-face routine interaction but operates without frontiers in a commonality of domestic space and gendered knowledge. The technology of localism with its promise to bring democracy back home has licensed practices in which household management

FIGURE 5.3 Domestic politics: women from a local tenants' association in Huddersfield prepare for a housing protest

Photo provided by Kirklees Federation of Tenants and Residents Associations

becomes the driver of national mobilisation to imagine a tenants' movement that privileges the local because it is universal.

Localism and the tenants' movement

Movement building among tenants is a fragile process that must celebrate the local and the particular even as it attempts to construct the semblance of shared interests and motivate collective action across space and distance. Tension between national organisation and community action has been a constant theme in the movement's history and these two poles exert opposite attractions in the narratives of the tenants' movement. Since the National Council of Corporation Tenants was set up in 1937 (Schifferes 1976), there has been a series of attempts to organise tenants nationally, sometimes with several groups competing with each other for national dominance. While each attempt can claim its successes, effective representation of tenants in national policy issues has seldom, if ever, been achieved (Oxley 1986; Grayson 2010).

The tension between localism and national organisation appears in the following debate among members of a tenants' federation in the north of England (ID 5). These federation members have been closely involved in the promotion of a national movement, and two of them have served on the governing bodies of the national tenants' organisation. In their discussion they are attempting to accommodate the distinctiveness of locality-based organisations and local needs with the development of an effective national movement that can make universal demands:

JULIA: It can't be a proper tenants' movement if nobody, all works together, we've all got to work together, all sing from the same hymn sheet, otherwise it won't work. I mean, what tenants want in one part of the country, probably they won't want in another part

RON: All the needs are different aren't they?

JULIA: The needs are different

MICHAEL: Yeah

JULIA: But unless everybody's working together, [pause] it won't work.

MICHAEL: Even if we are a national tenants' organisation, you cannot come and give me what I want, because you need to address my needs.

The discussion appears to conclude in agreement that a vertical organisational structure necessarily abstracts from local autonomy and fails to represent local needs. Another member of the group, Theresa, then offers the view that the irreconcilability of scales can be resolved through horizontal mobilisation, where each organisation can retain its autonomy but lend its support.

THERESA: As tenants, we would support what London needs, just as London would support us on what our needs are. And that's the basis of everybody working together: realising there is different needs, but supporting the tenants when the needs are still different.

This proposal is challenged, however, by another participant in the discussion, Dave, who clearly believes that operating away from his 'own little corner' results in an inevitable loss of identity. As Dave continues this argument, voices are raised and the majority of members force his acquiescence, evidencing the contested nature of national organising among the subjects of localism.

DAVE: I think you have a better chance of doing this in smaller communities than going national, myself.
HARRY: Well
RON: We need to know what we're doing national
THERESA: The bigger the voice
DAVE: The bigger the voice, what?
HARRY: You can't have a national voice that.
RON: You could become isolated, then.
DAVE: Pardon?
RON: Smaller communities could become more isolated
HARRY: Yes
DAVE: I think you've a better chance of achieving your goal in your area, than, you know? You've just said, everybody need different things in their areas. Well you can't have it all ways; if we've got one national voice we're all going to be the same
SEVERAL VOICES [shout]: No
HARRY: You can have a national voice and you can still fight for your own little corner
THERESA: And therefore that's when all tenants is working together.

The localism of the tenants' movement has been identified as its core weakness, or Achilles heel. It is the fundamental flaw that leaves the movement incapable of formulating effective strategy. 'The whole character of housing struggles is precisely that of their isolation and disparateness' wrote John Cowley (1979: 128), while Peter Saunders (1979: 125) dismissed tenant action as 'specific, short-lived and far from solid', as largely unco-ordinated defensive actions, with limited objectives, taking place in isolation from each other. Ian Cole and Rob Furbey (1994: 153) took up this refrain, describing the tenants' movement as 'typically limited, localised, occasional and defensive'. Tenants are clearly capable of engaging in national co-ordinated action, and this has been evidenced in the rent strikes of the early 1970s, the campaign against the 1988 Housing Act and in the campaigns against stock transfer after 2000, to choose just three examples. However, tenant organisations have never developed a political movement that articulates a long-term strategy, beyond the repeal of a specific act of legislation or change in policy initiative. The strategic weakness ascribed to tenant localism is that it provides its participants with no influence over questions of housing costs, housing supply or access to housing, and no protection against the effects of national housing and social policy decisions. Tenants' organisations have taken over the management of their estates, have voted for stock transfer or arm's-length management in order to see investment in their homes. Meanwhile, these initiatives have served to undermine municipal housing, local democracy and the values of public ownership, and have distracted attention from the centralisation of housing policy and the fragmentation of its delivery. Martin Wood (1994: 153) lamented that the tenants' movement as a whole 'seem to have their heads buried firmly in the sand'. The housing powers of the municipality have been eroded through a long process of reductions in subsidy and restriction on borrowing, centralised rent setting on market principles and stock transfer to housing associations. Local authorities that have retained their housing stock, or established arm's-length management companies, have very limited capacity for investment and the development of new affordable housing (Malpass 2005; Walker and Marsh 2003). Housing associations have not been exempt from this loss of autonomy, and regulatory authorities like the Housing Corporation and Homes and Communities Agency have exercised compelling influence over everyday management practices, while reductions in development grants, and prescriptions on bidding, have led to the creation of commercial group structures from mergers and take-overs. Tenants addressing themselves to the directors of their housing organisation in order to bring about change may find that strategic asset management, investment and service delivery are decisions controlled by parent boards, located miles from the local estate, and are in any case influenced by the requirements of institutional lenders and global bond markets (Malpass 2000; Pawson and Sosenko 2011). Commitment to localism has prevented a tenants' movement from adapting to these new relations of housing governance. At the meeting at London Tenants Federation (ID 6), Susan argued that tenants appear incapable of shifting their strategy to address the complexity and connectivity of the power relations that govern the locality:

SUSAN: When you, when you speak to tenants, I mean, tenants in my borough that have been around for donkeys years and probably should have retired many, many years ago, will recall when their main kind of remit, and where they got things done successfully, was lobbying their local councillor

JANE: Yeah

NAJINDER: Hmm

SUSAN: And I think the movement is still, in a sense, built up on that kind of premise, you know that you have a group of people on an estate who, you go in and you lobby a local councillor, but there's increasingly that kind of understanding that actually that doesn't work any more, because it's not even from the local authority that it's, it's, yes there's mismanagement, there's failure to address, there's failure to consult, and all those kind of things, but actually

> underneath there's this kind of sneaking suspicion, or at least understanding, that it comes from somewhere else, which is too far away to kind of address anyway.

Considered as fields of collective action, the local and the national/global often appear as mutually exclusive; the local being synonymous with the particular, and associated with conservative tendencies (Harvey 1996), while the national/ global is conflated with the universal, and with autonomous militant mobilisation (Featherstone 2005). This viewpoint privileges the nationally organised social movement or the globally connected campaign with the potential to achieve change, and regards the local tenants' group as inconsequential, or even as reactionary. Social movement theorists tend to counsel a middle path, advising that local protests need to negotiate between scales of activism (Routledge 2003), concluding that the local group must be 'nested within a distinctive counter-hegemonic movement at national and international scale' (Somerville 2004: 149). There may, however, be advantages in maintaining a local focus if the aim is to mobilise a popular movement that can attain influence on a national and even international scale. The feminist geographers Doreen Massey (1994), Julie Graham and Katherine Gibson (Gibson-Graham 2002) have pointed to the social construction of these geographies of scale and stressed the global consequences of place-based politics. The development of political strategies of localism in the UK over the last ten years has provided political opportunities to a locally mobilised tenants' movement through entry into local strategic partnerships and involvement in aspects of municipal governance (Somerville 2004). In tenant management and other initiatives around the outsourcing of public services, ownership of public assets and the promotion of active citizenship, tenants discern opportunities to advance participatory and direct models of democracy and modify power imbalances at a local scale. It would be foolish to gloss community localism as wholly progressive, and the resident-led housing organisations featured in this research invoke a new and divided public from the socialised provision of welfare services. However, in conflating the local community with a widening of democracy and the transfer of political power, localism licenses an imaginative reordering of public space and its socio-spatial positioning. It provides the regulatory licence that authorises tenant management, community-led housing companies and tenants' associations to make a scalar jump from the private to public realm and, in challenging power relations, enables them to 'resist the givenness of place' (Dikec 2012). By instituting relations of democracy and participation in the locality, tenants envisage a wider social transformation, imagining hierarchies flattened and relations of power brought within reach. This is a retelling of localism that rehearses the spatial practices through which empowered participatory democracy might be realised and demonstrates the desire for a more fundamental reshaping of political space. Community action in the locality could therefore be the most effective strategy for a tenants' movement that seeks to extend the principles of direct democracy to public services and to construct the local through the principles of co-operation, reciprocity and an ethic of neighbourly care. The most successful national mobilisations of tenants have arguably been those that were initiated in specific locations, campaigning on particular issues that developed as networks of grass-roots groups. In the 1980s the National Anti-Dampness Campaign, the National Tower Blocks Campaign and the People's Asbestos Action Campaign were all mobilised by local groups who realised that the problems they identified were more widespread than one particular block or city (Oxley 1986: 218). The National Tenants and Residents Federation developed in 1989 out of the battles of city tenants' federations who joined forces in campaigns against tenants' choice legislation and later compulsory competitive tendering of housing management (Hood and Woods 1994; Grayson 2010). Campaigns in the locality have the potential to mobilise national movements and retain the dynamism of grass-roots leadership. Susan, a member of London Tenants Federation (ID 6), argues for the potential of community action to mobilise a militant movement and advocates a return to local campaigning. She argues that conflict and direct action allow local tenants' organisations greater leverage than participation in partnerships governed by dominant groups (Davies 2007). Participation with landlords, becoming expert in the specialised and refined language of the professional, all these concerns are depicted as a sideshow in the following extract, as Susan recalls the time when her association had real impact:

> Probably that was our most successful time as a tenants' association because there were very physical things, and very practical things relating to our housing that we focused on. We took no notice of their, their meetings, focused on ours, did the campaigning, did the door-knocking, and didn't care who we bit at, whichever political party, whichever officer, we just bit and said 'we pay our rent' [. . .] We're still lost without the kind of things that the tenants' associations used to do, which was about their community. So it's that kind of thing: our homes, our communities stuff; it's not just about the practicalities of what happens, you know, in terms of the HRA [Housing Revenue Account], or how much money they're going to dish out or whether they want us to be consulted or whether that actually means little to most people on our estates, [. . .], but its actually a bit more of the kind of, and we've lost a bit of that; I think we've lost a bit of that and it's stuff we have to renew, which is about how we bring our communities together as, as communities, and maybe have to focus a bit less on attending all those damn meetings.

Mobilisation around immediate material issues in a defined locality, campaigning for a localised conception of social justice, 'our homes, our communities', here is the strategic vision that exerts a powerful attraction for the tenants' movement. Susan outlines a strategy of community action in which the development of reciprocal relations of solidarity, co-operation and neighbourliness motivate an oppositional movement. It is a vision, as Susan points out, that requires tenants' organisations to distance themselves from the patronage and the co-opting influence of housing providers and governmental agencies. As if reflecting Susan's contentions, the tenants' movement has been associated with the contemporary demand for a 'Right to the City' (Lefebvre 1996), in which a range of anti-capitalist struggles express themselves in conflict over urban space, 'over who should have the benefit of the city and what kind of city it should be' (Mayer 2009: 367). This association draws on Manuel Castells's (1983: 319) characterisation of tenants as an urban social movement agitating for a city organised around use value 'in contradiction to the notion of the city for profit'. To claim the right to the city is to claim the power to shape justice spatially, to demand 'the fair and equitable distribution in space of socially valued resources and the opportunities to use them' (Soja 2008: 3). The identity work evidenced among tenants in this chapter is distinctive in its concern for participatory and direct democracy, grass-roots governance and the transgression of socio-spatial boundaries; it seeks to extend a domestic ethic of care into the public sphere to foster social relations of co-operation and reciprocity. The assertions of this collective action frame provide a territorial basis for reflections on social justice. This territorialisation of social policy by tenants is explained by Stella Capek and John Gilderbloom in their discussion of the tenants' movement in the United States:

> Tenants must be understood as urban social actors linked to particular conceptions of space. The importance of space or territoriality for tenants' movements is striking since they lay their claims according to a reinterpretation of spatial justice.
>
> (Capek and Gilderbloom 1992: 5)

This chapter has identified the third collective action frame through which the collective identity of a tenants' movement is shaped. It has analysed the construction of a distinctive organisational culture shared among tenant participants, one that motivates collective action in the locality and suggests the structures and democratic principles around which a wider social movement might be mobilised. In actively producing 'nearness' through participation, tenant identity work lays claim to the public space of neighbourhood to enact more co-operative and neighbourly social relations. In asserting an organisational model of direct democracy as a potentially prefigurative programme for the participatory governance of public services, the collective identity of a tenants' movement provides mobilising narratives around a sense of territorial or spatial justice. The next chapter offers an assessment of the effectiveness of this mobilisation and examines the obstacles to the development of a distinctive tenants' movement in housing policy.

6

MOBILISING TENANTS

The three collective action frames examined in the previous chapters have evidenced a distinctive belief system or the collective identity of a tenants' movement. In the canon of social movement theory the purpose of collective action frames is to 'activate adherents, transform bystanders into supporters, exact concessions from targets and demobilise antagonists' (Snow 2004: 384). They are collective *action* frames because they provide the 'guides to action' that mobilise individuals into a movement and into a contentious challenge to the status quo (Tarrow 1992: 177). An analysis of the frames constructed by a movement should make clear its 'dynamics of recruitment and mobilisation' (Williams 2004: 94). This chapter extends the analysis of tenant identity work to assess the mobilising impact of these frames, the action plans and recruitment strategies they indicate, and the contentious action that they trigger. It examines the resources and opportunities available for mobilisation, and assesses the effectiveness of the national tenants' organisation, and its aims and tactics. It applies a rigorous definition of collective identity to evaluate the extent to which there exists a contemporary tenants' movement in England with aims, goals and plans for action.

We all want the same things

The collective action frames of a tenants' movement construct an emotional identification rather than a tangible organisation. The movement is expressed in an idealised litany of common cause, or combatively manifested in the language of struggle and rights. It is conjured up as tradition, a history to be referenced and celebrated, a spirit of possibility, a movement that has momentum, and that slowly and surely evidences progress. The phrase 'tenants' movement' is often used to suggest a sense of shared identity across the entirety of tenants engaged in participation – for example, Barnsley Federation (2008: 2) says that it 'co-ordinates the role of the tenant movement within the borough'. This nebulous identity captures an assumption of common cause that is most apparent at events like the conference of the tenant participation consultancy TPAS, an assembly of over 800 tenants all involved in consultation mechanisms. At the 2008 convention (ID 2) Stephanie, a tenant director, defined her sense of the movement as:

> It's just, it is, er, I I think it, it's one big group, passionate group with a common goal to improve our homes the way we are treated by the government and also the community we live in.

Although she attributes three specific goals to the definition of movement, Stephanie's 'one big passionate group' is an emotional identification that conveys the feeling of being present at a convention of like-minded people. At another TPAS focus group in 2009 (ID 8), Barbara, the secretary of a tenants' association, cites the networking that occurs at the convention to indicate a sense of wider unity between tenants:

> I always feel amazed when you go to a meeting, er, somewhere perhaps for the first time and you're meeting a new group of people how you can sit around that table and you can talk, and at the end of it you realise you're all there for the same reason and that strength I think it g-gives you, well it gives you more strength to carry on because you're not alone.

Although the feeling of belonging to a movement gives Barbara strength, it does so intangibly; she is not describing a relationship of solidarity or shared action. There is no joint response, no agreed strategy arising from these meetings. Barbara returns to her neighbourhood feeling resolved, secure in the knowledge that elsewhere people are also acting locally. This feeling of distant communion (Bell and Newby 1978) is expressed clearly in the following reflection by the organisers of a borough-wide tenants' federation (ID 7) on attendance at their public meetings:

BRIAN: I find it a pleasure when you go to big meetings. When we used to go out to Sally Army hall and you know people used to come, I mean like Margaret from H [place name] and a, a couple from M [place name], 'oh, eh up, you're here again', you know, and it's just a joy, you know, this is how it is, you have fun and, and it's great and when they walk in here, 'everywhere I go I see you', and it's a

ELAINE: 'Not you again' ((laughs))

BRIAN: Yeah, like that, and it's so relaxing.

Here the federation acts to bring together a network of familiar people and its meetings are sociable occasions for encountering old friends and well-known faces. The sense of a united movement is assumed from an emotional identification of common cause rather than agreement on strategic purpose. Tenants' organisational events and conferences amplify the emotional investment and the passion that Alberto Melucci (1995) defined as key components of the collective identity of a social movement. These events act as 'safe havens' (Fantasia and Hirsch 1995) or protected social settings where the emotional bonds, those 'hot cognitions' (Gamson 1992) that express the feeling of collective action, can be nourished. Discussions of recruitment to the membership of organisations, like tenants' associations or federations, are conveyed in the same emotion-laden idealism in which the image of the tenants' movement is itself expressed. The following catalogue of shared interests is put together by a tenants' federation (ID 5) to provide a framework for mobilisation:

JULIA: No matter what kind of a tenant you are, whether you're housing association or whether you, you live in a council house, or ten-, or council property, eh, we all want the same things
HARRY: We have lighting issues
TERRI: Yep
JULIA: We want a decent home to live in
TERRI: Yep
HARRY: We have road issues, we have rubbish issues
TERRI: Yep
HARRY: We all have similar issues. We may have different landlords but we all have the same interests in the environment.
JULIA: So it doesn't matter w-what kind of property you live in, whether as you say being a house owner, or being a tenant, you just want somewhere decent to live and somewhere where you feel safe, and comfortable in your environment.

In this litany of common cause, the definition of a tenants' movement is extended to all residents irrespective of income, location or housing tenure. The lack of precision in this mobilisation strategy with its vague assumption of unifying bonds is reflected in a TPAS conference discussion where Karen (ID 2) contributes this optimistic reflection on door-knocking for recruits in her local tenants' association:

I mean it's like, yeah, its like when, if you door-knock, most will say 'oh God, we're not interested' but then you say, 'ah, but would you be interested if *this* was going to happen or *that* was going to happen?' and 'Well, yeah, you can't let *that* happen!' Well, come on, then, do something about it.

The mobilisation strategy that is being advanced here is founded on the belief that an intrinsic propensity for collective action lies dormant in social housing communities. This is clearly an extension of the widely shared contention that social rented housing carries collectivising attributes. Translated into a mobilisation strategy, this frame, with its assumption that a contentious movement will emerge unbidden from common tenure and shared space, becomes woefully thin. Yet it is possible to see at the core of this frame a reflection of the social base of collective action that Stuart Lowe contended was manifest among the tenants of public housing. This supposed social base, 'the common material interests' shared by residents of council housing (Lowe 1986: 83), is transposed without challenge to contemporary estates, where decades of privatisation, resales, transfers and demolition have removed the ingredients of cohesion. Members of a regional tenants' federation (ID 3) acknowledge these divisions as they debate recruitment strategies:

ANDREW: There's a least four different categories of tenants
RON: Yeah
ANDREW: There's your housing association tenant, council stroke ALMO tenant. There's your shared ownership tenant and there's your leaseholder tenant
RON: Tenant
ANDREW: All have slightly different issues
THERESA: Yeah
RON: Well, they all have different issues completely.

Despite identifying this recruitment impasse, these participants again fall back on optimistic assumptions about the potential mobilising power of shared public space.

TERESA: You go to focus groups and you've got tenants you know the community issues, that the state of the estate is absolutely rife, there's anti-social behaviour, you know, we're sick of the dogs barking and all of that, there's a lot'll have them common, in common, you know what I mean
ANDREW: Yes
RON: The majority, yes
ANDREW: Yeah, the community issues yes, uhh, I'll agree completely that we've all got, doesn't have to be on an estate, it can be the nicest private estate going and they've still got anti-social behaviour and dog fouling.

This credulous belief in common ground, shared even with 'the nicest private estate', is the reassuring message advanced in the dominant model of participation, which admits of no structural obstacles to involvement and dismisses divisions of power and status as of no account to rational actors. On the contrary, taking part is the responsible thing to do and to participate is the act of the citizen. The discourse of responsible participation colours the mobilisation strategies of the tenants' movement, where engagement is presented as a moral duty and the refusal to participate is dismissed as apathy. As a responsible course of action participation is associated with hard work and personal endeavour and contrasted with its supposed

FIGURE 6.1 Mobilising a movement: the banner of Wakefield Tenants Federation suggests links with trade unions

Photo provided by Kirklees Federation of Tenants and Residents Association

polar opposite: dependency on welfare. The 'responsible tenant' can escape the stigmatised character of social housing by attributing to those tenants who do not participate, the 'irresponsible, workshy and undeserving' stereotype of welfare dependents (Card 2006: 54). A tenants' movement expressed through the language of participation thus absorbs welfare dependency discourse into its collective action frames. It views mobilisation as a responsibility and attributes any failure to recruit participants to the apathy of its constituency. Participation thus becomes the distinguishing mark that separates the responsible, and therefore deserving, from the apathetic, undeserving tenants. The 'apathetic tenant' becomes the disciplining example that serves as a moral lesson of the duty to participate.

Not everybody is capable of that

'They just can't be bothered,' John (ID 15) says in despair about turnout at his tenants' association meetings:

> You cannot get young tenants involved, no matter what you do. I mean it's their future: the estates now are their future. But you just cannot get them involved. It's too much trouble for them. They can't be bothered. All they want is a roof over their head and they can't be bothered.

Mourning at another empty tenants' association meeting, Henry (ID 6) agrees:

> It's very hard with the way people live now. They want to see their soaps, when you say there's a meeting, it's very hard to get the younger people [. . .] Now it's like, there's a lot of the older part and they're dying out in some cases and you're not getting them replaced, so there's like the very few doing the bulk of the work now.

'The biggest problem is apathy,' Andrew (ID 3) concurs:

> When there's a big issue you can get lots of tenants come out to a meeting, once it's sorted out, they all go home again. You're lucky if you can get one person in 500 who's any interest whatsoever in being on a tenants' group. They all want somebody they can use as a mouthpiece but they don't want to do it themselves.

The apathetic tenant is an identity that has become totemic; it is rooted so inextricably in the movement that it can be conjured immediately by a tangential reference. In this excerpt from a focus group drawing together members from three tenants' associations (ID 4), the identity is activated in response to perceived criticism from the moderator of the effectiveness of the organisations:

MODERATOR:	What things could a tenants' association do to put pressure on the landlord?
BOB:	The biggest let down [to me]
GRETA:	[They never turn up]
BOB:	You can't get enough [people to be involved]
GRETA:	[You can't get them]
BOB:	It don't matter what you do
SARAH:	No, no.

To an outside observer, Bob's response was unforeseen in that it did not appear to answer the moderator's question. Greta, however, anticipated the conclusion of his statement and interrupted him, correctly assuming that Bob intended to mobilise the identity of the apathetic tenant to avoid any deliberation of the effectiveness of the organisation. Apathy has become the automatic excuse for a failure of mobilisation and recruitment as Julia confirms from her federation (ID 5):

> General apathy is something that you're fighting all the time. I mean, when we go campaigning we get a lot of people and they say 'won't get you anywhere', don't they? You know, or 'we're not signing this' or 'we don't agree with you because no matter what you do, they won't do anything about it'.

The majority of tenants support the idea of involvement in housing services but do not believe it will lead to any real change (Ipsos MORI 2009b). Tenants labelled apathetic tend to pick and choose the issues in which they get involved, and balance the time commitment and their personal interest against the likelihood of achievement (McKee 2009b). A lack of confidence in their abilities to bring about change, combined with a keen awareness of the refusal of housing providers to yield control, supply strong reasons for tenants to withhold their active involvement from tenants' organisations. In deploying the welfare discourse of apathy to explain the failure of their mobilisation strategies, participating tenants evidence unease about the efficacy of their actions. The totemic identity of the apathetic tenant conceals misgivings about the capability of tenants to mobilise a social movement that can effect change. This short exchange at a regional tenants' federation meeting (ID 3) illustrates this disabling disposition:

RON: The tenants are used to the landlords telling them what they expect, not the other way around, which it should be. Tenants should be telling them what they expect.

ANDREW: Yeah, but for a tenant to be able to do that, he needs a basic level of understanding of what is and isn't possible.

The assertion here that tenants generally lack a basic level of understanding is symptomatic of a collective self-doubt that appears to undermine any serious attempt to mobilise a social movement. In discussion at a TPAS conference in 2009 (ID 8), Fran and Muriel attempt to construct a motivational frame to inspire militant collective action. This is contested rigorously by the third participant, Mary, who maintains that tenants are not capable of challenge. Mary's determination to block a discussion around collective action is shown by her disregard for the normal turn-taking mode of conversation; she interrupts three times in order to prevent further discussion about mobilisation.

FRAN: I believe we all have the power to get things changed. We just need to be j-joined as one voice to get things changed.

MARY: But not everybody has got the confidence to do that and that has to be recognised.

MURIEL: But you have to learn. [You have]

MARY: [But not] everybody can learn that

MURIEL: No [but]

MARY: [It's not] within them to be able to speak out

MURIEL: Not [necessarily]

MARY: [Doesn't mean] to say that they will be able to do so.

At the conference in the previous year (ID 2), a protracted argument developed over the opportunities for tenants in participation. One participant, Ted, promoted the idea that tenants should take control of their estates through tenant management organisations, or community-led housing associations rather than be dependent on housing staff for involvement in decision-making. Karen argued against Ted's advocacy of tenant control and repeatedly attempted to interrupt him, finally making clear her low opinion of tenants' abilities.

TED: It's just, you're looking at the housing associations, councils and whatever. We're still doing it for them

KAREN: But looking at it the other way

TED: Why shouldn't we say to them, do your job?

KAREN: ((Clears throat))

TED: This has got to change, hasn't it? Because it's us that's paying them

KAREN: Umm

TED: You can't, you can't accept that what we've got now we've got to live with it, you can't

KAREN: Well, no, but I'm actually ((tut))

STEPHANIE: So, so what are you saying? That housing, that tenants take over and run housing associations?

TED: Yeah, why not?

KAREN: Because not everybody is capable of that.

Stephanie's intervention seems to encourage Karen to make her point a little more forcefully than she, perhaps, intends. As the discussion continues, Paul joins in support of Karen and turns the debate into an undisguised criticism of the failings of tenants.

PAUL: I think if we can go on that line it's going to take years, unless the tenants change their attitude. Some of the tenants, really, they've a 'don't care' attitude.

STEPHANIE: Uh, huh

PAUL: You see, they just come in, live there; they don't care what is happening. They don't participate. Don't do, put any effort. So I think the tenants themselves need to change their attitude.

In this excerpt Paul, Stephanie and Karen identify social housing tenants as essentially apathetic in order to counter Ted's motivational argument and his attempt to mobilise support in favour of community control. In a similar discussion, a collection of tenants' association members at a TPAS conference discussion (ID 9) share their dismay at the failure of collective action.

CLARE: I think tenants are their own worst enemy because they put up with it. They don't challenge enough.

MODERATOR: Is that because it's what they're used to?

CLARE: Yes

LINDA: Sometimes it's just because it's too much trouble. You know there are tenants that just think it's easier to let the, let the

YVONNE: Yes, let someone else do it

WENDY: What um, the problem is, they have tried for years to solve problems. The result is that, um, they've given up and for me as their representative that makes them unreachable, because they just say 'Oh, no, I'm not talking about it. I can't be bothered'

CLARE: 'Nothing changes', yeah

WENDY: 'Nothing changes. I don't care what you say, they won't do anything, so just go away and leave me alone'

YVONNE: That's playing into the landlord's hands

CLARE: Yeah, it is, instead of a group of you really strengthening up so you can challenge it.

These participants have already reconciled themselves to the impossibility of mobilising support; they believe that apathy and a lack of efficacy are essential to the character of social housing tenants. Although they display a low opinion of the capacity of other tenants to engage in collective action, they have no problem in defining themselves as activists and express support themselves for contentious demands. All aged in their sixties or over, their involvement in collective action is based on an experience of housing radically different from that of many of the tenants they attempt to mobilise and whose capacities they disdain. They grew up in the high-quality municipal housing of post-war Britain amid the aspirations and comparative affluence of an economy of full (male) employment. According to *Growing Up in Social Housing in Britain* (Lupton *et al.* 2009), the last generation to experience social renting as a boost to their aspirations and confidence, and as an overwhelmingly positive experience, were those born in the 1940s for whom a council house meant their first indoor toilet, a bathroom and hot water, and quite likely a garden, amenities that made the municipal housing sector a step up from private renting and even homeownership. Many of the tenants contributing to the research for this book fall into the age range represented by this generational study. Their positive experience of public housing, before the impact of policies intended to reduce the sector to a welfare safety net, may have contributed to their support for social renting and encouraged belief in their capacity to bring about change. At the same time, the contrast between their memories of high-quality social housing and the experience of subsequent generations may explain their poor opinion of the capacity of other tenants to mobilise collectively. Jane, an articulate and thoughtful member of her regional federation (ID 6), remembers when a council tenancy was a symbol of social mobility. She associates herself with the generation that benefited from the quality of post-war general needs municipal housing, built for families in full-time employment, where Bevan's vision of different classes and income groups living in the same street was indicative of a rise in living standards and an increase in confidence and aspiration among better-off sections of the working class. She has watched the social status of tenants debased and charts the decline:

> I think the press and the politicians definitely try and make out that we're all a load of scroungers who don't work. And of course, their policy over the last few years, the last twenty, thirty years since they stopped building council houses, has allowed them to create that sort of situation because the only people who get housed now are the desperate, you know, who have to live on housing benefit in order to qualify to get a council house. Of course, historically that's not been the case and I come from the generation where you actually were considered one step up if you lived in a council house, because you had a decent home.

Jane implies in this excerpt that the capabilities of tenants have declined along with the status and quality of the social housing sector, and she is not alone in that contention. Eleven people from a borough-wide tenants' federation (ID 21), the majority born in the 1940s or 1950s, reminisce about their early experiences of municipal housing:

MIKE: I was brought up in a council house, er, my father worked for the post office, but five, six doors away, his triple-senior boss, if you understand, three grades higher than him,

PATRICIA: Yeah

MIKE: Lived in an equally the same council house. There was no stigma. A few doors further on was a teacher. So there was a cross section of normal people living in a row of council houses, and they were fine, wonderful houses.

LESTER: In 1969 we moved to council accommodation and it was a beautiful house, brand new estate, real nice people. The front lawns were all open plan. And there was no stigma. It was like, it was a step up. I mean our house before. We had an outside toilet. We had to get bathed in a little galvanised bath. But the thing is, we moved into a centrally heated house, two toilets, one downstairs, bathroom upstairs, three bedrooms, radiators, and the people on the estate were polite. I think actually they felt in awe of living there from wherever they'd been living before, so they took more care of it. And it were mixed, mixed group, schoolteachers, various businessmen, you know all sorts, sales reps, stuff like that.

These personal connections between council housing and social progress demonstrate the important role social housing played in post-war British childhoods (Lupton *et al.* 2009) and recount, too, a familiar and ubiquitous narrative of urban decline, a nostalgic tale of the loss of a golden age. The narrative is constructed around two frames of comparison. One is overtly stated: experience of poor housing standards in the private sector. The other is implied by the references to the lack of stigma of those first remembered council estates, the reference to 'normal people', who took care of their homes. This reference point, though unstated, appears readily understood by all the participants. The tale of two council housings, one the ideal, general needs provision, the other a residual welfare service, is a consistent theme in housing studies, where the 'ideal' appears to refer both to the quality of the houses and the quality of the tenants, 'the better-off members of the working class' (Clarke and Ginsburg 1975: 5; Cole and Furbey 1994). These narratives attribute the decline of council housing to a change in the social composition of tenants, with increasing numbers of households not in full-time paid employment, and to a redirection of subsidies from house-building to personal housing allowances to reduce rents for those rehoused from slum clearance and overcrowding. The decline of council housing is clearly associated, in this discourse, with the arrival of a different class of tenant.

The discussion in the tenants' federation (ID 21), continued from above, narrates the tale of two council housings around the key point of the 1980 Right to Buy, the sale of council homes at huge discounts to sitting tenants. The account of the consequences of the policy articulated in this discussion and the radical change in the social composition of tenants that supposedly ensued is also recounted by tenant campaign groups (DCH 2006; DCH 2008). Right to Buy was targeted specifically at those general needs tenants in the best quality homes with the most financial means and successfully removed 2.5 million council houses from public supply, skimming off the best quality stock and most affluent tenants, and dedicating the residue of council homes as an ambulance service for the low paid and unpaid (Jones and Murie 2006). The first speaker presents the change in the composition of council tenants as a migration of the more affluent into home ownership.

JIM: The problems really started when Mrs Thatcher became PM of this country. She was the one who brought in the Right to Buy. Before that time, people who lived in council houses, as they said, they were mixed, teachers and all sorts of people, lived together in a community. But when they started to get their mortgages and move out, we were left with the people who were more poor than those who moved out.

MICHAEL: When Maggie Thatcher's Right to Buy came along, all the – I don't mean this in the, the right way – all the decent people, the people who did look after their houses were encouraged to move off the council houses and buy their own houses away from the council estates. So sadly this is what is left, is all the people who are in social housing are on unemployment benefits and are subject to outbursts of crime.

The second speaker, Michael, makes it clear that the difference between two sets of tenants is not about income. Instead, it is characterised by behaviour. There are the 'decent people' who look after their houses, and there are those who do not, as he continues to explain.

MICHAEL: Unfortunately on these estates most of the people have found out, the teachers, the doctors, the nurses who used to live, who were brought up on these estates have, dare I say, have bettered themselves and moved away from the estates and they were the people that was the hope of, of the community. And they've all left and the estate is an empty shell.

The tenants' federation members taking part in this discussion make a clear distinction between their experience, as the generation that benefited from the 'general needs' council housing of post-war years, and were affluent enough to consider homeownership, and that of subsequent generations, rehoused from slum clearance areas and overcrowded inner-city streets. The concentration in the council housing sector of people on very low incomes and reliant on pensions and benefits was increasingly noticeable from the 1980s onwards, although the process began much earlier. An excluded section of the working class, particularly households headed by lone women, ethnic minorities and disabled people moved from the invisibility of the slums into the political spotlight of council housing, bringing with them the labels of undeserving, undesirable and unworthy that had been attached to these social categories since the Elizabethan Poor Law. The marginalisation and economic powerlessness of these tenants was reflected in the quality and terms of the housing service they received (Forrest and Murie 1991); the housing visitor quickly determined 'rough' from 'respectable', and made sure the former were housed in the worst properties, where stigmatising practices applied stigmatising labels to estates seen as 'dumping grounds' (Damer 1989). The council housing sector became a proxy for social policy initiatives aimed at disciplining, regulating and policing the poorest and most vulnerable (Somerville 2005a) but council housing did not change from an 'ideal' form to a poorer quality model; the change was in the loss of power and status of its tenants. The distinction between the affluent and confident generations of post-war council housing, and the poorer and less politically powerful households rehoused under criteria of housing need, is reproduced in the mobilising strategies of the tenants' movement. A division between activist organisers and apathetic followers is asserted, reproducing divisions between the respectable and the undeserving embedded in housing policy discourse, and indicating the effective barrier posed to the mobilisation of a tenants' movement by intraclass divisions and the discriminatory discourses of welfare dependency.

To be part of the system

Frances Fox Piven and Richard Cloward (1977) have explored the effects of collective disadvantage on the organisation of direct action in their concept of 'poor people's movements'. They identify the difficulties in mobilisation and in particular the obstacles to strategic planning that are a feature of protests among vulnerable and powerless groups such as homeless and unemployed people and that mean that 'mass defiance is neither freely available nor the forms it takes freely determined' (Piven and Cloward 1977: 23). When protest arises among these groups, it is often unplanned, undirected and opportunistic. The psychic effect of power on the down-trodden is well recorded in post-colonial literature (Butler 1997a). Paulo Freire (1993: 18) chronicled the challenges to mobilisation among colonial subjects, describing what he called a state of 'naïve transitivity' characterised by a type of reasoning founded on nostalgia, emotion and fancy, an oversimplification of problems and an avoidance of methods of investigation. Organisations of 'poor people' rarely challenge power relations overtly; instead they display deference to authority, and seek patronage and support. The powerless become 'socialised into compliance' (Gaventa 1980: 18), into dependence on authority; in the accounts of post-colonial literature the powerless seek to emulate those who exercise power over them (Freire 1990; Fanon 1986). Collective action among social housing tenants displays similar deference to authority; it is directed in pursuit of social recognition and seeks patronage and support rather than overtly challenging power relations.

At a meeting of a regional tenants' federation (ID 3) the phrase 'Yes Tenants' was used frequently in discussion. It was explained that 'Yes Tenants' referred to members of the National Tenants' Organisation. Andrew spoke scornfully of the secretary who had embraced the government Housing Minister at a recent public meeting.

ANDREW: Yeah, well, we've all made the, the point about, er, leading tenant activists cuddling Housing Ministers on the stage in public meetings, uhhh.
TERESA: Yeah
RON: That's right
ANDREW: That comfortable with, I won't say the enemy, but the opposition at times is not good
TERESA: No, to me a shake of the hand, you know, 'yes, thank you' and all that.

The desire to be recognised by authority figures is, of course, why tenants participate and there can be few stronger symbols of earned recognition than an embrace from the Housing Minister. Respect received from the politically and economically powerful is one of the few tangible benefits of participation. This desire to be close to the powerful, to be accepted, means that collective action in the tenant's movement rarely ventures into outright conflict or open disagreement, since the goal is not to alienate power holders but to gain their acceptance (Lipsky 1968). In the following extract from the 2008 TPAS focus group (ID 2) studied earlier in this chapter, Joy uses the language of struggle to launch a claim for the universal rights of tenants. When the moderator draws attention to the words used in the claim, the response from the other participants is significant.

JOY:	You have to keep on and on fighting for the rights of you and the people around you.
MODERATOR:	Is that how you see it, fighting for=
JOY:	Yep
MODERATOR:	=Rights?
PAUL:	Mmm
KAREN:	Not necessarily
STEPHANIE:	No, I don't see it
TED:	No, not so much a fight
KAREN:	No, we don't have to
TED:	Perhaps a matter of, ahh, I find it from our area a matter of discussion to come to the right [compromise].
STEPHANIE:	[Compromise]
BRUCE:	Yeah, compromise
KAREN:	Yeah, that's the word I was looking for.

The language of conflict has little place in these tenants' vocabulary. When asked what the strategy of a tenant's movement should be, another TPAS focus group (ID 1) gave the answer:

> To be consulted and not directed. To be considered at all time to be part of the system automatically.

This desire to be embraced by those with power and prestige is mirrored inside tenant's organisations where the exercise of authority can have a corrosive effect and result in tensions, intrigue and rivalry (Andrews 1979; Uguris 2004). Despite the need to construct shared identity positions and common interests among a disparate social base, a tenants' movement finds itself riven by rivalries and feuding. The complex relationship to authority among those accustomed to subjection is acknowledged in the following group discussion (ID 9):

CLAIRE:	Power is an awful word really because some people it's straight away 'up you'.
YVONNE:	Yeah. Frightens them.
CLAIRE:	And it makes, it's 'I'm the chair of this, and I'm the chair of that'. You know what I mean?
WENDY:	They don't know how to use it. They see power as a different thing, don't they? Power to me is the ability to change and influence whereas for some residents power is telling people what to do.

If a little authority has corrosive effects within the committees of tenants' associations, it can be devastating when reflected at a wider level where it is demonstrated in a history of feuding and factionalism among national tenants' organisations. The National Tenants' Organisation, launched in 1977, was contested by the development in 1989 of the National Tenants and Residents Federation (Hood and Woods 1994) and the merger of these two organisations in 1998 into the Tenants and Residents Organisations of England (TAROE) was contested immediately by the formation of the Housing Association Residents and Tenants Organisation of England (HARTOE), which, until that organisation's demise, confined TAROE to the municipal housing sector. The legitimacy of TAROE was challenged again in 2002 by the launch of the Tenants' Union, which attained sufficient government recognition to be included on the national Tenants' Sounding Board set up by the Labour government in 2003 (Millward 2005; Mayo and Tickell 2006). The regional tenants' organisations established to accompany the 1997–2010 Labour government's structure of regional authorities also contested the national role played by TAROE. Michael, Chair of the Tenants and Residents Organisations of England (TAROE), explained this rivalry (ID 18):

> The regions are threatening, because the regions believe together that they should represent the nation, and I don't see that as the function of the regions. The regions are there to support the regional organisations within them, not the other way round. They have their glass ceiling which is the region. Our glass ceiling is England.

Accepting that the national organisation does not enjoy wide recognition from tenants, Michael blames this on rivalry between key individuals and their competitive 'empire building'.

> The negativity from the tenant movement is a problem and there are people out there that, that, it's far easy to destroy than to create something, and there's a lot of people out there who are destroyers [. . .] A lot of the people I see are in it for themselves. Er, and that's quite sad. Um, it's more about them than it is the organisation, and it's more about them than it is tenants generally.

The construction of a tenants' movement is hampered at every step by divisions and factions. Its mobilisation strategies lack definition; its organisations are splintered and competitive. Distinctions between 'the responsible tenant' and 'the apathetic tenant' effectively militate against the mobilisation of contentious action while social identities steeped in stigma, disadvantage and deprivation are 'built into talk' (Wilkinson and Kitzinger 2003: 171) and are continually reproduced by tenants who proceed to undermine the potential for movement mobilisation. Michael Lipsky (1968: 1144) once observed: 'extremely powerless groups, lacking cohesion, will not even appear for observation'. Something less than a tenants' movement has appeared for observation so far in this chapter. What has emerged is resonant of Paulo Freire's 'naïve transitivity': a 'poor people's movement' (Piven and

FIGURE 6.2 Insurgent spirit: children from an estate in Huddersfield protest against the planned demolition of their homes

Photo supplied by Kirklees Federation of Tenants and Residents Associations

FIGURE 6.3 Oppositional identities: the children and their parents take the protest to the municipal authority

Photo supplied by Kirklees Federation of Tenants and Residents Associations

Cloward 1977), vulnerable, dependent and disabled by the effects of power. What has been observed may be the construction of a movement identity, but not yet of a social movement.

Singing from the same hymn sheet

The theory of collective identity operates as the symbolic yardstick of social movement processes. It sets out the three dimensions that are, supposedly, essential for the formation of a unified collective actor. While emotional commitment and the recognition of shared values form part of the definition, the content of a collective identity consists of an action system based on agreement on goals, means or tactics, and strategies for action (Melucci 1989; Mueller 1994). This identity is not a static framework or a written constitution; it is the effect of a network of relationships and negotiations between individuals, but the outcome is unity: the formation of a collective that can be defined as a social movement. It is manifested in the perceptions of participants, their framing activity and discourse (Melucci 1995; Gamson 1992), but together they must develop a shared assessment of the possibilities and limits of collective action (Klandermans 1992). Embracing collective identity theory as a robust framework for assessing progress towards the achievement of a social movement, the task for the remainder of this chapter is to investigate considerations of 'the goals, means and environment of action' in tenant identity work (Melucci 1989: 35).

In a TPAS focus group in 2008 (ID 1), a discussion about tenant organisation leads to the following exchange:

MODERATOR: Do you feel you belong to a tenants' movement?
GRAHAM: If you want to call us a movement we've got to have a national strategy.
MODERATOR: Do you have a national strategy?
MARY: We have a national wish to have a national strategy.
Winston: It would make the landlords sit up if all the tenants and all the panels were all singing from the same hymn sheet.

The idea that they might belong to a movement appears new to these participants, and the proposal that tenants might agree a joint strategy is received as a novel suggestion that is worthy of consideration. Later in the discussion, Sonia follows up this point:

> We need a manifesto, a link between all the many organisations. A statement of intent.

While Sonia refers to 'all the organisations', Winston's definition of a tenants' movement should be noted; he says 'all the tenants and all the panels'. He does not say 'all the tenant organisations'. The reference to panels is to customer panels:

the sounding boards, focus groups and service review groups that are initiated by landlords to enable tenant participation. The movement, for Winston, is not a network of autonomous tenants' organisations but a loose assemblage of individuals who are recruited by their landlords. The amorphous nature of the contemporary movement is reflected in a lack of coherence or collective agreement over goals. The stated aims of the National Tenants' Organisation are to improve the quality, affordability and accessibility of social housing, but it also, and more generally, aims 'to improve and protect the quality of life, social and environmental conditions for everyone in our local communities' (TAROE 2008). A desktop survey of the publicity of twelve tenants' federations across the country finds that the majority define themselves as community development agencies. One federation describes itself as 'a catalyst for community action' (Barnsley Federation of Tenants and Residents 2008: 7); another is 'community focused' (Plymouth Federation of Tenants and Residents 2009: 2). Only two out of twelve surveyed related their aims to questions of housing policy or tenants' interests. Most tenants' organisations define themselves in uncritical relation to the current policy definition of participation and are concerned with their successes in influencing the standards of housing organisations and in developing community capacities in ways that complement the empowerment aims of governmental strategies (for example, DCLG 2006, 2007b, 2008; Localism Act 2011). A similar audit of publicity issued by twelve tenants' organisations in 2013 following the imposition of cuts in welfare benefits for social housing tenants, a controversial measure dubbed the 'bedroom tax' that plunged thousands of tenants into rent arrears (Brown 2013), evidenced the apparent absence of contention on this or other measures included in the Coalition government's social housing and welfare reforms. The national tenants' organisation, TAROE, made no public statement on the bedroom tax, while borough-wide tenants' federations confined themselves in the majority to giving advice on the changes to benefits. One of the few signs of active campaigning against welfare cuts from a tenants' federation (Camden Fed 2013) was accompanied by notice that their local authority funding had been terminated. In contrast to the absence of outright contention from formal tenants' organisations, isolated protests against the bedroom tax quickly mobilised into a network of grass-roots campaign groups, resulting in a national day of action and the formation of what one commentator called a 'significant new tenants power bloc' (Halewood 2013).

A common theme in the study of contemporary urban movements has been their ensnarement in government strategies of collaboration and partnership and the co-option and moderation of contentious politics. The domesticating effect of patronage on previously disruptive movements has been extensively studied (Mayer 2000; Kavoulakos 2006). Tenants' organisations are keenly aware of the benefits that patronage can bring and recognise the importance of resources to movement viability (Cress and Snow 1996). They value access to meeting space, transport, training and publicity resources (Furbey *et al.* 1996). Ron, speaking at a regional tenants' federation meeting (ID 3), displays the acute appreciation of the need for financial resources that occupies his, and most other, strategic organisations.

I think quite honestly I think it's raw cash that stops you from achieving anything. It's just raw cash. We ain't got it.

The withdrawal of funding from many autonomous tenants' organisations over the last decade has reversed the upward growth in the number of tenants' groups that once seemed an inevitable outcome of the spread of participation across housing organisations. Research by the Tenant Services Authority and Audit Commission published in 2010 showed funding for tenant participation from municipal authorities to be declining. Tenants' organisations that continue to receive a yearly grant from municipal authorities are contracted through service level agreements to achieve specified performance targets in return and become, in effect, arm's-length agencies of the local state (Nicholls and Beaumont 2004). Susan, from a regional federation (ID 6), explains:

> There's more and more of this kind of, like we are, as a regional organisation, the kind of funding agreements so like you're commissioned to do something on their behalf rather than, or being something that is completely independent and something separate.

While a small number of autonomous tenants' organisations have been funded from a tenants' levy, through ring-fenced contribution from rents, most traditionally have received their core funding from their landlord, whether local authority or housing association. A borough-wide tenants' federation (ID 5) confided that this funding relationship compromised their independence; they were frequently reprimanded by their local authority for the views they expressed in their newsletter, and were forced to assess the risk to their sources of finance whenever they articulated contentious views.

LINDA: We're not 'yes' people to the Council.
DAVE: But it can't be right that they can hold us to ransom over money
TERRI: Umm
DAVE: If we say the wrong word to them
TERRI: Yeah
DAVE: They can pull our funding. What would happen to our committee then? That's a proper question. What would happen to our committee?

They looked, optimistically, to national regulatory bodies for alternative sources of funding:

HARRY: If they had a different source of money they could do a lot better. Their hands are tied by being reliant on the council, er, for money. The local groups are reliant on the council for money. Whereas if they had a national something that would give them money, they'd have the freedom to speak as they like and not be dictated to, say what you could write, what you couldn't write, what information you could put out there and what information you couldn't. The fact is we are being

MINA: Manipulated?

HARRY: Not manipulated, no. We're being gagged

RICHARD: Constrained

HARRY: The tenant is being gagged because of the political awareness of the councils. So therefore if we had another funding stream, it would be far better. And that's something we could do and it would benefit all tenants.

In 2011 the national tenants' organisation, TAROE, lost its funding from the government-administered Tenant Empowerment Fund and became reliant on what income it could attract from membership fees, landlord accreditation and training services. In 2013 the organisation registered as a charity in order to improve the likelihood of attracting donations. Government funding had enabled it to employ staff and run three annual conferences, free to tenants, but the organisation's reliance on public grant was criticised, and these conferences were dismissed as conventions rather than opportunities for democratic policy making among member organisations (Grayson 2010). In an interview, the Chair of TAROE, Michael, compared the insecure finances of the tenants' movement with the healthy funding arrangements of the housing professional associations and landlord trade bodies. These organisations are funded by social housing organisations from tenants' rents, without tenants' agreement, he claimed.

How many tenants out there in the housing association world know that altogether the 2,300 housing associations give the National Housing Federation £7.1 million a year? [. . .] It's a trade body, er, it takes £7 million out of rents to fund it, that's the affiliation fee without. It's a levy but we don't talk about that; the LGA [Local Government Association] gets £15 million from local authorities to run it, and we [TAROE] got £124,000. But those levies aren't talked about with tenants or council tax payers, they're just done, just done deals.

The National Housing Federation lobbies on behalf of the interests of social landlords and campaigns on housing issues. Michael argues that if this trade body requires £7.5 million to talk to its membership of 1,200 housing associations (National Housing Federation 2010), there is a strong case to argue that financial support for a body communicating with 5 million tenants should also come from a landlord levy. The comparison between the national tenants' organisations and the landlord and housing trade associations was first made in 1985 by the National Tenants' Organisation, backed by the National Consumer Council, which identified a lack of consumer representation in housing (Oxley 1986). This consumerist manifesto was revived in 2006 when the National Consumer Council (Mayo and

Tickell 2006) pointed to the lobbying power of producers through the Chartered Institute of Housing, the Local Government Association and the National Housing Federation. The establishment of the National Tenant Voice, recommended by Martin Cave (2007), was intended as a consumer watchdog to act as a counterweight against the producer interest. Speaking before the abolition of the National Tenant Voice in July 2010, Michael, Chair of TAROE argued for the need for a single consumer organisation to represent tenants.

> I would like to see one trade body for tenants in England. I think there's far too many. You've got TPAS, you've got CCH, you've got the Nat Fed of TMOs, you've got the Nat Fed of ALMOs, even though they're landlord organisations, or agent organisations, they're still tenant focused. We've got TPAS, we've got TAROE, we've got now the National Tenant Voice, it's just far too many, it's a plethora, far too many, confuses people, there should be one trade body [. . .] I mean, you've got the Nat Fed for Housing Association, er, employees and you've got the LGA for local authorities and we need a body for tenants. And only then will people take us seriously. But at the moment if we're too good landlords will go and talk to somebody else and not us, so we don't want that, we want one body.

Following the abolition of the National Tenant Voice an attempt was made by TAROE, working with the national federations for tenant management and co-operative housing, and the consultancy TPAS, to present a united consumer voice as the National Tenants Organisations Policy Forum. The trade body, or consumer watchdog model, adopted by the national organisation, appears to signal a break with the value-identities of community action and direct democracy that characterise the local tenants' movement. In 2007 the horizontal model of direct democracy underpinning TAROE's governance structure was overhauled to enable its board of directors to be elected as individuals rather than representatives. Individual membership was allowed without the requirement to belong to a tenants' organisation, cutting the lines of accountability between TAROE directors and the regional, federal and local structures of the tenants' movement. The governance model pursued by TAROE seemed to jettison the values of accountability and democracy that appear as the defining identification of the tenants' movement, with its foundation in 'housewives networks' (Baldock 1982) and its commitment to grass-roots decision-making. Michael acknowledges TAROE's departure from the movement's roots in collective representation and associates it with the decline in numbers of autonomous tenants' federations and the rise of the discourse of consumerism:

INTERVIEWER: Would you agree that one of the defining things about the tenants' movement is its representative structure?

MICHAEL: I think it is defining, but I think it is changing, because, umm, we have to change, er, because society changes, er, and we should

> never be scared of change. We should embrace change, and we should make change work for us. Er, there used to be a lot more federations around, but, umm, er, so if we were based ourselves on federations and that, that, that model, we would be dying. Because we hadn't changed. So we had to change.

The effectiveness of TAROE as an organisation, its ability to lobby government, and to influence landlords and their associations, depended, for Michael, on the development of a more professional image.

> We've tried to professionalise what we do, the way we dress, er, the way we speak, the way we research now before we go to meetings, to be informed about the subject matter.

In part this was the consequence of running an organisation that now had a small staff team and premises, but Michael's language is significant because it appears to distance TAROE further from the more chaotic and informal networks that characterise a tenants' movement. The Chartered Institute of Housing's (CIH) annual conference, usually held in Harrogate, is an important event in the calendar of the social housing sector, where trade bodies, contractors and consultants exhibit. TAROE received a free exhibition stand, courtesy of the Chartered Institute of Housing, and Michael described how tenants visiting the exhibition from across the country, and collecting their free gifts, pens, mugs and coasters from the well-provisioned displays of housing construction companies or building contractors, would leave their full carrier-bags at the TAROE stand to collect later, and how, as he says, 'it just looked like a dumping ground sometimes'.

> Last year we had to put a diktat out, and if there's any bags on the stand, they will be removed and dumped. Because it's not a resting place for tenants: 'Oh, we're back at the TAROE stand. Leave all your bags here and we'll go off and have a cup of tea.' It's, we're a professional organisation.

This glimpse of domesticity in the midst of a trade exhibition is indicative of the value-identities of the movement, its ability to navigate on both sides of the artificial boundary between domestic and public spaces, and to draw its strength from face-to-face interaction. In seeing the TAROE stall as 'a resting place for tenants', as Michael's narrative indicates, tenants visiting the CIH exhibition evidenced that they recognised the national organisation as part of the movement, and felt comfortable in that space. The TAROE stall appeared as a safe place, a social movement haven (Fantasia and Hirsch 1995) in the bustle of the marketplace. However, an exhibition stall that has domestic appeal does not project an image that is comprehensible to the corporate institutions who have power and influence in that market. Michael contends:

I represent all these organisations who have within them five million people. There is an expectation if you do that, you need a suit, you need a collar and a tie, you need to act in a more mature way, and, and wouldn't you be proud of being part of an organisation that looks good in the marketplace – and Harrogate is the marketplace. So, no, I don't think we're losing something, I think we're actually gaining, and, and people want to be part of a professional organisation but we still have that human touch. We can still come and make people laugh. We can still have a joke. And we can still look foolish sometimes. But, we do that in-house, but not out there, because they look for the chink, and they go for the chink, so we have to be professional all the time. So, there's, there's ways and means and we got, gotta be, we gotta change colour, haven't we, er, and that's what we do.

In this symbolic language Michael indicates the antagonism that constructs a tenants' movement in opposition to 'them', a hostile group here undefined but associated by implication with the landlord and housing provider lobby. In addressing this opposition, and in seeking to defend the tenant consumer against them, Michael and the National Tenants' Organisation feel constrained to take on a different identity, to model themselves on the styles of dress and behaviour associated with commerce, and they seek to discipline and conceal the domestic and informal systems that underpin collective action in a tenants' movement. The strategy adopted by the national organisation has distanced TAROE from the 'bundle of narratives' (Fine 1995) that provides the movement with its identifying themes, its celebration of experiential knowledge against professionalism, its insurgent spirit of democracy, and its roots in the 'nearness' of domesticity and neighbourly interaction. In adopting the profile of the consumer watchdog or trade body, the national organisation has substituted the generic interests of the consumer for the specific contentions of tenants, in a significant loss of oppositional identities.

It's going to take a long, long time

Alberto Melucci, writing in 1995, maintained that social movement theory had yet to answer the question of 'how social actors form a collective and recognise themselves as part of it' (Melucci 1995: 42). His collective identity theory addressed precisely that issue: it explained the construction and maintenance of organisational unity. Unity, however, eludes the tenants' movement. As a movement it is characterised as a network of panels, rather than autonomous groups. It has four national organisations, none of which enjoys more than partial support. The goals it expresses are indistinct; its national organisations appear detached from the values that motivate the grass-roots; it avoids confrontation and craves the acceptance of those who exercise power. Its ability to influence the direction of housing policy appears negligible, as the TAROE Chair concedes:

INTERVIEWER: How would you assess the achievements of the tenants' movement?

MICHAEL: I don't think it's very successful. 'Cause it hasn't got the power to be successful. You've got to have money, and then you've got to have charismatic leaders, um. [. . .] So I don't think, er, we have been very good at influencing the direction of housing policy.

Melucci pointed to three dimensions necessary for the construction of collective identity: the formation of cognitive frameworks concerning the goals, the means and the strategies of collective action; the development of group relationships through processes of communication, negotiation and decision-making; and the emotional commitment of participants to the collective and to each other (Melucci 1989: 35). Carol Mueller (1994: 246) made it clear that for these three dimensions of social movement collective identity to be claimed:

> Specific individuals must be identified who have formed emotional bonds from their interaction, negotiated a sense of group membership and made a plan for change (or a series of plans) however tentative, with goals, means, and a consideration of environmental constraints.

Evaluated against Melucci's definition of collective identity, the tenants' movement lacks clear goals and has no plan for change; it is an action system without strategies, without means and with little appreciation of constraints. Tenant identity work evidences an emotional commitment to a collective idea, but the development of group relations is inhibited by failures of efficacy and mobilisation, and mediated by discourses of welfare dependency and divisions between deserving and undeserving. The regulatory policy of participation has swallowed almost all collective action and the idea of a network of autonomous tenants' organisations campaigning in the neighbourhood has metamorphosed into a myriad of panels and forums enveloped in a landlord-administered participation process that promises eventual, although continually receding, recognition. Individualising discourses of consumerism have disengaged the national tenants' organisation from the traditions of democracy and collective representation that motivate local action, while the articulation of community as an instrument of government has channelled tenants' federations and associations into activities deserving of patronage. This is a social movement with little confidence in its own efficacy, seemingly lacking the ability to think strategically; it is divided and fractious. These are not failings or flaws in the tenants' movement; instead they are the consequences of immersion in the individualising discourses and divisive themes of public service reform expressed as participation. Participation, it seems, awards the tenants' movement its power and at the same time embodies in it an inability to realise that power.

The tenants' movement is a domesticated movement; it exists in, and through, the regulated processes of participation and it is made intelligible only in the language of participation and according to its rules. What can be called a movement is the expression of a collective and continuous attempt to expand the boundaries of this regulation, to widen the vocabulary of its voice and to find exceptions to its rules. The problems of evaluating the continuing contention of domesticated movements, like the tenants' movement, are not assisted by the definitional vagaries of social movement studies and the lack of specificity around what is meant by collective action, or what a social movement that is not co-opted should look like. Charles Tilly (1985: 736), the pioneer in this field, defined social movements without reference to the militancy of their mobilisation as 'a series of demands or challenges to power holders in the name of a social category that lacks an established political position'. More recently, the concept of 'contentious politics' (McAdam *et al.* 2001) has been advanced to apply to any extra-parliamentary influence exerted on governments. A more stringent definition appears to focus on the types of claims made by movements:

> Forms of contestation in which individuals and groups organise and ally, with various degrees of formality, to push for social change that challenges hegemonic norms.
>
> (*Leitner* et al. *2007: 157*)

However, it is necessary to consider what is meant by 'social change' when collective action is authorised by regulatory strategies, when organisations speak of compromise rather than contention, and their achievements are difficult to identify. In Judith Butler's thesis, the acts of resistance of social movements emerge in routine engagement with the exclusionary practices that provide them with intelligibility. 'Social transformation occurs', Butler (2000: 14) says, 'through the ways in which daily social relations are rearticulated.' This would suggest that the collective contentions of tenants can accomplish a 'critical subversion' of the regulatory norms and power relations of participation, and impact on the direction of social policy more generally (Butler 2004: 334).

In participation, tenants recognise a political environment that promises them the status and the equality of citizenship. The strategic opportunities of participation offer a substitute for movement mobilisation, a surrogate that awards recognition in return for compliance and that offers the impression of gradual, but inevitable, progress. Participation is a realm of possibility, where universal claims to rights and democracy may be articulated from market processes and governmental strategies. Despite its individualising discourses, participation has provided the cognitive frameworks, the forums and the opportunities for tenants to act collectively as subordinate partners in a project of governance. Participation has equipped tenants with a collective 'voice', and in its reiterative rituals, in landlord panels and board-room meetings or in the activities of tenants' organisations, it presents them with the opportunities to reclaim other voices and to force the return of antagonism in a discourse that has sought to exclude all notions of conflict. Tenants appear able to use the discourse of participation to launch contentions around social housing and social rights, and to challenge the direction of public service reform, as previous chapters have evidenced. They construct an image of a combative public engaged in a collective and long-term campaign for social change. By engaging in user participation, then, tenants may achieve some level of social change and amend or subvert the hybrid, and sometimes contradictory, discourses of social welfare policy. Certainly, a sense of patient optimism imbues much of tenant identity work, illustrated in this comment from Cheryl at a TPAS conference discussion in 2009 (ID 8):

> We're still in this, what the gentleman over there would call a class system, and my obs-, I've only been involved as a council tenant for about the last twelve or thirteen years, and my understanding is that people like us, now being given a voice, coming to conferences like this, etc. has only been a recent development historically and it's going to take a long, long time but hopefully one day it will come and things will be much better as how we're looked at as council or tenants of whatever organisations.

There is inevitability to this process; by taking part in the rituals of participation with social housing organisations, tenants expect to achieve, gradually but surely, fundamental social change. It is just a matter of time (ID 8):

CHERYL: It's just going to take a long time
ROBERT: It's a big wheel.

As Jean, in her tenant management organisation (ID 10), said:

> It'll be a long hard fight but we will certainly get there in the end.

This assessment of the capacity of a domesticated tenants' movement to achieve social change restates the assumptions in tenant participation about the power of 'voice' to change social relations simply through its utterance (Richardson 1983; Paul 1994). Voice, it will be remembered, is conceived as a market-like force (Hirschman and Nelson 1976: 386) that has performative power; the act of speaking brings about the change that is described. In the assumptions of market theory the simple presence of new players in participation influences the outcome. This market-like model has defined the menu of participation practices offered to tenants; through their involvement in these rituals tenants exercise voice and, supposedly, trigger change in the behaviour of housing providers. The defining discourses of participation therefore provide a path to social change. A tenants' movement emerges from the rituals of participation, given voice by individualising state practices and deeded by market theory with a pre-existing 'plan for change' (Mueller 1994): the performative power of its collective voice. The sense of optimism and belief in social progress evidenced in tenant identity work reflects the market assumptions evident in participation. Belief in the performative power of participation obviates the need for tenants to mobilise effectively as a social movement, or to express clear goals and action plans. Without a strategy, including 'goals, means and a consideration of environmental constraints' (Mueller 1994: 246), the collective identity of a tenants' movement fails to mobilise a unified collective actor. Instead, tenants construct a 'performative' tenants' movement, a movement that is talked into existence as an emotional unity and deeded with transformative potential. As a collective identity, it is called into being by the performative power of a tenant 'voice' to initiate the social relations it names. It is a movement of collective contentions rather than strategies for change – a movement, therefore, of possibilities, not plans.

This chapter has evidenced the failures of collective identity to mobilise a coherent tenants' movement with clear aims, objectives and a defined strategy. It has pointed to the disablement of mobilisation strategies caused by intraclass divisions and the absorption by the movement of the divisive discourses of apathy and responsibility carried by tenant participation policy. The crippling effects of economic and political powerlessness, the rivalry and in-fighting that prevent the organisation of unity, the constraints of patronage that domesticate the movement and undermine its contentions, and the strategic vulnerability of the national tenants' organisation in housing policy have been identified. What emerges as the contemporary tenants' movement is the passionate performance of a social movement, a loosely networked but resolutely shared contention of collective belief in the power of performative voice, the market-like dynamic of public participation, to challenge hegemonic norms, to transform relationships of inequality and oppression, and to bring about social change.

7

CONCLUSION

The aim of this book has been to investigate the tenants' movement of England and to articulate its distinctive voice. In the place of an autonomous social movement it has found a fragmentation of loosely networked organisations, dependent groups and disparate individuals whose collective action is channelled into partnership with social landlords and absorbed in the intricacies of participation in housing management. The influence of tenants' organisations in government policies or housing policy discourse more broadly is almost non-existent. The crisis of housing supply and affordability, the promotion of price inflation in homeownership, the expansion of the largely unregulated private rented sector, and the reduction in the security and status of social housing all advance to the accompaniment of little political agitation. Those who castigate the tenants' movement for its failure to build a sustained political programme have advanced no convincing strategy for how the conditions for radical social change might be engendered through housing and community action (Dickens et al. 1985). The action-image of a confrontational tenants' movement has proved an illusory framework to judge the effectiveness of locally based organisations that seldom demonstrate such opposition to authority. In contrast to the European social democracies, the tenants' movement of England has demonstrated only rarely the ability to co-ordinate national political action, reflecting the marginalisation of the social housing sector from housing policies promoting a dominant market bias. Contrary to the other Anglo-Saxon welfare regimes in the USA, Canada, Australia and New Zealand, however, the significance of the size of the social housing sector in England, particularly prior to its partial privatisation in 1980, has deeded the tenants' movement in England with a palpable social base, and the substantial contribution made by social housing to the aspirations and well-being of generations of working-class households has bequeathed a weight of values and traditions that constitute the English tenants' movement as a unique social movement.

The voice of a tenants' movement

The contemporary tenants' movement in England developed in the struggles of the 1960s and early 1970s in which the more affluent tenants of post-war municipal housing fought to maintain a model of collective housing provision, where capital subsidies for house building reduce the cost for all without the requirement of a stigmatising means test (Ginsburg 1979). This exceptional model of general needs social housing provision, which never secured more than short-term support from governments, was presented by the tenants' movement as potentially universal (Craddock 1975; CDP 1976; DCH 2006), although universality was mediated by strongly established traditions of allocation by merit and just deserts, perpetuated by disciplinary housing management practices (Clarke and Ginsburg 1975; Damer 1989; Flint 2006). The intraclass divisions and welfare dependency discourses that accompanied the exclusivity of the general needs model continued to operate as unacknowledged fault lines in the evolution of the English tenants' movement, promoting stigma and 'underclass' narratives at the same time as motivating collective action designed to achieve recognition and status, and attain the rights and entitlements of citizenship (Haworth and Manzi 1999; Watt 2008). By the 1970s, a third of all English households lived in municipal housing and for many the affordability, quality and comparative security of the tenure provided the confidence and new-found affluence that delivered a sense of collective social mobility (Forrest 2010). Contentions around social citizenship advanced by the tenants' movement are founded on an idealised and privileged memory of this mass public housing (Dunleavy 1981). The critical defence of this idealised model of provision, with its vision of communities of mutual aid and reciprocity encouraged by collectivism, delivered through a more democratic and participatory housing service, has been a consistent theme in the development of the English tenants' movement (Somerville 2012). In a desire for greater democracy in public services, and consequently for a more empowered and influential 'public', tenants find the opportunities to achieve the greatest change (Baldock 1977; Ravetz 2001).

In contrast to the image of a combative and oppositional social movement, the English tenants' movement is defined by its orientation away from confrontation, in its commitment to 'voice' not 'exit'; to working with public service managers to achieving change through supposed partnership, even when that change appears slow and intractable (Needham 2003). The movement is a demonstration of loyalty to the institutions of collective housing and to their potential transformation through participation and the exercise of 'voice' (Forrest 2010). A vision of a welfare state that is democratic and collectively empowering motivates this perseverance in the rituals of participation and signals a fundamental challenge to the individualism and market models of the new social settlement (Wainwright 2003; Somerville 2005a). The political opportunities of participation provide tenants with the institutional resources and licensed rituals in which collective action can be conceived, and present them with an authorised strategy in which change may be achieved. This is the politics of possibility (Gibson-Graham 2006); the belief that the development of new relationships between social landlords and tenants, and the delivery of new models of participatory governance, may have consequences that cannot be foreseen by the scale of the initiatives or judged by any immediate calculation of effectiveness. In the field of community action, and especially in tenant management, co-operative housing and community-controlled housing companies, the spatial divisions of labour, gender, ethnicity and class are being challenged and redrawn. The collective empowerment and feelings of efficacy associated with tenant participation have inspired a new politics of care in many localities, where experiments in democratic engagement are modelled on an ethics of neighbouring that draws its strength from a transgression of the boundaries between the domestic and the public. Models of community ownership and management that might otherwise represent a fragmentation of public services are networked and federated to ensure the primacy of direct experience and local knowledge, and provide support and solidarity across difference and diversity. In its grass-roots localism, and in its democratic and participatory organisational behaviour, the tenants' movement represents something approaching a prefigurative social movement; in disparate projects that are largely unrecorded and unpublicised, it initiates a more democratic and accountable model of public services, and a new conception of a participatory public that is assertive in its engagement. It advances a vision of social justice practised through the daily interactions and face-to-face encounters of lived space, a spatial justice that is rooted in a sense of belonging and commitment to a field of care. In its partnerships with the providers of public services, and the quasi-public agencies and private institutions that now constitute the complexity of the welfare state, the tenants' movement is consistent in its support for collective provision, user-control and direct democracy. Despite all attempts to inculcate the values of individualism, private enterprise and personalised risk, the tenants' movement continues to promote the social relations of mutual aid, co-operation and solidarity. By persistently maintaining the benefits of the collective provision of housing and the principles of direct democracy and other excluded identities in the regulated reiterations of participation, tenant collective action resists the foreclosure of the new hegemonic settlement.

The social housing sector provides 18 per cent of all housing in England, ensuring decent quality homes for nearly 4 million households. Municipal and not-for-profit housing is in high demand, with over 1.8 million households registered on waiting lists, and most unlikely ever to acquire a tenancy (Wilcox and Pawson 2012). While government strategies to reduce the size and status of the sector continue unabated, and reflect broad public support for welfare reform, social housing still appears in popular discourse as a reward for merit and deserving behaviour, and there are strong tensions between its residual role as a stigmatised refuge for the poorest, and its promotion as the housing solution for more affluent households excluded from ownership (Fitzpatrick and Pawson 2007). Similar tensions can be seen in French and Swedish models of social housing where rent policies and bureaucratic selection increasingly favour better-off tenants. It is possible to perceive in this uncomfortable fission in policy a reminder of the defence of general needs social housing that provided the tenants' movement with its combative, yet divisive dynamic, and to see too the contradictory resilience of a belief in collective provision and socialised risk. The principle of collective housing continues to cast a long shadow over public policy in England through notions of housing rights and memories of 'homes fit for heroes' (Hanley 2007; Flint 2008). No government has attempted the privatisation of social housing without cloaking its intention as the promotion of tenants' choice or tenants' right to buy; the rights, and potential impact of social housing tenants are continuing matters of political significance. Even the Conservative-led Coalition government elected in the UK in 2010, resolved to increase the rate of attrition against social housing, and thought it prudent to promise that the rights of existing social housing tenants would not be threatened (Hodkinson and Robbins 2012). Many tenants in social housing continue to demonstrate an ingrained tendency towards collective action coupled with a passionate understanding of social justice. Fragmented by landlord, geography and individualist rhetoric, tenants nevertheless appear united by loyalty to collective provision and its collectivising social relations, by antagonism to the dominance of professional knowledge in the delivery of social housing, and adherence to grass-roots decision-making and a continuing tradition of direct democracy. The rise of participation has not dissolved the defining contentions of the tenants' movement; instead, those claims are rediscovered in the landlord–tenant relationship and become what shapes and motivates the contemporary movement.

Participation provides a discourse of rights that can empower and unite tenants. It supplies the vocabulary for the collective identity of a movement, an identity enunciated through shared and contentious beliefs, articulations of antagonism and an intrinsic sympathy for collective action. Three interpretive frames or identity constructions have been evidenced, shared widely among tenants that provide diagnostic, prognostic and motivational identities for a tenants' movement. These collective action frames present an image of a social movement demarcated by boundary markers, knitted together by emotional ties and expressed in claims to rights. There is a shared assumption that a tenants' movement exists and its general aims can be defined; the rituals and practices of participation provide the collectivising narrative and emotional unity of a movement, but they also channel the direction and undermine the mobilisation of autonomous collective action. Evaluated as a process of collective identity construction, this identity work fails to mobilise tenants around a coherent strategy, or enable agreement on aims and means. These collective action frames, though widely shared and sometimes oppositional, cannot sustain a unified collective actor. The tenants' movement may be talked into existence, but what appears is a collective wish for a tenants' movement; its plans are provided by partnerships dominated by more powerful collective actors, its antagonism is more than offset by its desire for social recognition, and its commitment to the associative relations of community makes it eminently adaptable to government projects that promote civic responsibility to reduce the provision of public services. Where this tenants' movement is most challenging is in propagating a collective identification of public services as a gift relationship (Titmuss 1970), the belief that collective provision encourages co-operation and mutual aid (Williams 1967), that it carves out spaces where the social relations of care can be nurtured as a process of participatory democracy, and models of collective or socialised services can be planned and delivered in ways that foster efficacy and collective empowerment.

Social movements operate in cycles of protest, where strategies of confrontation and direct action are followed by periods of lobbying, negotiation and partnership (Tarrow 1998). These cycles may include a latent stage when the movement exists only as a circuit of exchange in the beliefs shared by 'submerged' or informal networks (Melucci 1994) or as a sense of social movement 'community' (Taylor and Whittier 1992). The continuing identity work of these networks provides a degree of continuity to the challenge of a movement and enables it to emerge again as a visible and defined force. 'Latency is a sort of underground laboratory for antagonism and innovation,' claimed Alberto Melucci (1994: 127); it is where oppositional frames are maintained and rehearsed despite their repudiation in unreceptive and hostile political and social climates. These 'abeyance processes' (Taylor 1989: 761) help retain latent support for different social and economic models, and sustain a collective challenge under circumstances unfavourable for political mobilisation. Cycles of protest characterise the history of the English tenants' movement, with the emergence of campaigns against the bedroom tax in 2013 (Halewood 2013) only the latest in a sequence of confrontations involving popular direct action and disruption. However, periods of latency are the defining feature of the movement that most commonly appears as a communion of shared beliefs, exhibited and reaffirmed in scattered networks, groups and encounters between individuals. In the community action of tenants' associations and federations, the effective maintenance of an oppositional movement is evidenced in experiments with direct democracy that foster an ethic of neighbourly care. In its dogged participation with social landlords, the potential mobilisation of a contentious move-ment is asserted through claims to rights and justice, and the promotion of demo-cratic and participatory models of public services. The tenants' movement 'is a latent and powerful tradition' (Lowe 1997: 162), a spirit of collective action inspired by collective services that continues to express the potential for social change.

It appears from the research in this book that the shared experience of housing tenure can act as a basis for collective identity constructions, and that the aspects of collective citizenship implied in social housing may operate as an impetus for mobilisation. Janet Newman and John Clarke (2009) have pointed to the power of public services to constitute their public, and to act as a focus for public imagin-ations around the values of solidarity and commonality. In a similar manner, social housing appears to serve, at least potentially, as the inspiration for feelings of collec-tive belonging, and to enable the promotion of values of co-operation and a spirit of collective action. It can be articulated as an expression of public ownership and shared public space to construe the concept of community as a forum for direct democracy and mutual relations of care. In regenerating in ideal terms the concept of social housing as a universal service, and in extolling the virtues of mutuality in specific opposition to private ownership, tenant identity work prefigures more democratic models of community governance (Somerville 2005b) than those prescribed in governmental themes of 'big society' and the previous incarnations of active citizenship (Hancock *et al.* 2012). In continuing, persistently, to demand equality and recognition for the inhabitants of a stigmatised and residual social housing service, the tenants' movement makes claims to rights that cannot be honoured and gnaws at the contradictions in dominant definitions of citizenship (Mouffe 2000). In maintaining collective solidarities in the face of individualising strategies, the construction of a tenants' movement signals a submerged popular process in which the meanings of citizen and consumer, choice and voice and, out of these pairings, equality and justice are being contested and reimagined (Newman and Clarke 2009).

Challenging the hegemony of the market

While market-oriented strategies have been successful in establishing a hegemonic consensus over social policy in England, the resurgence of contentious collective identities in social housing provides tantalising evidence that the new welfare settlement remains potentially unstable and vulnerable to continuing change. The tenant identity work evidenced in this book through the construction of collective action frames, points to the political fragility of the hegemony of a programme of public service restructuring that has insinuated the transformative dynamics of choice and voice throughout the welfare state. Where a convergence of meaning was once achieved between the desires of social welfare movements and the dogma of the libertarian right (Williams 1994), floating concepts of empowerment, community and participation, though still functioning to connect the discourses of a hegemonic project, have the potential to point in new and radically different directions. Tenant identity work adopts the language of the market and the contractual rights of a customer relationship to endow these civil claims with a collective political voice. It constitutes a new public out of public participation, articulating a narrative of social struggle in the pursuit of rights of equality and invoking a collective that can be conceived of as a combative movement. This book has evidenced the performance of a tenants' movement from excluded narratives of collective provision, the construction of values of mutualism and co-operation, and the promotion of organisational principles of direct democracy. Goals of social citizenship and social justice, the traditional field of social welfare and urban movements, motivate the identity work of an English tenants' movement (Nicholls and Beaumont 2004; Roth 2000).

In returning social movement theory to housing studies, this book has identified the combative articulations of rights that emerge as an effect of tenant participation. These expressions of social citizenship may be generated, advanced and developed through the political opportunities of particular structures of governance. The rise to dominance of market ideologies since the 1980s and the subsequent restructuring of welfare states has resulted in the deployment of new technologies of public governance, and the scalar displacement of state functions into networks, partnerships and processes of collaboration among a range of agencies and agents. In this decentred network of institutional power, community organisations and urban movements have been hailed as agents of policy and allotted a role in the outsourcing and redefinition of public services; their supposed ethical and moral probity has provided a resource to address the more obvious failures of market supremacy (Tarrow 1998; Meyer 2004). These partnerships and collaborations provide particularly ambiguous opportunities for the development of contentious politics. The enmeshment of urban movements in networks of governance has been characterised traditionally as a process of co-option and institutionalisation in which previously disruptive contentions are rendered docile by state sponsorship. In this characterisation, community campaigns and urban movements are absorbed by regimes and reproduced in ways that do not threaten the stability of power relations (Mayer 2000; Pruijt 2003; Kavoulakos 2006; Böhm *et al.* 2010). This book, however, argues for a rethinking of the traditional narrative of social movement institutionalisation and co-option. It directs attention to the unintentional effect of collaborative governance in giving rise to contentious social movements and points to the domesticating discourses that may generate and sustain new contentious claims. As a subject constituted by regulatory discourse, rather than as an external force opposed to it, the domesticated social movement can be rethought in richer and more complex ways to deepen the theorisation of collective political engagement or contentious politics. Rather than theorising a social movement with a defined and structured identity that is institutionalised and co-opted by collaboration in the decentred systems of governance, it is possible to envisage movements that emerge as an effect of the technologies of governance and the discourses of citizenship and identity they propagate. In particular, regulatory discourses that promise to enhance service user influence, derived from market theories of performative voice (Hirschman 1970; Paul 1992), offer both the collectivising narratives and the belief in change that can generate the emotional identification of a social movement. In this way individualising State practices and regulatory schemes can provide the means through which challenging claims may be developed.

The concept of the 'performative social movement' is originated here to denote the contentious claims-making and oppositional identity talk that may be generated by the normative discourses of public service reform. State strategies of devolved governance, localism, partnership and participation may give rise to combative claims-making and oppositional identity talk that, in the field of social housing, is seen to generate a performative social movement among the network of tenants engaged in collaborative practices. The regulated discourse of participation supplies a vocabulary of rights-claims that enables tenants to overcome its individualising intent and to identify themselves as collective actors. It establishes the collective processes, unifying narratives and strategic framework for achieving social change in the performative power of voice to enact the outcomes it describes. It does so, however, only ideally, and there can be no guarantee of change (Butler 2000: 150).

A discourse is hegemonic to the 'extent that it can articulate different visions of the world in such a way that their potential antagonism is neutralised' (Laclau 1977: 161). Participation has been extremely successful in achieving this strategic task. In its consistent and repeated invocation it has achieved a wholesale inter-pellation of tenant participants as 'citizen governors' (Flint 2006: 24) and 'substitute managers' (Sullivan 2001: 34), hailing tenants as equals to generate new rule-governed identities (Clarke 2005). The tenant movement's orientation towards 'voice' and its enduring support for participation, has enabled it to be interpellated into a hegemonic project to introduce market forces and market provision into the welfare state. Tenant participation has been the state-sanctioned strategy through which the discourses of responsibility, self-reliance and enterprise have been embodied in institutional changes to the supply and management of social rented housing. The level of participation achieved in social housing through the course of this programme of welfare restructure has been far higher than evidenced in any other reformed public services and has effectively enveloped and encom-passed all social movement activity among tenants (Boyne and Walker 1999; Goodlad 2001). The dominance of these reform discourses is not under threat. The performative effect of voice has infused the sector and this immersion in participation has been enthralling; it dominates the lives of the social housing tenants who donate their voluntary resources as directors, inspectors or panel members (DCLG 2009c). In participation tenants have glimpsed the potential for a demo-cratic model of public services that empowers its public, and delivers respect and the status of citizenship (Craddock 1975; Croft and Beresford 1996). It has awarded them, in some instances, with the rights to appoint and manage housing staff, command budgets, direct operational policy, influence rent setting, run their own estates and design their own homes. These advances are unevenly distributed and have depended on changes in organisational culture, in particular social housing organisations in specific locations. As advances, they are extremely vulnerable to the edicts of national housing policy and legislation that might impact on rent and investment levels, security of tenure, housing allowances and income supplements. Progressive initiatives negotiated with one social landlord can be dissolved in the mergers and takeovers of housing associations, swept away by the appointment of a new chief executive, or their effect dissipated by regressive policies that make the social housing sector more conditional and temporary. The dominance of individualising discourses in which tenants are defined as customers and consumers has undermined the influence of democratic traditions of collective representation and replaced them with market models of accountability in citizen governance (Millward 2005; Morgan 2006). Where tenants' organisations still have influence with social landlords, the patronage they receive is exchanged for their compliance and quiescence, and formally recognised tenants' federations have almost universally retired from protest campaigns, leaving the field open to impromptu uprisings that receive limited support. An immediate future in which investment in affordable housing plunges, new social housing tenants lose their security of tenure, affordability worsens through cuts in housing allowances and social housing rents are set in relation to market prices offers little hope to the contentions of a social movement championing denigrated ideas of social citizenship (DCLG 2011a).

While the size and status of the social housing sector has been diminished, its disciplinary management policies amplified, and the economic powerlessness of tenants and their political marginalisation intensified, the hegemonic discourse of participation has provided the vocabulary of unity that has maintained the collective identity of a tenants' movement and kept alive a belief in the collectivising effect of public services. The direction of public service reform supplies a unifying narrative, delivering the means and defining the strategy for tenant collective action, and it is the dynamic of public service reform that now enables the positive attributes of collective housing provision and its principles of reciprocity and co-operation to be reclaimed. Participation is 'recognition at an expense', in Judith Butler's phrase (1993: 121); what can be achieved is clearly limited; what can be lost along the way may be unconscionable. The extent to which tenants are able to enlarge the political boundaries of a new social settlement by participating in its assemblage has to be weighed carefully against the cost they pay in subjection to individualising discourses and to the institutional erosion of collective services. There is little opportunity to gauge success and every possibility of failure, and practices that have radical intent may enact regulatory and regressive outcomes. For a tenants' movement to continue collectively to rehearse excluded identities and to resist the naming and containing power of hegemonic discourse, nevertheless, presents the ever-present possibility of change.

This research does not find a tenants' movement institutionalised or co-opted by public participation; it discovers the performative practices of participation that constitute a tenants' movement. This performative social movement is interpellated into hegemonic power relations and fully immersed in technologies of citizenship. It is both the subject and agent of governance (Cruikshank 1999), but in its engagement with regulatory discourse it articulates new contentions of social citizenship and, in reproducing the power relations of subjection, it advances new possibilities of democracy. Social movements can be constituted through the technologies of collaborative governance and in reproducing those technologies mobilise against them. Resistance, exemplified in this study of the tenants' movement, is an effect of the regulated repetition of power and the possibility of its reversal (Butler 1997a).

The politics of possibility

The tenants' movement that emerges from participation is not on the road to liberation from subjection, but it may be able to widen the possibilities available to tenants as subjects. Regulatory discourse can initiate collective and antagonistic claims, and can also provide a strategy whereby such claims may appear to be advanced. Contentious identities may develop, be maintained and find articulation inside the hegemonic discourses of governance, and movements can be mobilised through the discovery and reclamation of excluded narratives and voices. However, such domesticated movements rarely escape the subjection that undermines their potential and limits their possibilities. Service-user groups, welfare campaigns and locality-based associations that rise up without the support of well-resourced social movement organisations may be all but invisible as collective actors; their mobilisation leaves little trace and their quest for recognition and acceptance may speed their incorporation into local systems of governance (Piven and Cloward 1977; Mayer 2000).

The global roll back of social housing provision can be taken as evidence of the inability of even the strongest tenants' movements, those in the European social democratic tradition, to resist the triumphant advance of the interests of finance and property capital elites. In the dissolution of consensus around the norms of market liberalism triggered by the 2008 financial crisis, states across the globe have moved decisively against the remaining defences of an alternative social model. The tenants' movement in England has always been more poorly resourced than its European counterparts and it has never acquired the influence those organisations exercise over the discourses of housing policy. The diminishing size of the social rented sector, the corresponding expansion of private renting and the government strategies that forge equivalence between the two, underline the increasingly precarious position of an English tenants' movement that exists only in the minds of social housing tenants. Collective identities developed in the social housing sector that display tenacious support for models of collective provision and social insurance, may not survive an 'increasingly recalcitrant and punitive state' (Mayer 2000: 145) that threatens the continued existence of that sector. The tenants' movement persists in playing by the rules of the formal political game, even though the odds are stacked against it (Lustiger-Thaler and Maheu 1995). Its intermittent protests and 'visible' social movement action remains defensive and marginal while the political influence it exerts is negligible. The continued existence of a social housing tenants' movement that defends the collective provision of affordable housing is, however, a significant achievement in itself and one of urgent importance to study.

There is a clear and pressing need for an effective and combative tenants' movement. The purposeful inflation of housing costs by government pursuit of asset-based welfare strategies (Malpass 2005) and the aggrandisement of financial institutions (Harvey 2010) has triggered a worsening affordability crisis. The size of the private rental sector has tripled in just over ten years, while owner-occupation has continued to decline sharply (Wilcox and Pawson 2012). The reduction and capping of housing allowances in England from 2013 is likely to render central areas of the capital city, London, and a third of most other cities entirely unaffordable to anyone on low to average incomes (Ramesh 2012), creating a swaggeringly unequal landscape in which homeless households are transported beyond city limits by municipal authorities unable to access affordable accommodation, and essential workers are bussed into residential zones reserved for the most affluent (Fenton 2011). To secure the tenancy of increasingly inadequate and substandard property, private renters are expected to pay exorbitant administration fees, undergo background and credit checks, produce references, advance rents and deposits in their readiness to compete in a monopoly market (DCLG Select Committee 2013). There have been few attempts to extend the organisations of social housing tenants to private renters and, given the obstacles in mobilising such a temporary and individualised market sector, this is not surprising. It is largely left to homelessness charities, under-resourced environmental health officers from the municipality and housing law campaigners to advocate on behalf of the swelling throng of renters, but the provision of publicly funded advice and legal services for private tenants was drastically reduced in 2013 by government cuts to the legal aid budget (Bowcott 2013). There are growing signs, however, of popular protest against the injustices of a broken housing market. Parliamentary calls for the regulation of lettings agencies and the extension of municipal licensing powers over private landlords are signs of a mounting frustration that has already inspired private tenants to take direct action against property market monopolies (Booth 2013). The tenants' movement began in a wave of collective action against exploitation in the private rental sector in the nineteenth century, and it is likely that new mobilisations of tenants and new demands for affordable decent housing will emerge from the unregulated growth of this sector in the twenty-first century. Conflict in housing policy will continue around issues of affordability and supply, empowerment, localism and democracy. In maintaining a popular discourse around the community benefits of housing that is collective, democratic and partially decommodified, the tenants' movement offers new generations of renters the hope of a fairer and more just housing system.

It is not the intention here to author the 'plan for change' that Carol Mueller (1994) regards as essential to the definition of collective identity in a social movement but, faced with the spectre of a 'generation rent' (Shelter 2013) exposed to the exploitation of a property-owning monopoly, the priorities for a tenants' movement may be sketched as tentative suggestions for strategy. For a movement to develop from the local and the particular, and to formulate a collective challenge, its participants must have the desire to take that course of action, and those who share that desire must take the responsibility (Massey 2004; Cumbers *et al.* 2008). If the tenants' movement was a social movement confronting power rather than innate to it, the task would be to clarify its aims and beliefs, and initiate a strategy aimed at mobilising wider support. It would champion the cause of collective housing provision while extending its organisational activity to recruit tenants in the private rented sector. The national tenants' organisations set out a housing strategy for a 'post credit crunch world' (TAROE, NFTMO, CCH 2008) in which they envisaged a housing system that promoted co-operative and democratic models of provision and ownership. Translating this policy statement into a political mobilisation would mean concerted lobbying by tenants' organisations for the changes in government fiscal policies to enable the 'mass' development of a general needs social housing sector, accompanied by encouragement for ownership and management co-operatives. But the last time an organised tenants' movement marched out of a national conference chanting its support for investment in social house building was in 1995, when there was also concerted lobbying for a common tenancy across the public and private sectors to guarantee affordability and security (Hood 1997). Support for social house building is not, in any case, a unifying cause by itself. The continued development of municipal housing in Sweden and France has not provided egalitarian outcomes, but instead generated class tensions between discourses of need and desert (Turner 2007; Nativel 2009).

The legislative adoption of rights to housing in France in 2007 and, through homelessness legislation, in Scotland in 2012, demonstrates that measures to widen access must be accompanied by fiscal policy changes to allow increases in housing supply and provide opportunities not just for meeting housing need but to cater for housing choice. If the national tenants' organisations were to pursue their vision, they would need to champion mass and general needs affordable house building, promote co-operative and mutual ownership models of provision, strengthen the democratic networks of community housing initiatives and guard against the fragmentation and unequal development of services, campaign for affordability and security in the private rented, as well as the social housing, sector and engage in open debate over issues of need and desert. There are potential allies for such a mobilisation in social movements that demand more popular control over political and economic institutions (Polletta 2002), in citizens' organisations and the demand for a living wage, in the campaign against corporate tax avoidance, and in the growing popular concern for an ethics of responsibility in the private sector. The mobilisation of this campaigning tenants' movement would require the locality-based groups, informal tenants' panels and focus groups to acknowledge their cohesion as a movement and to take responsibility for brokering solidarities between individuals and localities, and for inspiring feelings of efficacy not submission. To retain the movement's values of direct democracy, this process of networking would need to be led from below, to amplify the contentions of the localities with the intent to develop a movement that articulated a distinctive challenge to the hegemonic settlement of social policy. Even if it remained marginalised and ineffective, such a movement at least would be distinguishable as an oppositional force. There are inevitable obstacles to the development of such a political programme from the identity work of tenants, however. The individual and organisational rivalries would be difficult to overcome. The requirement to obtain resources free of the controlling patronage of local government or social housing providers is a major challenge. The need to extract and distil a series of oppositional claims from framing narratives that are dominated by themes of welfare reform could prove an even more significant barrier. A movement that is so resolute in its denial of politics (Grayson 2010), its avoidance of conflict and in its determination to represent tenants rather than lead them, may, in any case, be constitutionally unable to metamorphose into a campaign with an explicit strategy for social change (Ravetz 2001).

A unique social movement

The global tenants' movement has its origins in a popular offensive against extremes of housing market exploitation in the cities of the industrialising world and in the demand for the collective provision of affordable housing free from the injustice of market forces and the speculation of private capital. Its greatest success has been in the development of municipal, state or not-for-profit social housing that has provided generations with decent secure homes. In co-operative housing, tenant management and local tenants' associations, networked in federations and national organisations, a tradition of grass-roots tenant democracy has evolved, and carved for itself an enduring influence in housing policy. In countries where social housing provision has been grudgingly rationed as a minimal safety net, tenants' movements have agitated for rent control, security and quality in the private landlord sector, providing legal advice services to private tenants supported by local mobilisation and direct action. Where they achieved influence over the direction of social policy in alliance with the organised labour movement, tenants' movements have championed the development of social housing, tenure neutrality in public policy and the regulation of private renting in the face of the powerful interests fuelling the promotion of home ownership. In the social housing sectors that they helped to establish, tenants' organisations have pressed for local control over strategic and operational policy, and in shaping the costs, standards and provision of housing supply and management, promoting democratic models of public governance and community ownership, and championing the role of experiential knowledge in public policy making.

In England, the significance of the social housing sector in popular culture, coupled with its marginalisation from political policy, resulted in the evolution of a tenants' movement focused almost exclusively on social housing and in developing and promoting the benefits of living in that tenure. This is a social welfare movement committed to the defence, reform and the possibilities of collective housing as an aspect of the welfare state. To its weakness, it is not a campaign for housing rights, or for affordability in housing; it rarely addresses the issues of homelessness, or combines with campaigns in the private rented sector. As a mobilisation of social welfare users, the tenants' movement has developed a distinctive vision of a public inaugurated by the socialising provision of collective housing. The identity work of tenants revealed in this book, evidenced in the widely shared construction of its collective action frames and the generation of aspects of a combative collective identity, articulates a vision of public services and the public that competes with and opposes the dominant direction of welfare reform. The tenants' movement is defined by its belief in the benefits of the collective provision of housing, in the quality, affordability and security of social housing, and its potential to foster relations of solidarity and mutual aid around a sense of shared public space and public service. The tenants' movement adds to this declaration of loyalty to the welfare state a combative agenda for reform and improvement so that public services might empower and bestow status on their users rather than belittle and exclude them. It conjures a vision of public services designed in partnership with the users and sensitive to their self-defined needs, that is local and accountable and fundamentally participative and democratic. This vision of democracy through collective provision is developed and anticipated through an organisational model of grass-roots mobilisation that is non-hierarchical, that privileges direct experience in participative democracy, and that suggests not only the unifying effect but also the individual empowerment possible from collective provision and shared identification with a sense of neighbourhood and belonging.

The tenants' movement may be a performative enactment, a wish for a contentious movement rather than a practical mobilisation, but its latency and resurgence is demonstrated in the shared beliefs of its distinct identity work and manifested in the collective action that provides the dynamic for tenant participation with social landlords, and continuing traditions of conflict and community action in housing policy. Like other urban movements, social welfare movements and 'poor people's movements', the tenants' movement cannot be theorised through a study of its effectiveness alone. Only under exceptional circumstances will people who lack institutional power become defiant, Frances Fox Piven and Richard Cloward (1977: 7) argued. Defiance is, however, only part of the story. In the absence of an oppositional movement with a strategy for change, what appears as a tenants' movement emerges from inside a programme of welfare restructuring and is given voice by its regulated practices. That voice appears to speak of excluded narratives, different priorities and unmapped directions. In participation, and in the day-to-day repetition of that regulated ritual, tenants construct the outline of a movement that can challenge the contradictions at the heart of welfare reform. This is a 'domesticated' movement that, nevertheless, advances principles of direct democracy and new concepts of public good, and in its identity talk contests the enclosure of public space and the foreclosure of public spheres. The tenants' movement in England promotes the collective provision of human needs outside of market, transforming the exchange value of housing into the use values of home, community and collective belonging. Despite a global assault on these principles, the movement continues to offer a different vision of society in which housing affordability, security and quality are foundations for belief in democratic provision and the community management of human needs. In the face of a range of institutional reforms and discursive identity practices targeted on social housing and acting on the subjectivity of tenants, this tenants' movement is evidence of the persistence of concerted dis-identification (Butler 2000). The tenants' movement may be a movement of the powerless, but its articulation of collective identities signals the instability of power. The performative achievement that is the tenants' movement is evidence of a continuing contest over social citizenship and the restructuring of the welfare state.

APPENDIX 1

Transcription key

[ ]	Square brackets	Overlapping talk
=	Equals sign	No space between turns
here	Italics	Emphasis
((Laugh))	Word(s) in double round brackets	Sounds with transcriber comments
[. . .]	Three dots in square brackets	Material omitted for presentational purposes

APPENDIX 2

Participation in focus groups and interviews

Research ID	Date	Type of tenants' organisation	Participants
1	2 August 2008	TPAS national conference focus group	20 people: 14 women and 6 men, 4 BME, 8 housing association and stock transfer tenant board members, 2 arm's-length management tenant board members, 4 residents' groups, 4 tenant panels, 2 tenant forums
2	3 August 2008	TPAS national conference focus group	14 people: 10 women and 4 men, 2 BME, 4 residents' group, 6 housing association tenant board members, 3 tenant panels, 1 individual voice
3	13 March 2009	Regional tenants' federation	7 people: 4 women and 3 men, 3 housing association, 4 council tenants, 2 tenants' panels, 5 residents' groups, 1 stock transfer association tenant director
4	2 April 2009	Residents' associations	16 people: 10 women and 6 men, 14 council tenants, 2 owner-occupiers

Research ID	Date	Type of tenants' organisation	Participants
5	21 April 2009	Borough tenants' federation (active in Defend Council Housing and TAROE)	10 people: 7 women and 3 men, 1 leaseholder, 1 BME, 1 housing association and 8 council tenants
6	11 May 2009	Regional tenants' federation	6 people: 2 women and 4 men, 1 BME, council tenants and members of borough panels
7	28 July 2009	Borough tenants' federation	2 people: 1 man, 1 woman, council tenants
8	1 August 2009	TPAS national conference focus group	16 people: 10 women, 6 men, 4 BME, 6 housing association tenant board members, 4 residents groups, 2 tenant management organisations, 4 tenant panels
9	2 August 2009	TPAS national conference focus group	6 people: 6 women, 1 arm's-length management tenant board member, 3 tenant-led housing association board members, 2 federation chairs
10	5 August 2009	Tenant management organisation	4 people: 3 women and 1 man, 3 council tenants, 1 owner-occupier, 4 TMO board members
11	7 September 2009	Borough tenants' federation	8 people: 4 women and 4 men, 8 council tenants, 2 arm's-length management tenant board members
12	7 October 2009	Regional tenants' federation	1 man: retained council tenant
13	28 October 2009	Borough tenants' federation	1 man: council tenant, arm's-length management and board member of National Tenants' Organisation

Research ID	Date	Type of tenants' organisation	Participants
14	17 Nov 2009	Tenant director	1 man: council tenant and arm's-length management company director
15	23 November 2009	Residents' association	1 woman: council tenant
16	25 November 2009	Residents' association/ Tenants' panel	2 men: 1 former arm's-length management tenant board member, both tenant inspectors for council arm's-length organisation
17	1 December 2009	Regional tenants' federation	1 man: council tenant, former tenant director, active in Defend Council Housing
18	30 January 2010	National tenants' federation	1 man: chair of the national tenants organisation TAROE, housing association tenant, stock transfer tenant board member
19	5 February 2010	Tenant director	1 man: housing association tenant board, federation chair
20	12 February 2010	Tenant director	1 man: arm's-length management board member
21	4 May 2010	Borough-wide tenants federation and tenant panels	11 people: 7 women and 4 men, 7 council tenants, 2 housing association tenants, 1 owner-occupier, 1 private tenant
22	24 July 2010	TPAS national conference focus group	10 people: 6 women and 4 men, 2 housing association tenant board members, 1 council arm's-length tenant board member, 1 federation chair, 1 national federation member, 2 tenant panel members, 3 residents' group members

Research ID	Date	Type of tenants' organisation	Participants
23	19 November 2012	Borough tenants' federation	8 people: 4 women, 4 men: council tenants
24	5 November 2012	Borough tenants' federation	9 people: 7 women, 2 men, 7 council tenants, 1 housing association board member, 1 leaseholder

REFERENCES

Abel, E. and M. Nelson (1990) *Circles of Care: Work and Identity in Women's Lives*. Albany, NY: State University of New York Press.

Abercrombie, N. (1994) Authority and Consumer Society. In: Keat, R., N. Whitely and N. Abercrombie (eds) *The Authority of the Consumer*. London: Routledge.

Aldbourne Associates (2001) *A Study of Tenant Participation in Registered Social Landlords*. London: The Housing Corporation.

Allen, C. (2008) *Housing Market Renewal and Social Class*. London: Routledge.

Allen, J. and A. Cochrane (2010) Assemblages of State Power: Topological Shifts in the Organisation of Government and Politics. *Antipode*, 42 (5): 1071–1089.

Althusser, L. ([1971] 2001) *Lenin and Philosophy and Other Essays*. New York: Monthly Review.

Ambrose, P. (2006) What *is* the Housing Problem? In: *Defend Council Housing: The Case for Council Housing in 21st Century Britain*. Nottingham: Russell Press.

American Planning Association (2005) AICP National Planning Landmarks and Pioneers. *Planning Magazine*. Available at: www.planning.org. Accessed 6 July 2010.

Andrews, L. (1979) *Tenants and Town Hall*. London: HMSO.

Appleyard, R. (2006) *Growing Up: A Report of the Future Shape of the Sector Commission*. London: L&Q Group.

Arnstein, S. (1969) A Ladder of Citizen Participation. *American Institute of Planners Journal*, 35 (4): 216–224.

Audit Commission (2004a) *Housing – Improving Services through Resident Involvement*. London: Audit Commission.

Audit Commission (2004b) *Housing KLoEs*. Available at: www.audit-commission.gov.uk. Accessed 25 October 2005.

Austin, J. L. (1976) *How to Do Things with Words*. Oxford: Oxford University Press.

Baldock, P. (1977) Why Community Action? The Historical Origins of the Radical Trend in British Community Work. *Community Development Journal*, 12 (2): 68–74.

Baldock, P. (1982) The Sheffield Rent Strike of 1967–1968: The Development of a Tenants' Movement. In: Henderson, P., A. Wright and K. Wyncoll (eds) *Successes and Struggles on Council Estates*. London: Association of Community Workers.

Bandy, G., J. Drew and M. Sarantis (2007) *Tenants' Views: The Cave Review of Social Housing Regulation*. London: DCLG.

Barnes, M. (1999) Users as Citizens: Collective Action and the Local Governance of Welfare. *Social Policy and Administration*, 33 (1): 73–90.

Barnes, M. and D. Prior (1995) Spoilt for Choice? How Consumerism can Disempower Public Service Users. *Public Money and Management*, 15 (3): 53–58.

Barnes, M., J. Newman, A. Knops and H. Sullivan (2003) Constituting 'The Public' in Public Participation. *Public Administration*, 81 (2): 379–399.

Barnsley Federation of Tenants and Residents (2008) *Business Plan 2008–2010*. Available at: www.barnsleytaras.org.uk. Accessed 6 July 2010.

Barron, A. and C. Scott (1992) The Citizens' Charter Programme. *Modern Law Review*, 55: 526–546.

Bauman, Z. (1998) *Work, Consumerism and the New Poor*. Buckingham: Open University Press.

Bell, C. and H. Newby (1978) Community, Communion, Class and Community Action. In: Herbert, D. T. and R. J. Johnston (eds) *Social Areas in Cities*. Chichester: John Wiley & Sons.

Benford, R. and D. Snow (1988) Ideology, Frame Resonance and Participant Mobilisation. In: Klandermans, B., H. Kriesi and S. Tarrow (eds) *From Structure to Action: Comparing Social Movement Research Across Cultures*. London: JAI Press.

Benford, R. and D. Snow (1992) Master Frames and Cycles of Protest. In: Morris, A. and C. McClurg Mueller (eds) *Frontiers in Social Movement Theory*. London: Yale University Press.

Benford, R. and D. Snow (2000) Framing Processes and Social Movements: An Overview and Assessment. *Annual Review of Sociology*, 26: 611–639.

Bengtsson, B. (1995) Housing in Game-Theoretical Perspective. *Housing Studies*, 10 (2): 229–243.

Bengtsson, B. and D. Clapham (1997) Tenant Participation in a Cross-National Comparative Perspective. In: Cooper, C. and M. Hawtin (1997) *Housing, Community and Conflict*. Aldershot: Arena Ashgate.

Beresford, P. (1988) Consumer Views: Data Collection or Democracy? In: White, I., M. Devenney, R. Bhaduri, J. Barnes, P. Beresford and A. Jones (eds) *Hearing the Voice of the Consumer*. London: Policy Studies Institute.

Bernstein, M. (1997) Celebration and Suppression: The Strategic Uses of Identity by the Lesbian and Gay Movement. *Annual Journal of Sociology*, 103 (3): 531–565.

Bhabha, H. (1994) *The Location of Culture*. London: Routledge.

Bines, W., N. Pleace and C. Radley (1993) *Managing Social Housing*. London: HMSO.

Blagg, H. and N. Derricourt (1982) Why We Need to Reconstruct a Theory of the State for Community Work. In: Craig, G., N. Derricourt and M. Loney (eds) *Community Work and the State*. London: Routledge & Kegan Paul.

Bliss, N. and B. Lambert (2012) *Tenant Panels: Options for Accountability*. Birmingham: National Tenants' Organisation.

Boaden, N., M. Goldsmith, W. Hampton and P. Stringer (1982) *Public Participation in Local Services*. Harlow: Longman.

Böhm, S., A. Dinerstein and A. Spicer (2010) (Im)possibilities of Autonomy: Social Movements in and Beyond Capital, the State and Development. *Social Movement Studies*, 9 (1): 17–32.

Bolger, S., P. Corrigan, J. Docking and N. Frost (1981) *Towards Socialist Welfare Work*. Basingstoke: Macmillan.

Booth, R. (2013) Letting Agents must be Upfront about Hidden Fees and Charges, say MPs. *The Guardian*, 18 July. London. Available at: www.guardian.co.uk. Accessed 22 July 2013.

Bourdieu, P. (1986) The Forms of Capital. In: Richardson, J. E. (ed.) *Handbook of Theory of Research for the Sociology of Education*. Westport, CT: Greenwood Press.

Bourdieu, P. and J.-C. Passeron (1990) *Reproduction in Education, Society and Culture*. London: Sage.

Bowcott, O. (2013) Legal Aid Cuts Force Closure of Almost a Third of Shelter Offices. *The Guardian*, 11 March. London. Available at: www.guardian.co.uk. Accessed 24 July.

Boyne, G. and R. Walker (1999) Social Housing Reforms in England and Wales: A Public Choice Evaluation. *Urban Studies*, 36: 2237–2262.

Bradley, Q. (1997) *The Leeds Rent Strike of 1914: A Reappraisal of the Radical History of the Tenants Movement*. Leeds. Available at: www.tenantshistory.org.uk. Accessed 3 July 2013.

Bradley, Q. (1999) *The Birth of the Council Tenants Movement: A Study of the 1934 Leeds Rent Strike*. Available at: www. tenantshistory.org.uk.

Breines, W. (1989) *Community and Organisation in the New Left 1962–1968: The Great Refusal*. London: Rutgers University Press.

Brent, J. (2009) *Searching for Community*. Bristol: Policy Press.

Brown, C. (2013) Tenants Fail to Pay the Bedroom Tax. *Inside Housing*, 17 May. Inside Publications.

Brown, K. and R. Patrick (2012) Re-moralising or De-moralising? The Coalition Government's Approach to 'Problematic' Populations. Special Issue. *People, Place and Policy Online*, 6 (1). Available at: http://extra.shu.ac.uk/ppp-online. Accessed 31 January 2013.

Brownhill, S. (2009) The Dynamics of Participation: Modes of Governance and Increasing Participation in Planning. *Urban Policy and Research*, 27 (4): 357–375.

Bulmer, M. (1986) *Neighbours: The Work of Philip Abrams*. Cambridge: Cambridge University Press.

Burn, D. (1972) *Rent Strike: St Pancras 1960*. London: Pluto Press.

Butler, J. (1990) *Gender Trouble: Feminism and the Subversion of Identity*. London: Routledge.

Butler, J. (1993) *Bodies that Matter: On the Discursive Limits of Sex*. London: Routledge.

Butler, J. (1997a) *The Psychic Life of Power*. Stanford, CA: Stanford University Press.

Butler, J. (1997b) *Excitable Speech: A Politics of the Performative*. London: Routledge.

Butler, J. (2000) Restaging the Universal: Hegemony and the Limits of Formalism. In: Butler, J., E. Laclau and S. Zizek, *Contingency, Hegemony, Universality*. London: Verso.

Butler, J. (2004) Interview with G. A. Olson and L. Worsham. In: Salih, S. (ed.) *The Judith Butler Reader*. Oxford: Blackwell.

Cairncross, L., D. Clapham and R. Goodlad (1992) The Origins and Activities of Tenants Associations in Britain. *Urban Studies*, 29 (5): 709–725.

Cairncross, L., D. Clapham and R. Goodlad (1993) The Social Bases of Tenant Organisation. *Housing Studies*, 8 (3): 179–193.

Cairncross, L., D. Clapham and R. Goodlad (1994) Tenant Participation and Tenant Power in British Council Housing. *Public Administration*, 72: 177–200.

Cairncross, L., D. Clapham and R. Goodlad (1997) *Housing Management, Consumers and Citizens*. London: Routledge.

Cairncross, L., C. Morrell, J. Darke and S. Brownhill (2002) *Tenants Managing: An Evaluation of Tenant Management Organisations in England*. London: Office of the Deputy Prime Minister.

Cairncross, L. and M. Pearl (2003) *Taking the Lead: Report on a Survey of Housing Association Board Members*. London: Housing Corporation.

Camden Federation (2013) Protest at Genesis Eviction Threat. Camden Federation of Tenants and Residents Association. Available at: http://camdenfed.org.uk. Accessed 4 June 2013.

Cameron, D. (2009a) People Power: Reforming Quangos. Speech, 6 July. Available at: www.conservatives.com. Accessed 1 August 2010.

Capek, S. and J. Gilderbloom (1992) *Community Versus Commodity: Tenants and the American City*. Albany, NY: State University of New York Press.

Card, P. (2001) Managing Anti-social Behaviour: Inclusion or Exclusion. In: Cowan, D. and A. Marsh, *Two Steps Forward*. Bristol: The Policy Press.

Card, P. (2006) Governing Tenants: From Dreadful Enclosures to Dangerous Places. In: Flint, J. (ed.) *Housing, Urban Governance and Anti-Social Behaviour*. Bristol: The Policy Press.

Carr, H., D. Sefton-Green and D. Tissier (2001) Two Steps Forward for Tenants? In: Cowan, D. and A. Marsh (eds) *Two Steps Forward*. Bristol: The Policy Press.

Carr, S. (2007) Participation, Power, Conflict and Change: Theorising Dynamics of Service User Participation in the Social Care System of England and Wales. *Critical Social Policy*, 27 (2): 266–276.

Cary, L. (1970) Resident Participation: Dominant Theme in the War on Poverty and Model Cities Program. *Community Development Journal*, 5: 73–78.

Castells, M. (1976) An Experimental Study of Urban Social Movements. In: Pickvance, C. G. (ed.) *Urban Sociology: Critical Essays*. London: Tavistock.

Castells, M. (1977) *The Urban Question*. London: Edward Arnold.

Castells, M. (1978) *City, Class and Power*. Basingstoke: Macmillan.

Castells, M. (1983) *The City and the Grassroots*. London: Edward Arnold.

Cave, M. (2007) *Every Tenant Matters: A Review of Social Housing Regulation*. Wetherby: DCLG.

CCH (Confederation of Co-operative Housing), Chartered Institute of Housing and Cooperative Union (2003) *Empowering Communities: The Community Gateway Model*. Coventry: Chartered Institute of Housing.

CDP (Community Development Project) (1976) *Whatever Happened to Council Housing?* London: CDP Information and Intelligence Unit.

CIH (Chartered Institute of Housing) (2006) *Empowering Communities: The Community Gateway Model*. Available at: www.cih.org. Accessed 20 August 2010.

Clapham, D. and M. Satsangi (1992) Performance Assessment and Accountability in British Housing Management. *Policy and Politics*, 20 (1): 63–74.

Clapham, D. and K. Kintrea (2000) Community-based Housing Organisations and the Local Governance Debate. *Housing Studies*, 15 (4): 533–599.

Clapham, D., B. Franklin and L. Saugeres (2000) Housing Management: The Social Construction of an Occupational role. *Housing, Theory and Society*, 17: 68–92.

Clark, E. and K. Johnson (2009) Circumventing Circumscribed Neoliberalism: The System Switch in Swedish Housing. In: Glynn, S. (ed.) *Where the Other Half Lives*. London: Pluto Press.

Clark, H. (1994) Taking Up Space: Redefining Political Legitimacy in NYC. *Environment and Planning A*, 26: 937–955.

Clarke, J. (2005) New Labour's Citizens: Activated, Empowered, Responsibilized, Abandoned? *Critical Social Policy*, 25: 447–463.

Clarke, J. (2007) Unsettled Connections: Citizens, Consumers and the Reform of Public Services. *Journal of Consumer Culture*, 7: 159–177.

Clarke, J. (2009) Community, Social Change and Social Order. In: Mooney, G. and S. Neal (eds) *Community: Welfare, Crime and Society*. Maidenhead: Open University Press.

Clarke, J., J. Newman, N. Smith, E. Vidler and L. Westmarland (2007) *Creating Citizen-Consumers: Changing Publics and Changing Public Services*. London: Sage.

Clarke, M. and J. Stewart (1994) The Local Authority and the New Community Governance. *Local Government Studies*, 20 (2): 163–176.

Clarke, S. and N. Ginsburg (1975) The Political Economy of Housing. *Political Economy and the Housing Question*. Papers presented at the Housing Workshop, London. Conference of Socialist Economists.

Cochrane, A. (2003) The New Urban Policy: Towards Empowerment or Incorporation? In: Imrie, R. and M. Raco (eds) *Urban Renaissance? New Labour, Community and Urban Policy*. Bristol: Policy Press.

Cockburn, C. (1977a) *The Local State*. London: Pluto Press.

Cockburn, C. (1977b) When Women Get Involved in Community Action. In: Mayo, M. (ed.) *Women in the Community*. London: Routledge & Kegan Paul.

Cohen, P. (1997) Beyond the Community Romance. *Sounding*, 5, Spring: 29–51.

Cole, I. (2007) What Future for Social Housing in England? *People, Place and Policy Online*, 1(1): 3–13. Available at: http://extra.shu.ac.uk/ppp-online/wp-content/uploads/2013/06/future_social_housing_england.pdf. Accessed 10 July 2010.

Cole, I. and R. Furbey (1994) *The Eclipse of Council Housing*. London: Routledge.

Cole, I., P. Hickman, L. Millward, B. Reid, L. Slocombe and S. Whittle (2000) *Tenant Participation in England: A Stocktake of Activity in the Local Authority Sector*. Sheffield: Centre for Regional Economic and Social Research.

Cole, I., P. Hickman, L. Millward, B. Reid, L. Slocombe and S. Whittle (2001) *Tenant Participation in Transition: Issues and Trends in the Development of Tenant Participation in the Local Authority Sector in England*. London: Department of the Environment, Transport and the Regions.

Cooper, C. and M. Hawtin (1997) *Housing, Community and Conflict*. Aldershot: Arena Ashgate.

Cooper, C. and M. Hawtin (1998) *Resident Involvement and Community Action*. Coventry: Chartered Institute of Housing.

Corkey, D. and G. Craig (1978) CDP: Community Work or Class Politics. In: Curno, P. (ed.) *Political Issues and Community Work*. London: Routledge & Kegan Paul.

Corr, A. (1999) *No Trespassing: Squatting, Rent Strikes and Land Struggles Worldwide*. Cambridge, MA: South End Press.

Council House Building (2008) HC Early Day Motion 355. Available at: www.parliament.uk/edm/2008-09/355. Accessed 10 July 2010.

Cowley, J. (1979) *Housing for People or for Profit?* London: Stage 1.

Cowley, J., A. Kaye, M. Mayo and M. Thompson (1977) *Community or Class Struggle?* London: Stage 1.

Craddock, J. (1975) *Tenant's Participation in Housing Management: A Study of Four Schemes*. London: Association of London Housing Estates.

Cress, D. (1997) Nonprofit Incorporation Among Movements of the Poor: Pathways and Consequences for Homeless Social Movement Organisations. *The Sociological Quarterly*, 38 (2): 343–360.

Cress, D. and D. Snow (1996) Mobilisation at the Margins: Resources, Benefactors and the Viability of Homeless Social Movement Organisations. *American Sociological Review*, 61 (6): 1089–1109.

Croft, S. and P. Beresford (1996) The Politics of Participation. In: Taylor, D. (ed.) *Critical Social Policy: A Reader*. London: Sage.

Cruikshank, B. (1999) *The Will to Empower: Democratic Citizens and Other Subjects*. London: Cornell University Press.

Cumbers, A., P. Routledge and C. Nativel (2008) The Entangled Geographies of Global Justice Networks. *Progress in Human Geography*, 32 (2): 183–201.

Daly, G., G. Mooney, L. Poole and H. Davies (2005) Housing Stock Transfer in Birmingham and Glasgow: The Contrasting Experiences of Two UK Cities. *European Journal of Housing Policy*, 5 (3): 327–341.

Damer, S. (1989) *From Moorepark to 'Wine Alley': The Rise and Fall of a Glasgow Housing Scheme*. Edinburgh: Edinburgh University Press.

Damer, S. (2000) 'The Clyde Rent War!' The Clydebank Rent Strike of the 1920s. In: Lavalette, M. and G. Mooney (eds) *Class Struggle and Social Welfare*. London: Routledge.

Davies, J. (2007) The Limits of Partnership: An Exit-action Strategy for Local Democratic Inclusion. *Political Studies*, 55: 779–800.

Davis, C. and A. Wigfield (2010) Housing: Did it Have to Be Like This? A Socialist Critique of New Labour's Performance. Nottingham: Spokesman Books.

Davis, M. (2006a) *Planet of Slums*. London: Verso.

Davis, M. (2006b) *City of Quartz*. London: Verso.

DCH (Defend Council Housing) (2006) *The Case for Council Housing in 21st Century Britain*. London: Defend Council Housing.

DCH (2008) *Dear Gordon 2: Investment in First Class Council Housing Makes Sense*. London: Defend Council Housing.

DCLG (Department for Communities and Local Government) (2006) *Strong and Prosperous Communities: The Local Government White Paper*. Cm 6939-I. Norwich: HMSO.

DCLG (2007a) *Tenant Empowerment: A Consultation Paper*. Wetherby: DCLG.

DCLG (2007b) *An Action Plan for Community Empowerment: Building on Success*. Wetherby: DCLG.

DCLG (2008) *Communities in Control: Real People, Real Power*. Cm 7427. Norwich: The Stationery Office.

DCLG (2009a) *Directions to the Tenant Service Authority*. London: Communities and Local Government Publications.

DCLG (2009b) *Evaluation of the Mixed Communities Initiative Demonstration Projects: Initial Report: Baseline and Early Process Issues*. London: DCLG.

DCLG (2009c) *Place Survey 2008, England: Further Results*. London: DCLG.

DCLG (2009d) *2007–2008 Citizenship Survey Empowered Communities Topic Report*. London: DCLG.

DCLG (2009e) *Fair and Flexible: Draft Statutory Guidance on Social Housing Allocations for Local Authorities in England*. London: DCLG.

DCLG (2010) *Review of Social Housing Regulation*. London: DCLG.

DCLG (2011a) *Laying the Foundations: A Housing Strategy for England*. London: DCLG.

DCLG (2011b) *Allocation of Accommodation: Guidance for Local Housing Authorities in England*. London: DCLG.

DCLG (2011c) *Neighbourhood Planning Regulations*. London: DCLG.

DCLG (2012) *National Planning Policy Framework*. London: DCLG.

DCLG Select Committee (2013) *The Private Rented Sector*. HC 50. London: The Stationery Office.

Dean, M. (1999) *Governmentality*. London: Sage.

Delaney, D. and H. Leitner (1997) The Political Construction of Scale. *Political Geography*, 16 (2): 93–97.

Della-Porta, D. and M. Diani (2006) *Social Movements: An Introduction*. Oxford: Blackwell.

Derricourt, N. (1971) Community Work on Housing Estates in the United Kindom. *Community Development Journal*, 6 (1): 38–42.

Derricourt, N. (1973) Tenants and Housing Management. In: Hatch, S. (ed.) *Towards Participation in Local Services*. London: Fabian Society.

DETR (Department of the Environment, Transport and the Regions) (1999) *National Framework for Tenant Participation Compacts*. London: DETR.

Dickens, P., S. Duncan, M. Goodwin, and F. Gray (1985) *Housing States and Localities*. London: Methuen.

Dikec, M. (2012) Space as a Mode of Political Thinking. *Geoforum*, 43 (4): 669–676.

Dreier, P. (1984) The Tenants' Movement in the USA. *International Journal of Urban and Regional Research*, 8 (2): 254–279.

Dunleavy, P. (1980) *Urban Political Analysis*. Basingstoke: Macmillan.

Dunleavy, P. (1981) *The Politics of Mass Housing in Britain, 1945–1975: A Study of Corporate Power and Professional Influence in the Welfare State*. Oxford: Clarendon Press.

Durant, R. (1939) *Watling: A Survey of Social Life on a New Housing Estate*. London: P. S. King.

Durose, C. and J. Rees (2012) The Rise and Fall of Neighbourhood in the New Labour Era. *Policy and Politics*, 40 (1): 39–55.

Dwelly, T. and J. Cowans (2006) *Rethinking Social Housing*. London: Smith Institute.

Edgell, S. and V. Duke (1991) *A Measure of Thatcherism: A Sociology of Britain*. London: HarperCollins Academic.

Elton, Sir L. (2006) *Review of Regulatory and Compliance Requirements for RSLs*. London: Housing Corporation.

Englander, D. (1983) *Landlord and Tenant in Urban Britain, 1838–1918*. Oxford: Clarendon Press.

Escobar, A. (2001) Culture Sits in Places: Reflections on Globalism and Subaltern Strategies of Localization. *Political Geography*, 20 (2): 139–174.

Fanon, F. (1986) *Black Skin, White Masks*. London: Pluto Press.

Fantasia, R. and E. Hirsch (1995) Culture in Rebellion: The Appropriation and Transformation of the Veil in the Algerian Revolution. In: Johnston, H. and B. Klandermans (eds) *Social Movements and Culture*. London: University College London Press.

Featherstone, D. (2005) Towards the Relational Construction of Militant Particularisms. *Antipode*, 37 (2): 250–271.

Featherstone, D., A. Ince, D. Mackinnon, K. Strauss and A. Cumbers (2012) Progressive Localism and the Construction of Political Alternatives. *Transactions of the Institute of British Geographers*, 37: 177–182.

Fenton, A. (2011) *Housing Benefit Reform and the Spatial Segregation of Low-income Households in London*. Cambridge: Cambridge Centre for Housing and Planning Research.

Fine, G. (1995) Public Narration and Group Culture: Discerning Discourse in Social Movements. In: Johnston, H. and B. Klandermans (eds) *Social Movements and Culture*. London: University College London Press.

Finlayson, A. (2003) Public Choice Theory: Enemy of Democracy. *Soundings*, 24: 25–40. London: Lawrence & Wishart.

Finnigan, R. (1984) Council Housing in Leeds 1919–1939: Social Policy and Urban Change. In: Daunton, M. (ed.) *Councillors and Tenants: Local Authority Housing in English Cities 1919–1939*. Leicester: Leicester University Press.

Fitzpatrick, S. and H. Pawson (2007) Welfare Safety Net or Tenure of Choice? The Dilemma Facing Social Housing Policy in England. *Housing Studies*, 22 (2): 163–182.

Fitzpatrick, S. and M. Stephens (2008) *The Future of Social Housing*. London: Shelter.

Fleetwood, M. and J. Lambert (1982) Bringing Socialism Home: Theory and Practice for a Radical Community Action. In: Craig, G., N. Derricourt and M. Loney (eds) *Community Work and the State*. London: Routledge & Kegan Paul.

Flint, J. (2003) Housing and Ethopolitics: Constructing Identities of Active Consumption and Responsible Community. *Economy and Society*, 32 (4): 611–629.

Flint, J. (2004a) The Responsible Tenant and the Politics of Behaviour. *Housing Studies*, 19 (6): 893–909.

Flint, J. (2004b) Reconfiguring Agency and Responsibility in the Governance of Social Housing in Scotland. *Urban Studies*, 41 (1): 151–172.

Flint, J. (2006) *Housing, Urban Governance and Anti-social Behaviour*. Bristol: The Policy Press.

Flint, J. (2008) Welfare State Institutions and Secessionary Neighbourhood Spaces. In: Flint, J. and D. Robinson (eds) *Community Cohesion in Crisis: New Dimensions of Diversity and Difference*. Bristol: Policy Press, pp. 159–176.

Foot, M. (1973) *Aneurin Bevan: A Biography* (Vol. 2). London: Davis-Poynter.

Forrest, R. (2010) A Privileged State: Council Housing as Social Escalator. In: Malpass, P. and R. Rowlands (eds) *Housing, Markets and Policy*. London: Routledge.

Forrest, R. and A. Murie (1991) *Selling the Welfare State: The Privatisation of Public Housing*. London: Routledge.

Forrest, R. and J. Lee (2003) *Housing and Social Change*. London: Routledge.

Foster, J. (1975) Working with Tenants. In: Lees, R. and G. Smith (eds) *Action Research in Community Development*. London: Routledge & Kegan Paul.

Foucault, M. (1982) The Subject and Power. In: Dreyfuss, H. and P. Rabinow. *Michel Foucault: Beyond Structuralism and Hermeneutics*. Brighton: Harvester Press.

Foucault, M. (1991) Governmentality. In: Burchell, G., C. Gordon and P. Miller (eds) *The Foucault Effect: Studies in Governmentality*. Chicago, IL: University of Chicago Press.

Fraser, N. (1997) *Justice Interruptus: Critical Reflections on the 'Postsocialist' Condition*. London: Routledge.

Fraser, N. and L. Gordon (1997) A Genealogy of Dependence: Tracing a Keystone of the US Welfare State. *Signs*, 19 (2): 309–336.

Frazer, E. (1999) *The Problems of Communitarian Politics*. Oxford: Oxford University Press.

Freire, P. ([1972] 1990) *Pedagogy of the Oppressed*. London: Penguin Books.

Freire, P. ([1973] 1993) *Education for Critical Consciousness*. New York: Continuum.

Friend, A. (1980) The Post-war Squatters. In: Anning, N. (ed.) *Squatting: The Real Story*. London: Bay Leaf Books.

Fuller, C. and M. Geddes (2008) Urban Governance under Neo-Liberalism: New Labour and the Restructuring of State-Space. *Antipode*, 40 (2): 252–282.

Fung, A. and E. Wright (2003) *Deeping Democracy: Institutional Innovations in Empowered Participatory Governance*. London: Verso.

Furbey, R., B. Wishart and J. Grayson (1996) Training for Tenants: Citizens and the Enterprise Culture. *Housing Studies*, 11 (2): 251–270.

Fyfe, N. (2005) Making Space for Neo-Communitarianism? The Third Sector, State and Civil Society in the UK. *Antipode*, 37 (3): 536–557.

Gamson, W. (1992) *Talking Politics*. Cambridge: Cambridge University Press.

Gaventa, J. (1980) *Power and Powerlessness*. Oxford: Clarendon Press.

Gibson, K. (2001) Regional Subjection and Becoming. *Environment and Planning D: Society and Space*, 19 (6): 639–667.

Gibson, T. (1979) *People Power: Community and Work Groups in Action*. Harmondsworth: Penguin Books.

Gibson-Graham, J. K. (2002) Beyond Global vs Local: Economic Politics Outside the Binary Frame. In: Herod, A. and M. Wright. *Geographies of Power: Placing Scale*. Oxford: Wiley-Blackwell, pp. 25–60.

Gibson-Graham, J. K. (2006) *A Postcapitalist Politics*. Minneapolis, MN: University of Minnesota Press.

Gilroy, R. (1998) Bringing Tenants into Decision-making. In: Cowan, D. (ed.) *Housing, Participation and Exclusion*. Aldershot: Ashgate.

Ginsburg, N. (1979) *Class, Capital and Social Policy*. Basingstoke: Macmillan.

Ginsburg, N. (1989) The Housing Act, 1988 and its Policy Context: A Critical Commentary. *Critical Social Policy*, 9: 56–81.

Ginsburg, N. (2005) The Privatisation of Council Housing. *Critical Social Policy*, 25 (1): 115–135.

Glynn, S. (2005) East End Immigrants and the Battle for Housing: A Comparative Study of Political Mobilisation in the Jewish and Bengali Communities. *Journal of Historical Geography*, 31: 528–545.

Glynn, S. (2009) *Where the Other Half Lives: Lower Income Housing in a Neoliberal World*. London: Pluto.

Goetschius, G. (1969) *Working with Community Groups*. London: Routledge.

Goffman, E. (1974) *Frame Analysis: An Essay on the Organization of Experience*. Boston, MA: University Press of New England.

Goodlad, R. (2001) Developments in Tenant Participation: Accounting for Growth. In: Cowan, D. and A. Marsh. *Two Steps Forward*. Bristol: The Policy Press.

Grayson, J. (1997) Campaigning Tenants: A Pre-history of Tenant Involvement to 1979. In: Cooper, C. and M. Hawtin (eds) *Housing, Community and Conflict: Understanding Resident Involvement*. Aldershot: Ashgate.

Grayson, J. (2007) Independent Tenants Organisations or 'Consumer Panels'. In: Defend Council Housing National Conference. London, 12 July.

Grayson, J. (2010) Against the Market: Tenant Movement Resistance to Housing Privatisation. Conference paper presented to Housing Privatisation, 30 Years On: Time for a Critical Reappraisal. University of Leeds, 26–27 July.

Greg, M. (2004) New Social Movements and Democracy. In: Todd, M. and G. Taylor (eds) *Democracy and Participation*. London: Merlin Press.

Habermas, J. (1981) New Social Movements. *Telos*, 49: 33–37.

Hackworth, J. (2009) Destroyed by HOPE: Public Housing, Neoliberalism and Progressive Housing Activism in the US. In: Glynn, S. (ed.) *Where the Other Half Lives*. London: Pluto Press.

Hague, C. (1990) The Development and Politics of Tenant Participation in British Council Housing. *Housing Studies*, 5 (4): 242–256.

Halewood, J. (2013) Bedroom Tax and the Significant 'Tenant Power Bloc' that's Forming – Landlords and IDS Beware! SPeye Keeping an Eye on Supporting People and Housing. 30 May. Available at: http://speye.wordpress.com. Accessed 4 June 2013.

Hall, S. (1988) *The Hard Road to Renewal: Thatcherism and the Crisis of the Left*. London: Verso.

Hall, S. and D. Massey (2010) Interpreting the Crisis. *Soundings*, 44, Spring: 57–71.

Hambleton, R. and Hoggett, P. (1988) *Decentralisation and Democracy: Localising Public Services*. Bristol: School for Advanced Urban Studies.

Hamel, P., H. Lustiger-Thaler and M. Mayer (eds) (2000) *Urban Movements in a Globalising World*. London: Routledge.

Hammar, M. (2013) *Global Tenant*. April edn. Stockholm: International Union of Tenants.

Hampton, W. (1970) *Democracy and Community: A Study of Politics in Sheffield*. Oxford: Oxford University Press.

Hancock, L., G. Mooney and S. Neal (2012) Crisis Social Policy and the Resilience of the Concept of Community. *Critical Social Policy*, 32 (3): 343–364.

Hanley, L. (2007) *Estates: An Intimate History*. London: Granta.

Hanmer, J. (1977) Community Action, Women's Aid and the Women's Liberation Movement. In: Mayo, M. (ed.) *Women in the Community*. London: Routledge & Kegan Paul.

Harloe, M. (1995) *The People's Home?* Oxford: Blackwell.

Harries, A. and P. Vincent-Jones (2001) Housing Management in Three Metropolitan Boroughs: The Impact of CCT and Implications for Best Value. *Local Government Studies*, 27 (2): 69–92.

Harrison, M. and K. Reeve (2002) Social Welfare Movements and Collective Action: Lessons from Two UK Housing Cases. *Housing Studies*, 17 (5): 755–771.

Hart, C., K. Jones and M. Bains (1997) Do People Want Power? The Social Responsibilities of Empowering Communities. In: Hoggett, P. (ed.) *Contested Communities: Experiences, Struggles, Policies*. Bristol: Policy Press.

Harvey, D. (1996) *Justice, Nature and the Geography of Difference*. Oxford: Blackwell.

Harvey, D. (2003) *The New Imperialism*. Oxford: Oxford University Press.

Harvey, D. (2010) *The Enigma of Capital*. Oxford: Oxford University Press.

Haworth, A. and T. Manzi (1999) Managing the 'Underclass': Interpreting the Moral Discourse of Housing Management. *Urban Studies*, 36 (1): 153–166.

Hayes, J. (1988) The Development of the Association of London Housing Estates 1957–1977. *The London Journal*, 13 (2):156–161.

Hayes, J. (1989) The Association of London Housing Estates and the 'Fair Rents' Issue. *The London Journal*, 14 (1): 59–67.

Haywood, S. (2007) London Tenants Federation Response to the Cave Review of Social Housing Regulation. In: *Communities and Local Government (CLG) Responses to the Cave Review*. London: DCLG.

Held, D. (2006) *Models of Democracy*. Cambridge: Polity Press.

Hewitt, M. (1996) Social Movements and Social Needs: Problems with Postmodern Political Theory. In: Taylor, D. (ed.) *Critical Social Policy: A Reader*. London: Sage.

Hickman, P. (2006) Approaches to Tenant Participation in the English Local Authority Sector. *Housing Studies*, 21 (2): 209–225.

Hildreth, P. (2011) What is Localism, and What Implications do Different Models have Managing the Local Economy? *Local Economy*, 26 (8): 702–714.

Hills, J. (2007) *Ends and Means: The Future Roles of Social Housing in England*. London: ESRC Research Centre for Analysis of Social Exclusion (CASE).

Hilton, M. (2003) *Consumerism in Twentieth-century Britain*. Cambridge: Cambridge University Press.

Hirschman, A. (1970) *Exit, Voice and Loyalty*. Cambridge, MA: Harvard University Press.

Hirschman, A. and R. Nelson (1976) Discussion. *The American Economic Review*, 66 (2): 386–391.

Hirst, P. (1997) *From Statism to Pluralism*. London: University College London Press.

HM Treasury (2010) *Spending Review 2010*. Cm 7942. London: The Stationery Office.

Hodkinson, S. (2012) The New Urban Enclosures. *City: Analysis of Urban Trends, Culture, Theory, Policy Action*. 16 (5): 500–518.

Hodkinson, S. and G. Robbins (2012) The Return of Class War Conservatism? Housing under the UK Coalition Government. *Critical Social Policy*, 33 (1): 57–77.

Hodkinson, S., P. Watt and G. Mooney (2013) Introduction: Neoliberal Housing Policy: Time for a Critical Re-appraisal. *Critical Social Policy*, 33(1): 3–16.

Hoggart, R. (1957) *The Uses of Literacy*. London: Chatto & Windus.

Homes and Communities Agency (2012) *The Regulatory Framework for Social Housing in England from April 2012*. London: Homes and Communities Agency.

Hood, M. (1997) The Governance Revolution from the Tenants' Perspective. In: Malpass, P. (ed.) *Ownership, Control and Accountability: The New Governance of Housing*. Coventry: Chartered Institute of Housing.

Hood, M. and R. Woods (1994) Women and Participation. In: Gilroy, R. and R. Woods (eds) *Housing Women*. London: Routledge.

House of Commons Public Administration Select Committee (2005) *Choice, Voice and Public Services 2004–2005*. HC 49-I. London: The Stationery Office.

House of Lords (2008) *Local Democracy, Economic Development and Construction Bill*. HL Bill 2. 54/4. London: The Stationery Office.

Housing Corporation (1998) *Making Consumers Count: Tenant Participation, the Next Five Years.* London: Housing Corporation.

Housing Corporation (2007) *National and Regional Tenant Bodies.* Available at: www.housing corp.gov.uk. Accessed 11 July 2008.

Housing Quality Network (2002) *Best Value in Housing, Self Assessment Toolkit – Tenant Involvement.* Housing Quality Network. Available at: www.hqnetwork.org.uk. Accessed 25 October 2005.

Howarth, D. and Y. Stavrakakis (2000) Introducing Discourse Theory and Political Analysis. In: Howarth, D., A. Norval and Y. Stavrakakis (eds) *Discourse Theory and Political Analysis: Identities, Hegemonies and Social Change.* Manchester: Manchester University Press.

Hutton, W. (2007) Open the Gates and Free People from Britain's Ghettos. *The Observer,* 18 February.

Imrie, R. and M. Raco (2003) Community and the Changing Nature of Urban Policy. In: Imrie, R. and M. Raco (eds) *Urban Renaissance? New Labour, Community and Urban Policy.* Bristol: Policy Press.

Ipsos MORI (2009a) *Understanding Tenant Involvement.* London: Tenant Services Authority.

Ipsos MORI (2009b) *Existing Tenants Survey 2008: Tenant Involvement.* London: Tenant Services Authority.

IRIS Consulting (2010) *Regional and National Tenants' Organisations.* London: DCLG.

IUT (International Union of Tenants) (2013). *About IUT.* Available at: www.iut.nu. Accessed 3 July 2013.

Jacobs, K., J. Kemeny and T. Manzi (2003) Privileged or Exploited Council Tenants? The Discursive Change in Conservative Housing Policy from 1972 to 1980. *Policy and Politics,* 31 (3): 307–320.

Jacobs, S. (1981) The Sale of Council Houses: Does it Matter? *Critical Social Policy,* 1: 35–48.

Jenkins, J. C. and C. Eckert (1986) Channelling Black Insurgency: Elite Patronage and Professional Social Movement Organisations in the Development of the Black Movement. *American Sociological Review,* 51 (6): 812–829.

Johnston, C. and G. Mooney (2007) 'Problem' People, 'Problem' Places? New Labour and Council Estates. In: Atkinson, R. and G. Helms (eds) *Securing an Urban Renaissance: Crime, Community and British Urban Policy.* Bristol: Policy Press.

Johnstone, C. (2000) Housing and Class Struggles in Postwar Glasgow. In: Lavalette, M. and G. Mooney (eds) *Class Struggle and Social Welfare.* London: Routledge.

Jones, C. and A. Murie (2006) *The Right to Buy: Analysis and Evaluation of a Housing Policy.* Oxford: Blackwell.

Jupp, E. (2008) The Feeling of Participation: Everyday Spaces and Urban Change. *Geoforum,* 39 (1): 331–343.

Jupp, E. (2010) Private and Public on the Housing Estate. In: Mahony, N., J. Newman and C. Barnett (eds) *Rethinking the Public.* Bristol: Policy Press, pp. 75–90.

Karn, V. (1993) Remodelling a HAT: The Implementation of the Housing Action Trust Legislation 1987–1992. In: Malpass, P. and R. Means (eds) *Implementing Housing Policy.* Buckingham: Open University Press.

Kavoulakos, K. I. (2006) The Emergence, Development and Limits of the Alternative Strategy of the Urban Movements in Germany. *City,* 10 (3): 343–354.

Kaye, A., M. Mayo and M. Thompson (1977) The United Tenants Action Committee. In: Cowley, J., A. Kaye, M. Mayo and M. Thompson. *Community or Class Struggle?* London: Stage 1.

Kearns, A. (1992) Active Citizenship and Urban Governance. *Transactions of the Institute of British Geographers,* 17 (1): 20–34.

Kearns, A. (1997) Housing Association Management Committees: Dilemmas of Composition. In: Malpass, P. (ed.) *Ownership, Control and Accountability: The New Governance of Housing*. Coventry: Chartered Institute of Housing.

Kearns, A. and M. Parkinson (2001) The Significance of Neighbourhood. *Urban Studies*, 38 (12): 2103–2110.

Kemeny, J. (1995) *From Public Housing to the Social Market*. London: Routledge.

Klandermans, B. (1992) The Social Construction of Protest and Multi-organisational Fields. In: Morris, A. and C. McClurg Mueller (eds) *Frontiers in Social Movement Theory*. London: Yale University Press.

Kolarska, L. and H. Aldrich (1980) Exit, Voice and Silence: Consumers' and Managers' Responses to Organisational Decline. *Organisation Studies*, 1 (1): 41–58.

Kothari, U. (2001) Power, Knowledge and Social Control in Participatory Development. In: Cooke, B. and U. Kothari (eds) *Participation: The New Tyranny*. London: Zed Books.

Laclau, E. (1977) *Politics and Ideology in Marxist Theory*. London: New Left Books.

Laclau, E. and C. Mouffe ([1985] 2001) *Hegemony and Socialist Strategy*. 2nd edn. London: Verso.

Lakoff, G. and M. Johnson (1980) *Metaphors We Live By*. Chicago, IL: University of Chicago Press.

Lambert, J. (1981) A Graveyard for Community Action? Housing Issues and the Community Development Projects in Britain 1968 to 1978. *Community Development Journal*, 160 (3): 246–253.

Larner, W. and D. Craig (2005) After Neo-Liberalism? Community Activism and Local Partnerships in Aotearoa New Zealand. *Antipode*, 37 (3): 402–424.

Laver, M. (1976) 'Exit, Voice and Loyalty' Revisited: The Strategic Production and Consumption of Public and Private Goods. *British Journal of Political Science*, 6 (4): 463–482.

Lees, R. and M. Mayo (1984) *Community Action for Change*. London: Routledge & Kegan Paul.

Lefebvre, H. (1996) *Writings on Cities*. Kofmaan, E. and E. Lebas (trans and eds). Oxford: Blackwell.

Leitner, H., Sheppard, E. and K. Sziarto (2008) The Spatialities of Contentious Politics. *Transactions of the Institute of British Geographers*, 33 (2): 157–172.

Lemke, T. (2001) 'The Birth of Bio-politics' – Michel Foucault's Lectures at the College de France on Neo-Liberal Governmentality. *Economy and Society*, 30 (2): 190–207.

Lemke, T. (2002) Foucault, Governmentality and Critique. *Rethinking Marxism*, 14 (3): 49–64.

Lent, A. (2001) *British Social Movements Since 1945*. Basingstoke: Palgrave.

Lipsky, M. (1968) Protest as a Political Resource. *The American Political Science Review*, 62 (4): 1144–1158.

Localism Act 2011 (c.20) London: The Stationery Office.

Loney, M. (1983) *Community Against Government: The British Community Development Project, 1968–1978: A Study of Government Incompetence*. London: Heinemann Educational.

Lovenduski, J. and V. Randall (1993) *Contemporary Feminist Politics: Women and Power in Britain*. Oxford: Oxford University Press.

Lowe, S. (1986) *Urban Social Movements: The City after Castells*. Basingstoke: Macmillan.

Lowe, S. (1997) Tenant Participation in a Legal Context. In: Cooper, C. and M. Hawtin, *Housing, Community and Conflict*. Aldershot: Arena Ashgate.

Lowndes, V. and H. Sullivan (2008) How Low Can You Go? Rationales and Challenges for Neighbourhood Governance. *Public Administration*, 86 (1): 53–74.

Lupton, R., R. Tunstall, W. Sigle-Rushton, P. Obolenskaya, R. Sabates, E. Meschi, D. Kneale and E. Salter (2009) *Growing Up in Social Housing in Britain: A Profile of Four Generations 1946 to the Present Day*. London: Tenant Services Authority.

Lustiger-Thaler, H. and L. Maheu (1995) Social Movements and the Challenge of Urban Politics. In Maheu, L. (ed.) *Social Movements and Social Classes: The Future of Collective Action*. London: Sage.

McAdam, D., S. Tarrow and C. Tilly (2001) *Dynamics of Contention*. Cambridge: Cambridge University Press.

McCarthy, J. and M. Zald (1977) Resource Mobilisation and Social Movements: A Partial Theory. *The American Journal of Sociology*, 82 (6): 1212–1241.

McCormack, J. (2008) Critical Pedagogy, Experiential Learning and Active Citizenship: A Freirean Perspective on Tenant Involvement in Housing Stock Transfers. *International Journal of Lifelong Education*, 27 (1): 3–18.

McCormack, J. (2009) 'Better the Devil You Know': Submerged Consciousness and Tenant Participation in Housing Stock Transfers. *Urban Studies*, 46: 391–411.

McCulloch, A. (1997) 'You've Fucked Up the Estate and Now You're Carrying a Briefcase!' In: Hoggett, P. (ed.) *Contested Communities: Experiences, Struggles, Policies*. Bristol: Policy Press.

McKee, K. (2009a) Post-Foucauldian Governmentality: What Does it Offer Critical Social Policy Analysis? *Critical Social Policy*, 29 (3): 465–486.

McKee, K. (2009b) The 'Responsible Tenant' and the Problem of Apathy. *Social Policy and Society*, 8: 25–36.

McKee, K. (2010) Sceptical, Disorderly and Paradoxical Subjects: Problematizing the 'Will to Empower' in Social Housing Governance. *Housing, Theory and Society*. First published on 21 May 2010 (iFirst). DOI: 10.1080/14036091003788120.

McKee, K. and V. Cooper (2008) The Paradox of Tenant Empowerment: Regulatory and Liberatory Possibilities. *Housing, Theory and Society*, 25 (2): 132–146.

McKibbin, R. (1998) *Classes and Cultures: England 1918–1951*. Oxford: Oxford University Press.

Malpass, P. (1990) *Reshaping Housing Policy: Subsidies, Rents and Residualisation*. London: Routledge.

Malpass, P. (2000) *Housing Associations and Housing Policy: A Historical Perspective*. Basingstoke: Macmillan.

Malpass, P. (2005) *Housing and the Welfare State: The Development of Housing Policy in Britain*. Basingstoke: Palgrave Macmillan.

Malpass, P. (2008) Housing and the New Welfare State: Wobbly Pillar or Cornerstone? *Housing Studies*, 23 (1): 1–19.

Malpass, P. and A. Murie (1999) *Housing Policy and Practice*. 5th edn. Basingstoke: Macmillan.

Malpass, P. and D. Mullins (2002) Local Authority Stock Transfer in the UK: From Local Initiative to National Policy. *Housing Studies*, 17 (4): 673–686.

Manzi, T. (2010) Promoting Responsibility, Shaping Behaviour: Housing Management, Mixed Communities and the Construction of Citizenship. *Housing Studies*, 25 (1): 5–19.

Marinetto, M. (2003) Who Wants to be an Active Citizen? The Politics and Practice of Community Involvement. *Sociology*, 37: 103–120.

Marris, P. and M. Rein (1974) *Dilemmas of Social Reform*. Harmondsworth: Penguin Books.

Marshall, T. H. (1950) *Citizenship and Social Class and Other Essays*. Cambridge: Cambridge University Press.

Marston, S. (2000) The Social Construction of Scale. *Progress in Human Geography*, 24 (2): 219–242.

Martin, D. (2002) Constructing the Neighbourhood Sphere: Gender and Community Organising. *Gender, Place and Culture*, 9 (4): 333–350.

Martin, D. (2003) Place-framing as Place Making: Constituting a Neighbourhood for Organising and Activism. *Annals of the Association of American Geographers*, 93 (3): 730–750.

Massey, D. (1994) *Space, Place and Gender*. Oxford: Polity Press.

Massey, D. (2004) Geographies of Responsibility. *Geografiska Annaler*, 86B (1): 5–18.

Mayer, M. (2000) Urban Social Movements in an Era of Globalisation. In Hamel, P., H. Lustiger-Thaler and M. Mayer (eds) *Urban Movements in a Globalising World*. London: Routledge.

Mayer, M. (2004) Urban Social Movements in an Era of Globalisation. In: Hamel, P., H. Lustiger-Thaler and M. Mayer (eds) *Urban Movements in a Globalising World*. London: Routledge.

Mayer, M. (2009) The 'Right to the City' in the Context of Shifting Mottos of Urban Social Movements. *City*, 13 (2): 362–374.

Mayo, E. and J. Tickell (2006) *A Consumer Audit of Social Housing*. London: National Consumer Council.

Mayo, M. (1972) Some Fundamental Problems of Community Work on Housing Estates in Britain. *Community Development Journal*, 7 (1): 55–58.

Melling, J. (1983) *Rent Stikes: People's Struggle for Housing in West Scotland 1890–1916*. Edinburgh: Polygon Books.

Melucci, A. (1989) *Nomads of the Present: Social Movements and Individual Needs in Contemporary Society*. London: Century Hutchinson.

Melucci, A. (1994) A Strange Kind of Newness: What's 'New' about New Social Movements. In: Larafia, E., H. Johnston, J. Gusfield (eds) *New Social Movements: From Ideology to Identity*. Philadelphia, PA: Temple University Press.

Melucci, A. (1995) The Process of Collective Identity. In: Johnston, H. and B. Klandermans (eds) *Social Movements and Culture*. London: University College London Press.

Melucci, A. (1996) *Challenging Codes*. Cambridge: Cambridge University Press.

Millward, L. (2005) Just Because We Are Amateurs Doesn't Mean We Aren't Professional: The Importance of Expert Activists in Tenant Participation. *Public Administration*, 83 (3): 735–751.

Millward, L., J. Beckford, A. Douglas and B. Reid (2003) *Encouraging Participation – A Toolkit for Tenants and Social Landlords*. London: Joseph Rowntree Foundation and the Chartered Institute of Housing.

Mitchell, G. D. and T. Lupton (1954) The Liverpool Estate. In: Mitchell, G. D. and T. Lupton (eds) *Neighbourhood and Community*. Liverpool: University Press of Liverpool.

Mitropoulos, A. (2005) Precari-us? *Mute*, 29. Available at: www.metamute.org. Accessed 16 February 2012.

Mohan, G. and K. Stokke (2000) Participatory Development and Empowerment: The Dangers of Localism. *Third World Quarterly*, 21 (2): 247–268.

Mooney, G. and L. Poole (2005) Marginalised Voices: Resisting the Privatisation of Council Housing in Glasgow. *Local Economy*, 20 (1): 27–39.

Mooney, G. and S. Neal (2009) *Community: Welfare, Crime and Society*. Maidenhead: Open University.

Moorhouse, B., M. Wilson and C. Chamberlain (1972) Rent Strikes – Direct Action and the Working Class. In: Milliband, R. and J. Saville (eds) *The Socialist Register*, pp. 133–156.

Morgan, P. (2006) Tenant Futures: The Future of Tenants in Social Housing. In: Malpass, P. and L. Cairncross (eds) *Building on the Past*. Bristol: Policy Press.

Mosse, D. (2001) 'People's Knowledge', Participation and Patronage: Operations and Representations in Rural Development. In: Cooke, B. and U. Kothari (eds) *Participation: The New Tyranny*. London: Zed Books.

Mouffe, C. (1993) *The Return of the Political*. London: Verso.

Mouffe, C. (2000) Hegemony and New Political Subjects: Toward a New Concept of Democracy. In: Nash, K. (ed.) *Readings in Contemporary Political Sociology*. Oxford: Blackwell.

Mueller, C. (1994) Conflict Networks and the Origins of Women's Liberation. In: Larafia, E., H. Johnston, J. Gusfield (eds) *New Social Movements: From Ideology to Identity*. Philadelphia, PA: Temple University Press.

Mullins, D., P. Niner and M. Riseborough (1995) *Evaluating Large-scale Voluntary Transfers of Local Authority Housing*. London: HMSO.

National Alliance of HUD Tenants (2013) *Mission*. Available at: www.saveourhomes.org. Accessed 3 July 2013.

National Housing Federation (2010) *Membership*. Available at: www.housing.co.uk. Accessed 8 July 2010.

National Tenants Voice Project Group (2008a) *The NTV Project Group's Emerging Proposals for the National Tenants Voice*. London: DCLG.

National Tenants Voice Project Group (2008b) *Citizens of Equal Worth*. London: DCLG.

Nativel, C. (2009) The Politics of Housing under France's New Right. In: Glynn, S. (ed.) *Where the Other Half Lives*. London: Pluto Press.

Needham, C. (2003) *Citizen-consumers*. London: The Catalyst Forum.

Newman, J. (2001) *Modernising Governance: New Labour, Policy and Society*. London: Sage.

Newman, J. (2012) Making, Contesting and Governing the Local: Women's Labour and the Local State. *Local Economy*, 27 (8): 846–858.

Newman, J. and J. Clarke (2009) *Publics, Politics and Power: Remaking the Public in Public Services*. London: Sage.

Newman, J., M. Barnes, H. Sullivan and A. Knops (2004) Public Participation and Collaborative Governance. *Journal of Social Policy*, 33 (2): 203–223.

Nicholls, W. (2008) Place, Networks, Space: Theorising the Geographies of Social Movements. *Transactions of the Institute of British Geographers*, 34: 78–93.

Nicholls, W. and J. Beaumont (2004) The Urbanisation of Justice Movements? Possibilities and Constraints for the City as a Space of Contentious Struggle. *Space and Polity*, 8 (20): 119–135.

Norval, A. (1996) *Deconstructing Apartheid Discourse*. London: Verso.

Norval, A. (2000) Trajectories of Future Research in Discourse Theory. In: Howarth, D., A. Norval and Y. Stavrakakis (eds) *Discourse Theory and Political Analysis: Identities, Hegemonies and Social Change*. Manchester: Manchester University Press.

ODPM (Office of the Deputy Prime Minister) (2004) *Housing Transfer Manual 2005 Programme*. London: ODPM.

ODPM (2005) *Citizen Engagement and Public Services: Why Neighbourhoods Matter*. London: ODPM.

Olechnowicz, A. (1997) *Working-class Housing in England Between the Wars: The Beacontree Estate*. Oxford: The Clarendon Press.

Oliver, M. (1990) *The Politics of Disablement*. Basingstoke: Macmillan.

Olson, M. (1971) *The Logic of Collective Action*. Cambridge, MA: Harvard University Press.

Oxley, M. (1986) Housing Policy and Tenants' Organisations in Great Britain. *Property Management*, 4 (3): 217–229.

Paddison, R., I. Docherty and R. Goodlad (2008) Responsible Participation and Housing: Restoring Democratic Theory to the Scene. *Housing Studies*, 23 (1): 129–147.

Painter, J., Orton, A., Macleod, G., Dominelli, L. and Pande, R. (2011) *Connecting Localism and Community Empowerment: Research Review and Critical Synthesis for the ARHC Connected Community Programme*. Project Report. Durham: Durham University, Department of Geography and School of Applied Social Sciences.

Pakulski, J. (1995) Social Movements and Class: The Decline of the Marxist Paradigm. In: Maheu, L. (ed.) *Social Movements and Social Classes: The Future of Collective Action*. London: Sage.

Pateman, C. (1970) *Participation and Democratic Theory*. Cambridge: Cambridge University Press.

Paul, S. (1992) Accountability in Public Services: Exit, Voice and Capture. *World Development*, 20 (7): 1061–1076.

Paul, S. (1994) *Does Voice Matter?* Policy Research Paper 1388. Washington, DC: The World Bank Finance and Private Sector Development Division.

Pawson, H. and F. Sosenko (2011) *The Supply Side Modernisation of Social Housing in England: Analysing Recent Dimensions and Impacts of the Financial Crisis 2007*. Housing Studies Association Annual Conference Housing in Hard Times. 13–15 April. York: University of York.

Pawson, H. and S. Wilcox (2013) *UK Housing Review 2013*. Coventry: Chartered Institute of Housing.

Peck, J. and A. Tickell (2002) Neoliberalising Space. *Antipode*, 34 (3): 380–404.

Pickles, E. (2010) Speech to the Local Government Information Unit Reception of the All Party Parliamentary Group for Local Government. London, 7 June. In: Townsend, S. Pickles: Localism is my Top Priority. *Regeneration and Renewal*. Available at: www.regen.net. Accessed 7 April 2013.

Pickvance, C. (2003) From Urban Social Movements to Urban Movements: A Review and Introduction to a Symposium on Urban Movements. *International Journal of Urban and Regional Research*, 27 (1): 102–109.

Pinkney, S. and E. Saraga (2009) Communities and Social Mobilisations. In: Mooney, G. and S. Neal (eds) *Community: Welfare, Crime and Society*. Maidenhead: Open University.

Piratin, P. (1948) *Our Flag Stays Red*. London: Thames.

Piven, F. F. and R. Cloward (1977) *Poor People's Movements*. New York: Pantheon Books.

Plymouth Federation of Tenants and Residents (2009) *Annual Report 2008–2009*. Available at: www.plymfed.org.uk. Accessed 6 July 2010.

Polanyi, K. (1957) *The Great Transformation*. Boston, MA: Beacon Press.

Polletta, F. (1999) 'Free Spaces' in Collective Action. *Theory and Society*, 28 (1): 1–38.

Polletta, F. (2002) *Freedom is an Endless Meeting*. Chicago, IL: University of Chicago Press.

Portes, A. (1998) Social Capital: Its Origins and Applications in Modern Sociology. *Annual Review of Sociology*, 24: 1–24.

Potter, J. (1988) Consumerism and the Public Sector: How Well Does the Coat Fit? *Public Administration*, 66 (2): 149–164.

Pruijt, H. (2003) Is the Institutionalisation of Urban Movements Inevitable? A Comparison of the Opportunities for Sustained Squatting in New York City and Amsterdam. *International Journal of Urban and Regional Research*, 27 (1): 133–157.

Purcell, M. (2006) Urban Democracy and the Local Trap. *Urban Studies*, 43 (11): 1921–1941.

Putnam, R. (2000) *Bowling Alone: The Collapse and Revival of the American Community*. London: Simon & Schuster.

Raco, M. (2003) Governmentality, Subject-building, and the Discourses and Practices of Devolution in the UK. *Transactions of the Institute of British Geographers*, 28 (1): 75–95.

Ramesh, R. (2012) Housing Benefit Cuts Will Put 800,000 Homes out of Reach, According to Study. *The Guardian*, 1 January. London. Available at: www.guardian.co.uk. Accessed 24 July 2013.

Rao, J. (1984) *Power and Participation in the Public Sector Housing*. London: London Borough of Hounslow Housing Department.

Ravetz, A. (2001) *Council Housing and Culture*. Abingdon: Routledge.

Rex, J. and R. Moore (1967) *Race, Community and Conflict*. London: Oxford University Press.

Richardson, A. (1983) *Participation*. London: Routledge.

Riseborough, M. (1998) More Control and Choice for Users? In: Marsh, A. and D. Mullins (eds) *Housing and Public Policy*. Buckingham: Open University Press.

Rodwin, M. (2000) *Promoting Accountable Managed Health Care: The Potential Role for Consumer Voice*. Bloomington, IN: Indiana University.

Rose, N. (1999) *Powers of Freedom: Reframing Political Thought*. Cambridge: Cambridge University Press.

Roth, R. (2000) New Social Movements, Poor People's Movements and the Struggle for Social Citizenship. In Hamel, P., H. Lustiger-Thaler and M. Mayer (eds) *Urban Movements in a Globalising World*. London: Routledge.

Routledge, P. (2003) Convergence Space: Process Geographies of Grassroots Globalisation Networks. *Transactions of the Institute of British Geographers*, 28 (3): 333–349.

Rowbotham, S. (1973) *Hidden from History: 300 Years of Women's Oppression and the Fight Against It*. London: Pluto Press.

Saunders, P. (1979) *Urban Politics: A Sociological Interpretation*. London: Hutchinson.

Saunders, P. (1981) *Social Theory and the Urban Question*. London: Hutchinson.

Saunders, P. (1990) *A Nation of Home Owners*. London: Unwin-Hyman.

Savage, M. (2000) *Class Analysis and Social Transformation*. Buckingham: Open University Press

Savill, D. (1982) Council Tenants and the 1980 Housing Act. In: Henderson, P., A. Wright and K. Wyncoll (eds) *Successes and Struggles on Council Estates*. London: Association of Community Workers.

Schifferes, S. (1976) Council Tenants and Housing Policy in the 1930s: The Contradictions of State Intervention. In: Edwards, M., Gray, F., Merrett, S. and Swann, J. (eds) *Housing and Class in Britain*. London. Papers presented at the Political Economy of Housing Workshop of the Conference of Socialist Economists.

Segal, L. (1979) A Local Experience. In: Rowbotham, S., L. Segal and H. Wainwright (eds) *Beyond the Fragments*. London: Newcastle Socialist Centre and Islington Community Press.

Shapely, P. (2006) Tenants Arise! Consumerism, Tenants and the Challenge to Council Authority in Manchester 1968–1992. *Social History*, 31 (1): 60–78.

Shapely, P. (2007) *The Politics of Housing: Power, Consumers and Urban Culture*. Manchester: Manchester University Press.

Shelter (2013) 'Generation Rent' Locked Out of Property Market. *Shelter England News*, 19 June. Available at: www.shelter.org.uk. Accessed 3 July 2013.

Simmons, R., J. Birchall, S. Doheny and M. Powell (2007) 'Citizen Governance': Opportunities for Inclusivity in Policy and Policy Making? *Policy and Politics*, 35 (3): 457–478.

Sklair, L. (1975) The Struggle Against the Housing Finance Act. In: Milliband, R. and J. Saville (eds) *The Socialist Register*. Pontypool: Merlin Press, pp. 250–292.

Smith, A. M. (1998) *Laclau and Mouffe: The Radical Democratic Imaginary*. London: Routledge.

Smith, J. (1978) Hard Lines and Soft Options: A Criticism of Some Left Attitudes to Community Work. In: Curno, P. (ed.) *Political Issues and Community Work*. London: Routledge & Kegan Paul.

Smith, N. (1993) Homeless/Global: Scaling Places. In: Bird, J., B. Curtis, T. Putnam, G. Robertson and L. Tucker (eds) *Mapping the Futures*. London: Routlege, pp. 87–119.

Smyth, S. (2013) The Privatization of Council Housing: Stock Transfer and the Struggle for Accountable Housing. *Critical Social Policy*, 33 (1): 37–56.

Snow, D. (2004) Framing Processes, Ideology and Discursive Fields. In: Snow, D., S. Soule, H. Kriesi (eds) *The Blackwell Companion to Social Movements*. Oxford: Blackwell.

Snow, D. and D. McAdam (2000) Identity Work Processes in the Context of Social Movements: Clarifying the Identity/Movement Nexus. In: Stryker, S., T. Owens, R. White (eds) *Self, Identity and Social Movements*. Minneapolis, MN: University of Minnesota Press.

Snow, D., E. B. Rochford, Jr, S. Worden and R. Renford (1986) Frame Alignment Processes, Micromobilisation and Movement Participation. *American Sociological Review*, 51 (4): 464–481.

Soja, E. (2008) The City and Spatial Justice. Paper presented at the conference Spatial Justice, Nanterre, Paris, 12–14 March.

Somerville, P. (1998) Empowerment through Residence. *Housing Studies*, 13 (2): 233–257.

Somerville, P. (2004) State Rescaling and Democratic Transformation. *Space and Policy*, 8 (2): 137–156.

Somerville, P. (2005a) Housing, Class and Social Policy. In: Somerville, P. and S. Nigel (eds) *Housing and Social Policy*. London: Routledge.

Somerville, P. (2005b) Community Governance and Democracy. *Policy and Politics*, 33 (1): 117–144.

Somerville, P. (2012) Resident and Neighbourhood Movements. *International Encyclopedia of Housing and Home*. London: Elsevier Press.

Spivak, G. C. (1988) Can the Subaltern Speak? In: Nelso, C. and L. Grossberg (eds) *Marxism and the Interpretation of Culture*. Chicago, IL: University of Illinois Press.

Spivak, G. C. (2010) In Response: Looking Back, Looking Forward. In: Morris, R. C. (ed.) *Can the Subaltern Speak? Reflections on the History of an Idea*. New York: Columbia University Press, pp. 227–336.

Srebrnik, H. (1995) Class, Ethnicity and Gender Intertwined: Jewish Women and the East London Rent Strikes, 1935–1940. *Women's History Review*, 4 (3): 283–299.

Staeheli, L. (2002) Women and the Work of Community. *Environment and Planning A*, 35 (5): 815–831.

Stoecker, R. (1995) Community, Movement, Organisation: The Problem of Identity Convergence in Collection Action. *The Sociological Quarterly*, 36 (1): 111–130.

Stoker, G. (2004) *Transforming Local Governance, from Thatcherism to New Labour*. Basingstoke: Macmillan.

Sullivan, H. (2001) Maximising the Contribution of Neighbourhoods: The Role of Community Governance. *Public Policy and Administration*, 16 (2): 30–48.

Swyngedouw, E. (2004) Globalisation or 'Glocalisation'? Networks, Territories and Rescaling. *Cambridge Review of International Affairs*, 17 (1): 25–48.

Swyngedouw, E. (2005) Governance Innovation and the Citizen: The Janus Face of Governance-beyond-the-State. *Urban Studies*, 42 (11): 1991–2006.

TAROE (Tenants and Residents Organisations of England) (2008) *Tenants and Residents Organisations of England: About Us*. Available at: www.taroe.org. Accessed 6 July 2010.

TAROE (2012) *Annual General Meeting Annual Report*, Derby, 6 October. Available at: www.taroe.org.uk. Accessed 1 July 2013.

TAROE, NFTMO (National Federation of Tenant Management Organisations), CCH (Confederation of Co-operative Housing) (2008) *Developing Housing Strategy in a Post Credit Crunch World: Joint Submission to the Housing Reform Green Paper*. Runcorn: TAROE, NFTMO, CCH.

Tarrow, S. (1998) *Power in Movement: Social Movements and Contentious Politics*. Cambridge: Cambridge University Press.

Taylor, M. (1986) For Whose Benefit? Decentralising Housing Services in Two Cities. *Community Development Journal*, 21 (2): 126–132.

Taylor, M. (2003) *Public Policy in the Community*. Basingstoke: Macmillan.

Taylor, M. (2007) Community Participation in the Real World: Opportunities and Pitfalls in New Governance Spaces. *Urban Studies*, 44 (2): 297–317.

Taylor, V. (1989) Social Movement Continuity: The Women's Movement in Abeyance. *American Sociological Review*, 54 (5): 761–775.

Taylor, V. and N. Whittier (1992) Collective Identity in Social Movement Communities. In: Morris, A. and C. McClurg Mueller (eds) *Frontiers in Social Movement Theory*. New Haven, CT: Yale University Press.

Taylor, V. and N. Whittier (1995) Analytical Approaches to Social Movement Culture: The Culture of the Women's Movement. In: Johnston, H. and B. Klandermans (eds) *Social Movements and Culture*. London: University College London Press.

Thompson, E. P. (1968) *The Making of the English Working Class*. Harmondsworth: Penguin Books.

Tilly, C. (1985) Models and Realities of Popular Collective Action. *Social Research*, 52 (4): 717–747.

Titmuss, Richard (1970) *The Gift Relationship: From Human Blood to Social Policy*. London: George Allen & Unwin.

Torfing, J. (1999) *New Theories of Discourse: Laclau, Mouffe and Zizek*. Oxford: Blackwell.

Torgerson, U. (1987) Housing: The Wobbly Pillar under the Welfare State. In: Turner, B., J. Kemeny and L. Lundqvist (eds) *Between State and Market: Housing in the Post-Industrial Era*. Stockholm: Almqvist & Wiksell.

Touraine, A. (1985) An Introduction to the Study of Social Movements. *Social Research*, 52 (4): 749–787.

Townsend, J., G. Porter and E. Mawdsley (2004) Creating Spaces of Resistance: Development NGOs and their Clients in Ghana, India and Mexico. *Antipode*, 36 (5): 871–889.

Trentmann, F. (2004) Beyond Consumerism: New Historical Perspectives on Consumption. *Journal of Contemporary History*, 39 (3): 373–401.

Trentmann, F. (2005) Knowing Consumers – Histories, Identities, Practices: An Introduction. In: Trentmann, F. (ed.) *The Making of the Consumer: Knowledge, Power and Identity in the Modern World*. Oxford: Berg.

TSA (Tenant Services Authority) (2009) *Existing Tenants Survey 2008*. London: Tenant Services Authority.

TSA (2010) *The Regulatory Framework for Social Housing in England from April 2010*. London: Tenant Services Authority.

TSA/Audit Commission (2010) *Tenant Involvement: Assessing Landlords' Progess*. London: Tenant Services Authority.

Tuan, Yi-Fu (1979) *Space and Place: Humanist Perspective*. Netherlands: Springer.

Turner, B. (2007) Social Housing in Sweden. In: Whitehead, C. and K. Scanlon (eds) *Social Housing in Europe*. London: London School of Economics and Political Science.

Uguris, T. (2004) *Space, Power and Participation: Ethnic and Gender Differences in Tenant Participation in Public Housing*. Aldershot: Ashgate.

Vincent-Jones, P. and A. Harries (1998) Tenant Participation in Contracting for Housing Management Services: A Case Study. In: Cowan, D. (ed.) *Housing, Participation and Exclusion*. Aldershot: Ashgate.

Wainwright, H. (1979) Introduction. In: Rowbotham, S., L. Segal and H. Wainwright (eds) *Beyond the Fragments: Feminism and the Making of Socialism*. London: Newcastle Socialist Centre and Islington Community Press.

Wainwright, H. (1994) *Arguments for a New Left: Answering the Free Market Right*. Oxford: Blackwell.

Wainwright, H. (2003) *Reclaim the State: Experiments in Popular Democracy*. London: Verso.

Walker, B. and A. Marsh (2003) Setting the Rents of Social Housing: The Impact and Implications of Rent Restructuring in England. *Urban Studies*, 40 (10): 2023–2047.

Wallace, A. (2010) New Neighbourhoods, New Citizens? Challenging Community as a Framework for Social and Moral Regeneration under New Labour in the UK. *International Journal of Urban and Regional Research*, 34 (4): 805–819.

Ward, C. (1974) *Tenants Take Over*. London: Architectural Press.

Watmos Community Homes (2010) *How We Work*. Available at: www.watmos.org.uk. Accessed 9 October 2010.

Watt, P. (2008) 'Underclass' and 'Ordinary People' Discourses: Representing/Re-presenting Council Tenants in a Housing Campaign. *Critical Discourse Studies*, 4: 345–357.

Westwood, A. (2011) Localism, Social Capital and the 'Big Society'. *Local Economy*, 26 (8): 690–701.

Wilcox, S. and H. Pawson (2012) *The UK Housing Review*. Coventry: Chartered Institute of Housing.

Wilkinson, S. (1999) How Useful are Focus Groups in Feminist Research? In: Barbour, R. and J. Kitzinger (eds) *Developing Focus Group Research*. London: Sage.

Wilkinson, S. and C. Kitzinger (2003) Constructing Identities: A Feminist Conversation Analytic Approach to Positioning in Action. In: Harré, R. and F. Moghaddam (eds) *The Self and Others*. London: Praeger.

Williams, C. and J. Windebank (2000) Helping Each Other Out? Community Exchange in Deprived Neighbourhoods. *Community Development Journal*, 35 (2): 146–156.

Williams, F. (1992) Somewhere Over the Rainbow: Universality and Diversity in Social Policy. In: Manning, N. and R. Page (eds) *Social Policy Review 4 1991–1992*. Canterbury: Social Policy Association.

Williams, F. (1993) Women and Community. In: Bornat, J., C. Pereira, D. Pilgrim and F. Williams (eds) *Community Care: A Reader*. Basingstoke: Macmillan.

Williams, F. (1994) Social Relations, Welfare and the Post-Fordism Debate. In: Burrows, R. and B. Loather (eds) *Towards a Post-Fordist Welfare State?* London: Routledge.

Williams, R. (1967) *Culture and Society*. London: Chatto & Windus.

Williams, R. (2004) The Cultural Contexts of Collective Action: Constraints, Opportunities and the Symbolic Life of Social Movements. In: Snow, D., S. Soule and H. Kriesi (eds) *The Blackwell Companion to Social Movements*. Oxford: Blackwell.

Wood, M. (1994) Should Tenants Take Over? Radical Community Work, Tenants Organisations and the Future of Public Housing. In: Jacobs, S. and K. Popple (eds) *Community Work in the 1990s*. Nottingham: Spokesman.

Woodward, R. (1991) Mobilising Opposition: The Campaign Against Housing Action Trusts in Tower Hamlets. *Housing Studies*, 6 (1): 44–56.

Wright, T. (1997) *Out of Place: Homeless Mobilisations, Subcities, and Contested Landscapes*. Albany, NY: State University of New York Press.

Yelland, C. (1990) *The Gipton Story*. Leeds: The Gipton History Group.

Yeo, E. and S. Yeo (1988) On the Uses of 'Community': From Owenism to the Present. In: Yeo, S. (ed.) *New Views of Co-operation*. London: Routledge.

Young, M. and P. Wilmot (1962) *Family and Kinship in East London*. Harmondsworth: Penguin.

Zald, M. and R. Ash (1966) Social Movement Organisations: Growth, Decay and Change. *Social Forces*, 44 (3): 327–341.

INDEX